Saved by my Face

SAVED BY MY FACE

A TRUE STORY OF COURAGE AND ESCAPE
IN WAR-TORN POLAND

JERZY LANDO

MAINSTREAM
PUBLISHING
EDINBURGH AND LONDON

To the memory of my father and of all my friends and
relatives who did not survive the war.

First published in Great Britain in 2002 by
MAINSTREAM PUBLISHING COMPANY (EDINBURGH) LTD
7 Albany Street
Edinburgh EH1 3UG

ISBN 1 84018 546 5

A catalogue record for this book is available from the British Library

Typeset in Stempel Garamond and City
Printed and bound in Great Britain by
Butler & Tanner Ltd, Frome and London

CONTENTS

ACKNOWLEDGEMENTS

Many thanks to Danuta and Stefan Waydenfeld who persuaded me to embark on writing this book and without whose continuing encouragement and active help it might never have been written. Thanks also to Sonia Ribeiro who introduced me to the art of autobiography writing.

FOREWORD

Jerzy Lando survived the Warsaw ghetto, and took part in the Polish uprising in Warsaw in 1944. After his escape from the ghetto he survived with the help of Christian Poles. His memoirs are an important addition to the portrayal of those grim years by those – too few, alas – who survived them.

As Elie Wiesel has said, every memoir has its unique page, and there are many such pages in this book. I have no doubt that it will be incorporated in the Holocaust Memoir Digest, which is even now being prepared to bring the contents of survivors' memoirs to the attention of teachers and students worldwide.

The author of these pages was nearly 17 when the war began. He lived through the worst years in Jewish history as a young man who in normal times would have been at university and at work, exploring his own potential. Jerzy Lando's descriptions of each phase of the Holocaust are vivid. For him, the war began in Łódż, his birthplace. Later, he was expelled from Łódż to Cracow, and from there to Warsaw. His account of the Passover of 1940 in Cracow is memorable. So too is his account of the creation and early days of the Warsaw ghetto. His time in hiding, moving from place to place, is full of drama, including the ever-present risk of betrayal and exposure. Equally dramatic are his experiences during the Polish national uprising in 1944.

Deported to a camp in Germany, his liberators in 1945 were two British soldiers, the first a Scot and the second a Jew.

This is a story to be read, and then re-read.

Martin Gilbert
Merton College, Oxford
December 2001

PROLOGUE

At Christmas 1992 I was enjoying a self-catering holiday in Devon with my family. As is usual on such occasions, we soon got to know our neighbours, including the young family of a man called David Joseph from north London. While we were eating our mince pies, David told me casually that he was organising a six-day trip to Poland the following April for the commemorations of the 50th anniversary of the Rising in the Warsaw ghetto.[1] To his surprise I revealed to him that had it not been for my Aryan appearance, it would have been unlikely that I'd be with him to taste this traditional delicacy – I happened to be one of the few survivors of the Warsaw ghetto, having lived after my escape for two years under an assumed Christian identity. He immediately encouraged me to join his group and make a contribution to what they hoped to learn from their trip to Poland. I agreed.

The day after our arrival our group of some 30 people went to visit the Nożyk Synagogue in Twarda Street, restored 10 years earlier. The building, rather plain from outside, was crowded with people from all over the world, many of them non-Jews, and including representatives of the Church and of the Polish government. One enters the synagogue through a porch with richly ornamented columns on each side. Inside there are three aisles and, at the far end of the central aisle, behind a podium, an elaborate ark houses the Torahs, the sacred scrolls. Although the main illumination comes from the crystal chandelier hanging from the ceiling, bright sunlight filters through the stained-glass windows, casting multi-coloured hues on the faces and objects inside. The cantor, a middle-aged man with a serious demeanour, in a dark suit,

[1] There were two insurgencies in Warsaw during the occupation. First, the desperate Ghetto Rising of April 1943 and then the better prepared, longer but equally tragic Warsaw Rising of August 1944. The author took part in the latter.

enfolded in a white prayer shawl, and with a black cylindrical cap on his head, mounted the podium. In complete silence, punctuated by the sounds of sobbing, he chanted the moving words of a prayer for the dead, *El Male Rachanmim* (God Full of Mercy), followed by *Kaddish*, the prayer recited by mourners on the anniversary of death. A long procession of my relatives and friends who had perished under the occupation appeared before my eyes. To ensure that they were amongst the blessed ones I silently called their names.

When the cantor finished, a dignified, portly man standing next to him took over.

'Our prayer today is for the commemoration of the Rising which broke out in the Warsaw ghetto on 19 April 1943. It was directed against the Nazis who entered the ghetto to round up the small remnant of its original 400,000 inhabitants in order to deport them to the gas chambers of Treblinka. Mordechaj Anielewicz took command of some 800 men equipped with home-made guns and explosives smuggled in by the Polish Underground. They continued fighting the Germans equipped with artillery, tanks and aircraft until the last days of May. On 19 April the Jewish *Organizacja Bojowa*, the Fighting Organisation, issued the following declaration:

> Jews! The hour of deed and revenge against the occupant has struck. All those capable of carrying arms must join us. Old people and women must help. To arms!

'That day, the Germans, on entering the ghetto, were greeted with grenades and handgun fire and had to withdraw after a few hours. They soon responded by blowing up and burning all buildings, streets and whole districts one after the other. On 23 April the fighters issued another proclamation, which read:

> Amongst the fires, the smoke and the blood of the murdered in the ghetto we send our last address to the world outside: we may all perish but we shall not surrender. We fight for our freedom and yours.

'They fought in the name of human dignity. In the Ghetto Rising

7,000 Jews were killed, 5,000 burnt to death, 15,000 sent to perish in the gas chambers. They gained no military successes and did not live to enjoy the final victory of good over evil – but this first mass act of open resistance against the German occupants and its moral significance are written into Europe's history.'

'Soldiers of the ghetto,' the speaker called out, 'your sacrifice was not in vain! You are an inspiration for fraternity amongst nations and for a future that will know no wars. We salute your memory!' He continued: 'On this day we also remember the shoah, the annihilation of 6,000,000 innocent Jews. We remember the help given to us by our Polish brothers, and their proclamation of August 1943, urging all Poles to help the fugitives and inhabitants of the ghetto and warning those guilty of blackmail that they will be dealt with and punished in reborn Poland.'

The Archbishop of Warsaw, in a purple robe, a purple skullcap covering his head, his amiable face exuding warmth and sympathy, was the next to speak.

'As Catholics,' he said, 'we must understand the meaning of this event for us and for the future generations. We must pray to God that we may draw the right conclusions and the lesson we have learned is that we have all been blessed together as the sons of Abraham so that we shall become a source of blessing for others.'

He recited a psalm.

> . . . As I walk and look I see that no one cares for me, no one asks about me, I call for help but no one listens. Hear my cries, save me from those that persecute me and are stronger than I . . .

He ended with the words: 'To all those present here I say Shalom, my words of respect.'

In a drab, working-class district of Warsaw, enclosed on each of its four sides by Karmelicka, Anielewicza, Lewartowskiego and Zamenhofa streets[2], there is a large square covered with unkempt grass, weedy trees and bushes. Around it stand low-rise, cream-coloured, prefabricated apartment houses, separated from one another by patches of grass. They have been built over the compacted rubble, all that had remained of the Warsaw ghetto. Some

---

[2] Zamenhof is the founder of Esperanto, Anielewicz and Lewandowski are heroes of the Ghetto Rising.

of the rubble must have been left, some would have been carted away. But what about the thousands of bodies buried underneath it? Does anyone ever give them a thought? I left the place feeling empty and dejected. Was this because I witnessed so much of its past history?

During the day the square is deserted except for a few young children playing games and some old people sitting on wooden benches. Now and again a taxi or minibus brings a group of tourists accompanied by a guide. Only the guides now speak of what went on here 50 years ago, few others remember the desperate fighting, the blood that soaked into this little plot of land. The cheerless square has not yet even been named, but on its eastern side a vast monument dedicated to the memory of the Warsaw ghetto has been erected. It is a massive stone cube more than 30 feet high, of the same width and 15 feet deep, approached by a wide staircase along its full length, and bearing large stone menorahs (seven-branched sacred candelabras) on each side. Inscriptions in Polish, Hebrew and Yiddish read: JEWISH NATION TO ITS HEROES AND MARTYRS. On the front face an expressive sculpture, some 20 feet high and 10 feet wide, symbolises the struggle and martyrdom of the Jews. It shows a tall central figure, surrounded by a group of fighters, men and women of all ages who appear to be trying to tear themselves away from the burning ghetto, symbolising a nation attempting to set itself free. The other side of the monument shows, in bas-relief, a march to extermination. The figures, bent down in their hopelessness, follow one another on their deadly exodus. They are led by a rabbi carrying a Torah, a mother with a baby in her arms following close behind.

On my second evening in Warsaw I stood in the floodlit square, next to Boguś Howil, a Christian Pole, a man I had turned to in my hour of need 51 years earlier. This elderly man, ten years my senior, now stooping, has retained his open, smiling face, reminding me to this day of his once youthful good looks. We stood some distance from the monument as a crowd of thousands of people filled every inch of the square. A few hours earlier I had spoken to an invited audience, which included our group from England, about my experiences in that time of war. I introduced Boguś as one of the few

Christians who after my escape from the ghetto had helped me to survive, putting their own and their families' lives at risk. Asked now why he had helped the Jews, he replied simply that he could not bear the sight of injustice being done to them.

It was a bitterly cold night and I was shivering in spite of my warm anorak. Suddenly I saw a long procession, six deep, stretching into the distance as far as my sight could reach. They sang:[3]

> *We must never lose our courage in the fight,*
> *Though skies of lead turn days of sunshine into night.*
> *Because the hour for which we've yearned will yet arrive,*
> *And our marching steps will thunder: we survive!*
>
> *From land of palm trees to the land of distant snow,*
> *We have come with our deep sorrow and our woe.*
> *And everywhere our blood was innocently shed,*
> *Our fighting spirits will again avenge our dead . . .*
>
> *The golden rays of morning sun will dry our tears*
> *Dispelling bitter agony of yesteryears.*
> *But if the sun and dawn with us will be delayed –*
> *Then let this song ring out the call to you instead.*
>
> *Not lead, but blood inscribed this song which now we sing,*
> *It's not a carolling of birds upon the wing,*
> *But a people midst the crashing fires of hell,*
> *Sang this song and fought courageous till it fell!*
>
> *So we must never lose our courage in the fight,*
> *Though skies of lead turn days of sunshine into night,*
> *Because the hour for which we've yearned will yet arrive,*
> *And our marching steps will thunder: we survive!*

Young people, boys and girls, were marching by, proudly bearing the Israeli flags with the Star of David. I reflected how for them the blue star was a source of pride. When forced to wear it on my sleeve under the German rule, it had been a sign of humiliation and shame.

---

[3] *Zog Nit Keynmal!*, a Yiddish song.

'They don't look Jewish,' remarked Boguś. The last time he had seen Jews en masse was on a visit to the ghetto 51 years ago. They wore rags; they were pale, emaciated, starving and about to meet their deaths. Now, we were witness to a miracle; the words of the Scriptures were being fulfilled in our presence:

> The Lord set Ezekiel down in the midst of the valley, and it was full of bones, and there were very many in the open valley and they were very dry. Thus said the Lord God unto these bones: Behold I will cause breath to enter into you and ye shall live. And I will lay sinews upon you and will bring up flesh upon you and cover you with skin and put breath in you and ye shall live . . .
> [Ezekial 37]

I was too tired and too cold to listen to the speeches by the Polish President Lech Wałęsa, by the US Vice-President Al Gore, by many other Heads of State present. I had seen and have understood more than enough. I did not need any more lofty words. I said goodbye to Boguś and went back to my hostel.

On the third morning, as part of a vast crowd of people, I went to the Jewish cemetery in Okopowa Street in the suburb of Wola for the unveiling of a memorial to the children of the ghetto, the little smugglers who risked their lives every day to bring food for the starving inhabitants. It was another cold, dull day; I stood fairly close to the first row of graves that seemed to stretch forever in front of the cemetery wall. Here and there I saw large patches of brightness: a group of Polish girl guides standing patiently in formation, troops of Polish soldiers, guards of honour in their green uniforms, nuns in their black-and-white habits. A detachment of soldiers marched past bearing dozens of huge wreaths, flowers of all colours with ribbons carrying inscriptions from donors, seemingly from every part of the world. What a contrast to the grey, crumbling tombstones! Many speeches followed. Jewish songs known to me since my childhood were sung and I felt as if they were going to pierce my heart. It was not just my own sorrow and pain that I was conscious of, but that of those standing around me too. Blocked by the mass of people, I wasn't able to come any closer to the newly erected memorial, guarded on each side by a soldier with an expressionless face. I could read only half the inscription: THE LITTLE SMUGGLER GOES THROUGH A HOLE, THROUGH A CRACK OR A CRANNY, STARVING YET STUBBORN AND CANNY, SNEAKY AND SPEEDY LIKE A CAT. I DAILY RISK MY YOUTHFUL NECK BUT IF FATE WILL TURN AGAINST ME . . .

I left the cemetery and took a tram to Młocińska Street to look again at the railway siding along which 50 years earlier I had watched trains packed with their human cargo on their way to Treblinka, searching for a familiar face in the small barred window of a wagon. But even the railway track had disappeared.

On our last day in Poland the rest of my group made their way to Auschwitz to visit what remained of the infamous extermination camp. But I took a train to Treblinka. This is where most of my friends and family were gassed to death. Treblinka, some 60 miles north-east of Warsaw, is a hamlet situated on sandy hills, enclosed on the north by a small chain of lakes originating from an old bed of the Bug River. West of Treblinka, only a few miles from the extermination camp, lies an old village of Koscielna Prostyn, a small sanctuary of Saint Trinity and Saint Anne. From the tiny railway station of Treblinka meadows and peat bogs stretch out on the left-hand side of the tracks; along the right-hand side runs a tarmac road built by the Germans. Before Poniatowo the railway line divides again, the left line runs in the direction of Siedlce, the other leads through sand dunes, low hills and a small wood of small trees towards a massive gravel-pit. A few hundred yards further the track divides once more. One siding allows the goods trains access to the ramp of the extermination centre 'SS Sonderkommando Treblinks' (Treblinka II). The labour camp of Treblinka was some two miles away.

I had to be on my own. I needed to hear the rattle of the wheels, to see what they saw through the windows covered with barbed wire – the same fields, the same forests, the same farmyards, their last impressions of the outside world.

On 25 July 1993 the Special Commission for the Designation of the Righteous of the Yad Vashem[4] decided to confer upon Bogusław Howil and his late mother, Helena, its highest expression of

---

[4] The Holocaust Martyrs' and Heroes' Remembrance Authority in Jerusalem

gratitude: the title of the Righteous Among the Nations. This recognition entitled them to a medal and certificate of honour and the privilege of having their names inscribed on the Righteous Honour Wall at Yad Vashem Jerusalem.

For a long time after the war I could not bring myself to talk or write about what I found too painful to recall. It took me many years to be able to think of the past events calmly and coherently enough in order to write this memoir. But spurred on by friends and feeling ever more strongly that it was my duty as a witness, as a participant of the events and as a survivor to leave a record of the terrible years of the German occupation of Poland, I decided finally to delve into my past. I soon discovered that my emotions had not faded even after half a century; that I still mourned the dead and still vividly felt the old fears of one persecuted and mercilessly hunted. And that, more than anything, convinced me that this book had to be written.

1

THE STORM GATHERS AND ERUPTS

'Look, I am 16 years old, surely it's time that I should start spending my holidays with my friends, not with you?' I was trying to convince my mother as we were having breakfast on a bright Sunday morning in late June 1939. Mother looked at Father, hoping that he would come to her rescue and relieve her from having to express an opinion. I could hardly believe my ears when I heard his reply.

'I see no reason why you shouldn't, as long as I know who you are going with.'

'With Wiktor,' I replied, and there were no objections. Wiktor Szmulewicz was my best friend, a few months older than me and virtually at the top of our class at school. He was mature and streetwise. Much of my worldly wisdom came from him. He claimed that he could read peoples' minds. Once, when we were afraid of being late for a play sponsored by our school, we decided to take a droshky.

'How much to *Teatr Miejski* [the City Theatre]?' Wiktor asked the cabby.

'One złoty.' This was almost half of our week's pocket money. Having no choice we jumped in.

'I am not happy and neither is the cabby,' Wiktor revealed as we drove off. 'Now he is worrying that he didn't ask me for more. I might have agreed. On the other hand, I am sure that, had I haggled, he would have knocked 20 groszys off the price.'

We lived in Łódź, Poland's second largest city, with over 600,000 inhabitants; I was born there on 31 December 1922. The German border was 100 miles to the south-west and Warsaw was 75 miles to the north-east. According to one writer, Łódź was the only town in the world that nobody had ever visited for pleasure. Its life started in earnest in the 1830s and it grew rapidly to become the centre of the cotton industry, hence its nickname Polish Manchester, adopted in the pre-war years, when Manchester was the world capital of the cotton industry. Streets running parallel to each other north to south and east to west formed a giant chessboard. In absence of any town planning regulations, mills – ugly red-brick buildings, several storeys high – had been erected helter-skelter anywhere. Each had a tall chimney spewing clouds of black smoke into the sky.

So I now tasted freedom for the first time in my life. It was wonderful! I could do what I liked without interference from adults. Wiktor and I chose a remote mountain resort, a hamlet, close to Kołomyja in the Eastern Carpathians, near the Romanian border. On arrival, we rented two rooms with balconies in a modest pension, a plain wooden building. During the day we went for long walks in the wild, unspoiled countryside – between rugged mountain peaks, along green pastures, through dark forests, inhaling balsam-laden mountain air, without meeting a soul other than the odd shepherd tending his flock. The deep silence was broken only by birdsong, by the bleating of sheep and by the gurgling of fast-flowing streams swollen by recent rains. We had to cross these streams on primitive footbridges, often just a single plank of wood. In the evenings we would play chess or bridge with newly made friends. One memorable evening Wiktor invited me to join him for a drink of vodka, not the ordinary 70 per cent proof variety, but a generous measure of a spirit almost twice that strength, used generally for medicinal purposes.

'Don't sip it, throw it against the back of your throat and swallow it in one gulp,' Wiktor instructed me, pretending that he was an old hand. My throat was on fire, the clear liquid had a foul taste and left me breathless for a while. But Wiktor insisted that this was the best way to prove one's manhood. So how could I refuse? We continued with other new experiences, such as smoking mint-flavoured cigarettes – all just to prove how independent and grown-up we had become.

Before returning home at the end of August I first took a train to join Mother in Krynica, a summer resort and spa in southern Poland. She was spending her holiday there in the company of my former governess and now our housekeeper, Nacia. They were staying in the luxurious Hotel Patria owned by the famous Polish tenor, Jan Kiepura, and his film-actress wife, Martha Eggert.

Mother was an attractive blonde, 40 years old, vivacious and witty. She had two great passions: dancing and playing gin rummy. During our previous long summer holidays, the three of us – Mother, Nacia and myself – used to stay in popular mountain resorts, usually Zakopane or Krynica, in some of their best hotels. Now and again, Father would join us for a few days. In the afternoons and early evenings we would all sit at a table in the hotel ballroom, sipping drinks and listening to the jazz band. An excellent dancer, light on her feet and attractive, Mother was never short of a dancing partner. She caused me great embarrassment whenever she refused to dance with someone she did not fancy. At home, she indulged in playing gin rummy with her parents and sisters every evening. I adored Mother, even though she spent little time with me during my childhood.

The journey to Krynica along the Polish border with Slovakia, which was by then already under German occupation, was long and monotonous. Disturbing thoughts kept going round and round n my mind. Fragments of the overheard grown-ups' conversations, of radio broadcasts, the newspaper reports of the last few months, newsreels seen on my Saturday afternoon visits to the cinema, all these combined to produce a feeling of insecurity, uncertainty, a dread of the future. Poland, our newly independent country, was wedged between its two sworn historical enemies: imperial Russia, in its new guise as the Soviet Union, and Hitler's Germany. I knew a fair bit about Hitler and his credo as expressed in *Mein Kampf*, a work permeated by the most virulent brand of anti-Semitism. I have not experienced anti-Semitism personally, but in Poland it was also tangible. I couldn't but be apprehensive reading the occasional reports in the papers describing the so-called 'pogroms', when a mob would attack Jewish inhabitants of a town, beat them up, smash windows of Jewish-owned shops, loot and wreak destruction. The police usually stood idly by and made no attempt to restore order; in some instances they actually prevented Jews from defending themselves and their property. What would happen to us if the Polish Nationalist Party, known as 'Endeks', should come to power? Or would war break out first? Could it become another world war? And what were Poland's chances? Since the betrayal of Czechoslovakia in Munich in 1938 we had German armies on our southern, western and northern borders, with the Soviet Red Army lined up in the east.

And thus one black thought chased another. In March 1938, after some political machinations, Hitler had annexed Austria into his Thousand Year Reich – what we knew as the infamous 'Anschluss'. My mother happened to be in Vienna at the time, on one of her annual shopping expeditions. She used to come back laden with surprise gifts. A model aeroplane was what I cherished most; that was also where our two pet dogs, a Pekinese called Geisha and a white terrier called Puppi, came from. This time all she brought back was her fear. 'All over town,' she reported, 'wherever I went, I couldn't escape that constant chant: *"Deutschland erwache, Juda verrecke*! [Germany awake, perish the Jewry!]" And then I could not believe my eyes: a band of SA men (*Sturmabteilung*, Nazi Paramilitary Storm Troopers), in their brown uniforms with swastika armbands, stood in a busy street, surrounded by a crowd of civilians. They were all laughing at a group of smartly dressed Jewish men and women, down on their knees, being made to scrub the pavement by their tormentors. Again and again, during my short stay in Vienna, I kept coming across this dreadful spectacle. It was only my lapel badge of a Polish flag provided by the Polish Embassy that saved me from being molested.'

That terrible slogan would not leave my mind. Even the wagon's wheels kept rhythmically repeating it: '*Deutschland erwache, Juda verrecke*!'

And then, suddenly I recalled Hitler's speech, broadcast on 30 January 1939:

> *I have often made prophesies and people laughed at me . . . Today I am going to make another prophesy: should the Jewish international financiers succeed in involving the nations in another war, the result will be the destruction of European Jewry.*

Was this to be our fate if we ever fell into German hands?

At the start of 1939 no one knew where Hitler would strike next. He had already grabbed Austria and Sudetenland. His promise that Sudetenland would be his last territorial claim had already been proved worthless. On 15 March 1939 German troops occupied the rump of Czechoslovakia. This finally brought an end to appeasement in the West. It was only at this stage that the British Prime Minister, Neville Chamberlain, realised what kind of enemy the democracies were facing. Britain offered guarantees to Poland and on 31 March Neville Chamberlain informed the British Parliament that in the case of a threat to Polish independence, Great Britain and France would come to her aid. Events were now moving rapidly. At the end of April Hitler appeared before the Reichstag. This time he demanded that Poland give up her rights to the Free City of Danzig (guaranteed in the treaty of Versailles), that the city be returned to Germany and that an extraterritorial highway be built across the so-called Polish Corridor, the Polish territory separating Germany proper from East Prussia. Poland categorically rejected these demands and Germany responded by abrogating the 1934 German–Polish Non-Aggression Treaty. Our leaders displayed remarkable sangfroid in the face of German pressure.

Out of the train window I spied large detachments of our soldiers in horse-drawn vehicles or on horseback and the occasional horse-drawn gun raising dust on a typical Polish dirt road. Not an armoured vehicle, not even a lorry in sight. This is the same army which fought the 1920 war, I thought. Such a far cry from the motorised columns of the German Army, their tanks, their mobile guns, their totally modern weapons.

Only later did I realise how the Polish government must have underestimated the sophistication and overwhelming power of the modern German Army, having also a totally unwarranted confidence in the effectiveness of the infantry and cavalry, the bulk of our Forces. I heard at some stage that the British military attaché in Warsaw, when asked by London about our frontier defences, sent back his laconic report: 'There aren't any.' Were we really ready for anything more than sabre-rattling?

We got back to Łódż on 27 August, a week before school was due to start. This was to be my last year at school before *matura*, the Polish baccalaureate. Father met us at the station and told us that there was a surprise waiting for us at home. As we were sitting down to tea the door to the drawing room opened and my brother Michał walked in with a young girl I had never seen before. Michał was 20, blond, tall and good-looking. He was actually supposed to be in Manchester now, getting ready for his second year at the University. There was not much brotherly love lost between us; in fact we disliked one another. He always poked fun at me, calling me names that hurt, he was a bully. At school his performance had been uninspiring and he needed to be helped by a tutor at home. He played trumpet in the school band and just to annoy me he would bring the instrument home and play it on purpose whenever I wanted to go to sleep or practise the piano. As a child he had been hard to handle. During the school holidays my parents had usually packed him off to a holiday camp, where strict discipline was enforced, something my parents had failed to do. My father hoped that after university he would join the family business.

Our second surprise was Michał's girlfriend, Joan Parkinson, who had come with him. Both had arrived the day before our return. Joan was the daughter of Father's English business friend and she and Michał were never more than a foot apart. She was about 18 and looked like a blond doll just out of its box. Father was fuming.

'Joan is going back to England tomorrow,' he announced shortly after we arrived. 'The war may start any day now and Michał has no right to put her life at risk!' Thus the heart-broken Michał took Joan to the railway station the following day, but decided that he himself would stay at home for a few more days.

I was surprised to hear Father talk seriously about the likelihood of war. He was such an eternal optimist. As it happened, four weeks earlier, on their way home from England where they had spent a short holiday, my parents stopped for a day in Brussels with Father's sister and her family.

The first question Uncle Abek asked my Father on meeting them at the station was: 'Jakub, it looks like the Germans are about to invade Poland, have you made any contingency plans for such a day?'

Mother could never forget Father's reply in Yiddish: '*Abek, gesund bist di*? [Abek, are you feeling OK?]' as he changed the subject.

From one day to the next the news was getting increasingly disturbing. Only three days before our return home a partial mobilisation was announced. Reading the press and listening to the radio I was becoming increasingly concerned, though I was not yet frightened. Wasn't our eventual victory after all assured? Weren't the German bulletins nothing but propaganda?

In response to the appeal for volunteers broadcast by Jan Kwapinski, the Mayor of Łódż, crowds of people were digging trenches all over the town to serve as air-raid shelters. The diggers worked with enthusiasm and good humour. Our maid was busy masking tape across all the windows to prevent them shattering during air raids. I queued for a gas mask and then carried it with me for days.

On the afternoon of 31 August 1939, the day before the war broke out, I was sitting in an armchair reading a book. My room was both a bedroom and a study. A built-in wall unit in rich cherry wood, a wardrobe and bookshelves with sliding glass panels filled the whole length of the wall to the right of the door. Under the window opposite the unit stood a desk in matching wood. A deep sofa that served as a bed at night stood against the wall facing the entrance. Heavy damask curtains reached down to the parquet floor which was adorned by an oriental carpet. Outside the window the arrival of every new season was heralded by the changing appearance of the trees, like actors wearing different costumes for each new scene. I got annoyed with the buzzing flies beating against my window and decided to catch them and feed them to the fish in my aquarium. But then I changed my mind. At a time like this, when I wanted to throw myself before divine mercy as never before, how could I show no mercy to other living creatures?

Events were moving fast. All reservists up to the age of 40 were ordered to report to recruitment offices. The German threats were obviously being taken seriously. And yet I did not feel any fear. With no previous experience of war I had no idea of the infinite misery and human suffering it could bring. I also naively believed that righteous people would be spared and I hoped that I could count myself among them. Such childish faith would soon melt away.

On the morning of the following day, 1 September 1939, I switched on the radio. What we feared had happened. The German forces encircling Poland crossed its frontiers from four directions: East Prussia in the north, Pomerania in the north-west, Silesia in the south-west and Slovakia in the south. The Nazi Action Groups, Polish citizens of German origin, the so-called 'fifth column', were assisting the invaders, shooting our people without discrimination and spreading terror. The German army was advancing in spite of the valiant resistance of our troops, and enemy aircraft were attacking our cities – Warsaw, Częstochowa, Poznań and Cracow amongst many others. Lines of communication, bridges, railways, airfields were all targeted, as well as the civilian population. As if to confirm the news we suddenly heard the piercing wail of the siren, urging us to seek shelter.

We lived in one of the most luxurious blocks of flats in Łódż. My father had it built two years earlier in the smart part of town, almost opposite Sienkiewicza Park. He imported the best ceramic tiles from Italy to cover its façade, but never thought of providing an air-raid shelter. Our spacious cellar had to serve as one. Unlike many basements it did not smell of damp and we sat comfortably on large slabs of concrete together with our neighbours from the other flats. We all tried to put on a brave face, but as the roar of engines and noise of explosions came closer, we would freeze in terror until the all-clear was sounded. We soon got used to sleeping with our clothes on, instantly ready to grab our gas masks and rush downstairs. As soon as it got dark we drew the heavy curtains across the windows so that no light would show outside. The street lamps were off, the streets looked dark and deserted.

For two long days, glued to the radio, we waited for news of the help promised by our Western allies. Surely they would not leave us to our fate, the way they had left Austria and Czechoslovakia not so long ago! At last, on 3 September, France and Britian declared war on Germany. Our spirits rose. But as days went by, there was no news of fighting in the West and it became clear that our allies were not going to launch the promised offensive. Meanwhile the German Luftwaffe bombers kept coming back and dropping bombs on us.

Our radio broadcasts continued to assure us that Polish forces were resisting and repelling the enemy. It was only later that we learned how we never had a chance to stop the Germans, in spite of the boastful statements of our own high command. The enemy had 2,600 tanks against the Poles' 150, and 2,000 modern warplanes against our 400 mainly old aircraft.

Friends would drop in now and again and every single event of the day would be dissected. We talked and we listened. Endless conversations revolved around the news broadcasts, the gossip and the often conflicting stories of eyewitnesses describing vividly what they had just seen or heard. There were voices of hope and voices of despair. We talked about the danger of gas attacks, about civilian casualties caused by the German Luftwaffe's indiscriminate attacks, about atrocities committed by the invaders and by their Polish-born compatriots, the *Volksdeutsche* (who were amongst the descendants of German settlers, some of whom came to live in Poland as long as 600 years ago).

On the night of 5 September a sudden panic seized Łódź. I woke up before dawn and saw my parents looking anxiously out of our third-floor window in the direction of the main road, Sienkiewicza Street. An endless procession of people was heading east. There were the rich and the poor, young and old, men, women and children all with a look of despair on their faces. Some were carrying bundles and rucksacks on their backs, others were pushing wheelbarrows or carts filled with food, bedding and clothing. Empty prams were stuffed to the brim with their belongings. The wealthier, dressed in smarter clothes, travelled in horse-drawn wagons, coaches, cabs and, in a few cases, in motorcars.

I heard Father's voice. He must have been listening to the radio for most of the night. He was talking to our neighbours. Like most people they wanted to get away as fast and as far as they could. It was now evident that the Polish Command had given up its plans to defend our frontiers and that Łódź had been abandoned by the army and by the city authorities. Rumour had it that the Germans were only a few miles away.

'What are we to do?' cried Mother, on the verge of hysteria.

'We certainly cannot stay here,' replied Father. 'We have to get away from the Germans. We ought to make our way towards the Romanian border and get out of Poland.'

That frontier was more than 300 miles away.

'And what about my parents?' asked Mother, choking with tears. 'What about my sisters and their families? What about your family?'

'There is nothing we can do for them. We must leave now! There is no time to go and find them, all we can do now is look after ourselves,' Father replied.

This was the first time in my life when I realised that only the selfish would survive, but it wasn't the last time. In the ensuing years I witnessed again and again the hard struggle between the opposing forces of self-preservation and loyalty and love.

My brother walked into the room. 'I am not coming with you,' he said. 'I shall make my own way to Warsaw with Uncle Edek and then try for a dash to England.'

Mother tried to preserve some calm but found it difficult. Arguments and counter-arguments followed, but nothing would change my brother's mind.

'There is no time to be lost,' said Father, 'we must hurry.' Just before going downstairs to the garage he explained to Mother and Nacia which essentials to load into our car for the long journey. While they were packing I rushed to my wardrobe and put on my school cadet uniform, the khaki trousers and tunic with a leather belt.

'You are not wearing those!' cried Mother. 'The Germans will shoot you on sight if they stop us.'

'I shall certainly wear them,' I replied. 'You will see – Polish soldiers will treat us quite differently if they see me in uniform. And anyway I shall join the army as soon as I have a chance.' I won the argument.

There was an old black Chevrolet saloon in our basement garage that used to be at the disposal of Father's sales manager. Our brand-new Buick, the car that made people turn around admiringly in the streets of Łódż, had been requisitioned a few days earlier by the army, like most other roadworthy vehicles in the country.

It did not take long to pack the car and we were ready to go; the four of us, Mother, Father, Nacia and myself got inside. With Father behind the wheel, the heavily loaded Chevrolet drove out into the street, slowly making its way through the crowds of refugees. Soon we were out of town. The sun was shining in the cloudless sky, and the Polish countryside in its late summer glory did not seem to be affected by the upheaval brought about by the folly of man. Long columns of people were making their way in the same direction. Some of them tried to stop us, pleading for a lift, although there was visibly no room for more passengers.

Suddenly there was a roar of engines low overhead. Father stopped the car, we ran out and dropped down flat in a ditch. There was a rat-tat-tat of machinegun fire and a German plane flew past us virtually at treetop level. We could clearly see not only the black crosses on its hull, but even the pilot's face. More planes followed, strafing everyone in sight. It was over in a few seconds and yet it had felt like a lifetime. Bodies were strewn on the ground, screams reverberated in our ears. We rushed back to the car and drove off. My heart was pounding. This terrifying experience was repeated several times during our journey.

Our progress between the attacks was painfully slow. We had to stop at several Polish army posts, but after a short exchange of questions and answers, we were allowed to go on. By mid afternoon we passed Kielce, some 80 miles south-east of Łódź, full of hope that in a day or two we would reach the Romanian border, the only available escape route. We had just left Kielce when a complete stranger leapt out in front of the car and tried to stop us. Before we managed to pick up speed he jumped onto the running-board and refused to get off, determined to get a lift. The car was now progressing more slowly, its engine hardly coping with the extra burden. We went on like this for a few miles when suddenly a crunching noise coming from somewhere in the back made Father stop the car. He got out, looked underneath it and his face sagged with a kind of hopelessness that I had never seen before. 'The axle is broken,' he said. We all knew that this meant the end of our journey.

Father went looking for help, leaving us to wait by the roadside. A few hundred metres away he came across a farmer's cottage. A sturdy fellow appeared in the doorway and after some negotiations he disappeared, then returned with another man, the local blacksmith-cum-mechanic. He too looked underneath the car, then shook his head and walked away promising to fetch some help from a garage. After what seemed like an age he returned with yet another man. This time they both crawled under the car and a tapping noise proved that some kind of inspection was taking place. 'Nothing doing,' said the first man, emerging and shaking his head, 'the axle is broken, it's beyond repair.' There was no question of finding a replacement within a reasonable distance and our car had to be abandoned to join many other wrecks littering the countryside.

We walked away in silence, aware that our chance of escape had gone. The farmer agreed to give us temporary shelter, while Father went seeking a horse and cart for sale, hoping against hope that perhaps we could reach our destination by other means. The four of us spent the night in makeshift beds, sharing one large room with the farmer, his wife and several children. I fell asleep straight away and did not wake till the following morning.

The day was bright, we ate our breakfast and I went out to have a look at the farm. I came across a large plum orchard, with hundreds of ripe plums littering the ground. They were everywhere and no one was picking the fruit. I suppose that there were no buyers and there was nothing one could do with it. I tasted the plums, they were delicious and I gorged myself on them. From time to time the silence of the peaceful countryside was broken by the sound of planes high up in the sky, either on their way to targets or coming back from their bombing missions, but thankfully not interested in the farm and its inhabitants. In the evening we gathered around the radio. The Polish army was outflanked on all fronts; by the end of the second week of September Warsaw, the capital, was surrounded. On 17 September another disaster befell us: the Soviet army marched into Poland from the east without warning, making any further attempts at successful resistance impossible. It also cut off our last route of escape. The USSR, we heard, had joined forces with Nazi Germany by a prior secret agreement. Poland was to be divided in two between these new allies. Russian troops were already advancing westwards, meeting little resistance from the few Polish battalions not deployed fighting the Germans in the west, north and south. I remembered the words ascribed to Marshal Rydz-Śmigły, the Commanding Officer of the Polish forces, to the effect that there was little to choose between the Russians and the Germans: the Germans would annihilate our bodies and the Russians destroy our souls.

Father decided that we would stay where we were until the fighting was over and then try to make our way back to Łódź. He believed that his many German friends in the city would help protect us from the invaders. In any case, there was nothing else we could now do. For a few more days we went on eating plums and admiring the countryside, its brilliant yellows and greens contrasting against the bright blue sky. The war was effectively over. Only Warsaw was resisting the German invaders, defying the onslaught of bombers, tanks and ground forces. Russian and German troops met along the Bug River and rumours began to reach us of Russian and German atrocities.

2

THE NEW ORDER

A horse and cart were soon ready to take the four of us and our luggage back to Łódż. The roads were now empty. Only abandoned cars, shattered armoured vehicles, lorries and vans – many just burned-out wrecks – remained as grim reminders of the recent fighting. Numerous army trucks packed with German soldiers passed by, but no one took any interest in us.

Two days later we were back in Łódż. Curious, I looked around. The streets were largely deserted but for the occasional groups of Germans in green, khaki, brown or black uniforms and civilians with red armbands showing black swastikas against a white background. Now and again, an army lorry rumbled by, with two rows of soldiers facing one another under a canopy, rifles between their knees, steel helmets on their heads, grim faces beneath them. I recalled happier times when we used to drive back from a weekend in the country along the same route and all I had to worry about was the prospect of school the next morning. That school I had disliked and feared. Now a different kind of fear assailed me, that of an animal trapped in the lair of a predator about to devour it.

'Let's go home,' said Father, 'before anyone takes it.'

'No, no,' protested my mother, 'we must call on my parents first. I have to see whether they are all right, whether anything has happened to them,' and Father agreed.

We made our way to 24 Główna Street, a large block of flats built around a long courtyard with a small garden in the middle of it, owned by my grandfather and only half a mile away from where we lived. My father paid off the farmer for the transport, we took our belongings and climbed the stairs to the first floor off the courtyard.

Grandfather opened the door. He looked as stunned as if he had seen a ghost. My grandmother appeared behind him. What followed was total confusion: tears, embraces, everybody talking at the same time, no one getting a chance to finish a sentence.

Grandfather, a man in his early 60s, was immaculately dressed as usual in a three-piece suit, a white shirt with a stiff collar and a dark spotted tie. Mother called him *arbiter elegantiarum*. He was of slender build and completely bald, with a rather thin, slightly hooked nose and lively dark eyes. He was born into an orthodox Jewish family. As a child, like all orthodox Jews, he sported curly sideboards, wore a stiff black peaked cap, a *kapota* or silken black coat reaching just below his knees, and long white stockings. He looked just like his ghetto ancestors and spoke only Yiddish. In his early 20s he decided to 'assimilate' – he changed his garb, learned to speak Polish and started mixing with Christians. From modest beginnings, he prospered in his weaving business, which he sold after retiring and invested the money in the apartment house, where he lived with his wife and their son, Edek. My grandmother, with her large round face and thick, silver-white hair was of the same age as her husband, but looked much older. She was stout, quite tall and her somewhat hairy face used to put me off kissing her. Frequently unwell and unsteady on her feet, she was treated almost as an invalid. She found speaking Yiddish easier than Polish. She shared Mother's passion for gin rummy.

Anxious to hear the latest news, Father, Mother and Nacia followed my grandparents into the sitting room to the right of the entrance door, while I turned left into the dining room to play the piano. As I was about to start playing, I heard a doorbell ring, the sound of the front door opening and loud German voices. Then the doors were slammed with a bang. I was too frightened to move. A minute later, Mother rushed in, relieved to see me, but in tears.

'Thank God you are here!' she exclaimed. 'They took your father away,' she sobbed, and nothing I said would console her.

'He will be back soon,' I kept repeating, trying to sound confident. I followed her back into the sitting room, to wait for Father's return.

'You don't know how lucky you were,' said Nacia to me, 'being in another room when those beasts barged in. They would have taken you away too.'

In the meantime Grandfather continued his interrupted tale of recent events. 'When the German army arrived they did not bother civilians for the first few days, but then the German police, the SS[1] troops and our local Germans, the now-armed *Volksdeutsche*, took over the streets and Jew hunting began in earnest.' Many of the *Volksdeutsche* could hardly speak any German, most had German names and were Lutherans, unlike the majority of Poles who were Catholics.

'Now,' my grandfather continued, 'they welcome the invaders with open arms and are being rewarded with the looted property and lucrative jobs in administration and industry, taken away from Poles and Jews. They are responsible for some of the worst excesses perpetrated against us.' As the founders of Łódż were German weavers, it was not surprising that some 20 per cent of the city's inhabitants claimed to be German.

'Don't worry,' concluded Grandfather, turning to Mother and me, 'Jakub will come back. So far they have not held the detained Jews for long.'

At 50, my father was a handsome man of medium height and build. He had an open, jolly face and bright blue eyes and his receding hair made his forehead appear even higher than it was. Like many other Jews he had a hooked nose. With his upright posture and immaculate dress, he radiated self-confidence and looked exactly what he was – a captain of industry. He was a self-made man, the son of a struggling soda-water manufacturer with 12 children, who, like other strictly orthodox Jews, was separated by walls of language and custom from the Christian community. At 18 he left home and started work as a travelling salesman, covering large areas of Western Russia and Romania. He used to tell us about the Russian peasants he had travelled with in the same train compartment, bursting into deeply felt melodies, sung spontaneously in four parts. He told us about the Romanian drivers who would stop their train in the middle of nowhere and refuse to continue the journey until bribed by the passengers. Although the only school he ever went to was a *Cheder* – a purely religious establishment, where no language apart from

---

[1] SS – Police organisation independent of party and state, responsible to Hitler alone.

Yiddish was ever spoken and where only Hebrew texts were studied
– he managed to acquire a good command of Russian, German and
Polish. An avid reader, he became immersed in German literature.
Penniless to start with, he created a large textile manufacturing
business, employing hundreds of people. He was not easy to work for,
he was intolerant of other peoples' mistakes and with little
provocation he would scream and shout at his employees – not
unusual behaviour in pre-war Poland. At the same time he was
incredibly generous. Any relative of his or Mother's who happened to
be out of work would be found a job in his business. This in turn
would lead to incessant arguments, as Father invariably blamed
Mother for any of her relatives' shortcomings. Mother did not
consider her relatives any less competent than his, so loud altercations
would ensue, mainly in Yiddish, so that I would not understand.
Father belonged to the Masonic Lodge of Odd Fellows and on
Monday evenings, to Mother's great annoyance, he attended sittings –
Mother called them 'lie-downs' – which lasted late into the night.
Every year Father would go on at least a month's holiday abroad on
his own, but would never spend holidays with us. I hardly knew him.

Two hours went by before the doorbell rang. I could hardly
recognise Father when he walked in. He looked a broken man. His
hair had been roughly shaved off, his normally sun-tanned face was
pale. He told us how he was beaten and kicked, made to brush
floors, and how his captors, the Łódż *Volksdeutsche*, whose day of
triumph had arrived, laughed and insulted him.

'Yes, I know,' said Grandfather. 'Every day we hear similar
stories. Jews are stopped in the streets, dragged out of their
apartments, pulled out of trams and buses and forced into
humiliating work, such as cleaning latrines with their bare hands.
And as you see, the tormentors shave their victims' hair, cut off their
beards, subject them to every kind of indignity and ridicule they can
think of, and on top of that, they beat them up before letting them
go. And it's not even the uniformed Germans, but mostly civilians,
who do it with such relish.'

Obviously we were at the mercy of a ruthless enemy bent on
destroying us. There was no escape and not much hope; it seemed all
we could do was to resign ourselves to our fate.

We took leave of my grandparents and made our way home, about half a mile away in Świętokrzyska Street, a quiet cul-de-sac off Sienkiewicza Street. Our street took its name from the Church of Święty Krzyż or 'Saint Cross', at the corner of Sienkiewicza and Przejazd Streets, about 200 yards from where we lived. It was built in 1860, in the neo-Romanesque style, but its construction had been interrupted by the arrest and exile to Siberia for 'unpatriotic activity' of Father Jakubowicz, the priest behind the project, by the Russian occupants. The church, built on the plan of a cross, consisted of one long main aisle with a shorter one across it. Now, with the sun low on the horizon, the copper cross shone brightly above the slender octagonal spire.

Tall, majestic poplars, their leaves now just barely turning yellow, surrounded our five-storey apartment house, shielding it from the two-storey villa next door. Across the road there was an empty, grassed-over space, with a bench here and there for the weary walker. An iron gate stood guard over the path leading to our front door and to the sloping ramp to the garage in the basement. There was another entrance with a separate staircase for tradesmen and servants.

An armed soldier stood in front of the gate. He let us in. The janitor, Bogdan, a Catholic Pole who lived with his family on the ground floor, saw us returning and, visibly moved, came out to greet us. 'Most of the flats have been abandoned,' he explained. Father enquired about Jan Szyf, his close friend who lived on the second floor, and about Mr Gotlib from the third floor. 'They have not returned,' said Bogdan. 'Their apartments have now been assigned to German officers who have already started moving in, but, thank God, yours is still unoccupied.' He helped to carry our luggage and we took the lift to the third floor. Our five-room apartment looked exactly as we had left it, nothing seemed to have changed at all.

Father soon recovered from his ordeal and our life began returning to some kind of normality. The news on the radio was not encouraging, though. Disheartened, we vainly waited for our allies to open hostilities in the West, but neither the French nor the British seemed to have the heart for fighting. Indeed, instead of bombs, they were dropping propaganda leaflets on German cities. The Russians were now in control of Eastern Poland up to the Bug River, while the rest of the country, with the exception of Warsaw, was in German hands. Finally, after three weeks of heroic fighting and ruthless destruction, the defenders surrendered the heavily bombarded and burning capital. It had held out until 27 September, a great deal longer than the other European capitals – Copenhagen, Oslo, Amsterdam, Brussels, Paris, Belgrade and Athens – that were to surrender to the Germans later in the war with hardly any resistance.

During the long evenings, when the *Polizeistunde* (curfew) forced us to stay indoors, some of the German officers from the adjoining apartment would call on us and hold long discussions with Father. They were impressed by his wide knowledge of German literature and by his magnetic personality. They kept expressing regret for the treatment of Jews by the local Germans, the SA, SS and the police. They were appalled, they said, by what they saw, but were unable to intervene. They assured us that as long as we stayed indoors, we would not be harmed, as the building was now guarded and the guard on duty at the entrance was to keep strangers, marauders or predators out.

Father's business was put in the hands of an administrator, in the person of Herr Sachs, a *Volksdeutsche*. He was to dispose of the production according to the instructions of his German superiors. He found Father's assistance invaluable and in return showed him a great deal of consideration. Thanks to him no one dared to come into the factory or to the office, where my parents were working, to molest the staff. Every morning Herr Sachs would pick up Father, and occasionally Mother, in his car and would bring them home in the evening too.

Uncle Edek had been my idol throughout my childhood. We attended the same school, but just as I was starting my secondary education, he was completing his last form. He turned 28 at the outbreak of the war. Dark-haired, tall, slim, of athletic build and a marvellous swimmer, he was a true ladies' man. He was very conscious of his good looks, but even to me it seemed that no woman would be able to resist his masculine charm and sex appeal. There was one drawback: his looks were in no way matched by his enthusiasm for work. Sent by his parents to study engineering at the University of Liége in Belgium, he spent his time having fun and failed his qualifying exams. On Edek's return his father, my grandfather, set him up in business, but in spite of the family's help, the enterprise never succeeded. Edek married the daughter of Mr Alt, a wealthy woollen fabric manufacturer. Mr Alt was prudent enough to have invested some of his fortune in an apartment block in Allenby Street in Tel-Aviv; when the war broke out he was lucky enough to have found himself with his wife in Palestine, out of harm's way. When Edek married her, Mala Alt was 20. She was intelligent and well-educated, but plain, with a spotty face. My brother Michał, whose role model Edek had always been, and who saw a woman's good looks as her only important asset, never forgave Edek for marrying such a plain girl who was certainly no match for the glamorous women Edek used to go out with. However, what she lacked in good looks Mala made up for in the worldly wisdom that Edek lacked. A few weeks before the war broke out, Mala gave birth to a baby girl whom they called Krysia.

One day early in October, shortly after our return, my brother came home unexpectedly, though without Edek, with whom he had left for Warsaw earlier in September; they had lost touch somewhere on the way. A few days later Mala brought us the shattering news: Edek was imprisoned in the Radogoszcz concentration camp in a suburb, a notorious place dreaded by all. Mala, in a state of shock, was now left alone with their baby daughter.

Hard as they tried, my parents could not convince Michał that he should not venture outdoors without a good reason. He took no notice. His self-confidence bordered on arrogance and he had no fear. One day Michał came home, his usually spotless clothes covered in mud, his hair dishevelled, his face covered in bruises. He had been apprehended just outside our house by some German youths and taken next door to the new headquarters of a German organisation, where he was forced to scrub floors with a toothbrush. 'Make them shine like your Jewish balls!' they screamed at him. Before they let him go they made him clean the toilets with his bare hands and manhandled and humiliated him in every possible way.

The next morning he bade us goodbye and, ignoring our parents' pleas, left home to venture on a seemingly impossible journey back to England.

The academic year started late and I decided to go back to my old school. But even getting there had become hazardous. Every morning I would meet Wiktor and another school friend, Tadek Wolpert, about 100 yards from my home, opposite the entrance to Sienkiewicza Park. The park was a peaceful island of lawns interspersed with oak trees; it had a small lake in the centre, where narrow paths converged from all directions. On the other side of it, a few hundred yards away, was the entrance to Kiliński Street, with its ugly dwelling houses, thankfully screened from sight by the tall poplars. The park, once popular with young mothers and nannies pushing prams or looking after the older children playing with toy boats on the lake, was now deserted. The three of us walked in single file, the one in front looking out for Germans ready to pounce on Jews and the one at the back constantly turning his head to see what danger might be lurking behind. At the slightest suspicion of a trap we would repair to the nearest building and hide in the entrance or try to make ourselves scarce round a corner.

Walking with my friends north along Sienkiewicza Street, we passed large tenement houses erected before the First World War, designed to pack as many rooms as possible into the smallest area. A typical building here presented to the street an imposing four- or five-storey frontage of considerable architectural interest with fine masonry carvings and impressive balconies. Behind it, a 40-metre-long courtyard was surrounded on the remaining three sides by ugly, plain dwellings – a gigantic, hideous pit, several storeys deep, with its warren of staircases and doors to cellars, storage spaces and coal bunkers, which, however, could offer many useful hiding places. The rich lived in the front and the poor in the wings and in the back. Each apartment block had a live-in janitor, often with a large family, who performed the usual caretaking duties.

Further along Sienkiewicza Street at the approach to the railway station, Łódż Fabryczna, we would cross the street, turn right to get around the station and enter Narutowicza Street. This was an open space, providing little opportunity to hide or retreat in the face of any unwelcome encounter.

The Łódż Fabryczna station building had an imposing 50-foot-long façade with the name of the station spelled out in large letters. Many trains to various parts of the country started from here and it used to be an exciting point of departure for my holidays. In front of the station there was a small park with a few linden trees and a bare, neglected lawn, favoured by winos and other down-and-outs.

Having crossed Narutowicza Street, a wide main avenue with tramlines in the middle, we would turn right. My eyes would usually dwell with nostalgia on a large building on my left, where my family used to live before moving to our present flat. Our school was almost at the end of Narutowicza Street and it would take us all of five minutes to reach it from this point. On the way we passed on our left Plac Dąbrowski with the sand-coloured modern edifice of the main Law Courts, its large colonnade crowning the wide stairs leading to an impressive entrance. Plac Dąbrowski was another dangerous area with no place to hide and we did our best to leave it behind us in the shortest possible time. In an ugly, densely built-up industrial town like Łódż even Plac Dąbrowski, an airy space with a large green lawn in its centre, a few sad spruces and a number of usually empty benches, provided some attraction. Unfortunately, at the time, the aesthetic qualities of my city were far from my mind, as all I could think of was how to evade possible tormentors. Never before had I felt like a quarry and experienced a recurrent fear of such intensity.

The last section of Narutowicza Street between the law courts and my school bordered Staszica Park, the favourite place of my first nanny, Saba. While watching the three-year-old riding his tricycle, she could not foresee the agonies his older self would experience on his way to school some 13 years later.

Inside the school we were safe. Classes went on in the same way as before the war. Some of the younger teachers were missing, possibly taken prisoner or killed in the war, but almost all my friends were back. I now enjoyed school as never before. It was going to be my last year before matriculation; I was doing better than I ever had and was particularly keen on science subjects.

On 7 November it was announced that Łódż was to become part of

Wartegau, an eastern province of Germany, and that it was to be renamed Litzmannstadt in order to leave no trace of its Polish identity. One of the immediate effects was that Jews were forbidden to walk on the main artery, Piotrkowska Street. My friend, Tadek Wolpert, lived with his family at number 117, and had to pay five złoty, five times the usual cab fare, for a pass. It was further decreed that all Poles and Jews had to hand in their radios, and thus our remaining link with the outside world was cut. Jews were also ordered to step aside in the streets, giving way to uniformed Germans, while Jewish shops were made to display prominently a special sign denoting their ownership. No Jew was allowed to attend school. A week later the news reached us that the magnificent synagogue in Kościuszko Street had been burned down.

We plunged even deeper into the Middle Ages, when on 16 November the Germans issued an order forcing all Jews to wear a ten-centimetre-wide yellow band on their right arm to distinguish them from non-Jews, or 'Aryans' in Nazi terminology. By now I ought to have become fed up of suffering from a sense of injustice, but this new shock affected me badly. I was to be branded as someone belonging to a subhuman species for all to see and deprived of my remaining human rights. What had I done to deserve such humiliation? Barbarians had lawlessly invaded our land and were punishing us for an accident of our ancestry. I felt ashamed of being seen with a yellow band on my arm and frightened of the tormentors who would now find it easy to identify me. Forbidden to attend school, I decided to stay indoors and read, think and play the piano.

Winter was approaching. Brown leaves, tossed by the winds, were now lying thickly on the ground and before long would disappear under the cover of snow. These familiar sights seemed to prove that the world had remained unchanged, in spite of our enemy's efforts to turn it upside down. I tried to convince myself that what I was experiencing was only a nightmare from which I would wake up one day. I had to believe that real human values and moral laws, like the rules of nature, would remain unchanged.

Branded as a Jew I needed to review my links with the Jewish religion. Ours was not a very religious household. We did not observe Jewish dietary laws, my parents worked and I attended school on Saturdays. We went to the synagogue only five or six times a year on the most important holy days. As Father preferred to be a big fish in a little pond, we belonged to a small synagogue housed in a modest hall in an old people's home in Sterlinga (formerly Nowo Targowa) Street, a few doors away from where we had lived until 1936. The synagogue, like many other charities, had benefited from Father's generosity and he was well-known and respected by its members. By the time I was 13 we had moved house and joined another synagogue in Pomorska Street, next to a Jewish technical school. It was more spacious and a great deal less crowded. In accordance with Jewish tradition, Mother, with all the other women, sat separately from men on the balcony, while I sat downstairs, next to Father, close to the Ark.

There is a belief among Jews that on Yom Kippur, the Day of Atonement, the most important religious festival of the year, their fate for the year that follows is determined. As we stood praying next to each other, Father drew my attention to his favourite prayer:

> On Yom Kippur we need to consider how judgement will be sealed for all who pass away and for all who are born; for all who live and for all who die; for those who complete their normal span and for those who do not; for those who perish by fire or water, by the violence of man or beast, by hunger or thirst, by disaster, plague and execution . . .

How prophetic these words were when recited on the last Day of Atonement before the war . . .

3

WE ARE REFUGEES

We knew from German newspapers and from what our German neighbours told us that hardly anything was happening on the Western front. No real fighting was taking place (this period would be referred to later as the 'phoney war') but propaganda flourished: the Allies continued raining leaflets onto German cities.

In Łódź snow had fallen. It covered the city with a white blanket and not only did it completely transform the roofs, trees and grey pavements into the magic of an Andersen tale, but it muffled all sounds and, for a while, turned my home town into an enchanted land. It was snowing heavily on the day of Monday, 11 December 1939. I woke up and one look out of the window made me feel strangely excited. Late in the evening I sat down at the piano and played Beethoven's 'Sonata Pathétique'.

Mother always said that on hearing her play 'Für Elise' Father fell in love with her. She gave up the piano soon after the wedding, having, I suspect, achieved her purpose. Unlike my mother, I was not taught to play the piano for matrimonial reasons, but because it was fashionable for children of the 'intelligentsia' to play a musical instrument, usually either the piano or violin. I started learning at the age of six and my teacher, a man called Juliusz Meistermann, considered me a truly talented pupil right from the start. 'Professor' Meistermann, as he used to introduce himself, claimed to have graduated from that Mecca of pianists, the Moscow Conservatoire. He was a good-looking man in his early 30s, with curly brown hair and, being very short-sighted, he wore a pair of thick pince-nez secured by a golden clip to the bridge of his nose, where it left a deep red mark. He was in the habit of taking them off every few minutes to wipe the lenses. He regarded himself as the best piano teacher in Łódź. Whenever he wanted to display his virtuosity, he would play the same opening bars of Tchaikovsky's 'Piano Concerto in B-flat', a spectacular cascade of giant chords, with both hands, providing the accompaniment to this rousing tune, in the absence of a Symphony Orchestra, by singing. To this day I do not know why he always limited himself to the introductory theme.

By the time I was 11 or 12, 'Professor' Meistermann would devote a large part of his lesson to explicit descriptions of his amorous adventures with many women, who could not resist him. These tales impressed me as much as his accounts of the famous 'Miracle on the Vistula' battle of 1920, in which, as a captain, he claimed to have contributed to the defeat of the Soviet Red Army, who heavily outnumbered the newly formed Polish army. In reality the Polish victory did thwart the attempt of the Soviets to cross the Vistula river and thus stopped them taking the revolution to the simmering cauldron of vanquished Germany and then further west. The battle, classed with 'The Decisive Battles'[1] by General J.F.C. Fuller, had been commemorated by a great Polish artist in a giant painting displayed in the Warsaw National Art Gallery. Almost every schoolboy owned a postcard with its reproduction. When I asked 'Captain' Meistermann whether he could identify himself amongst the throng of soldiers, their heads no larger than pinheads and hardly visible through the confusion and smoke of the battle, short-sighted as he was, he had no difficulty in doing so. I was enormously impressed.

I worked hard at the piano but would easily lose patience with it when I hit a wrong note. On such occasions, in a fit of temper, I would stop, select the offending key and, as punishment, plunge a penknife into its wooden side. I must have found the procedure effective as I went on with it for quite a while. In time my upright piano was replaced by a new grand piano, but I doubt whether the person who eventually bought it had examined the sides of keys before completing the transaction; had he done so, the deep cuts in the wood might have made him change his mind.

When I was 12, my parents, on my teacher's recommendation, took me to Warsaw to meet Professor Turczyński, without doubt

---

[1] *The Decisive Battles of the Western World 1792–1944* by Gen. J.F.C. Fuller, Granada edition, Vol.2 pp.405–29.

the best piano teacher in Poland. We travelled in what was at that time the latest feat of technology, the so called *lux-torpeda*, a new kind of train consisting of only three carriages, capable of reaching the incredible speed of over 70 miles per hour, almost twice the speed of the ordinary steam train. We reached Warsaw in just over an hour. After Professor Turczyński heard me play a few pieces, he did his best to convince my parents that I ought to concentrate on a professional musical career without delay. He also insisted that I should not be allowed to play any more tennis, do any work at school which might expose my hands to the slightest risk of injury and, most importantly, that my piano teacher – whom he considered my greatest handicap – should be shown the door. He offered to see me once a month in Warsaw to supervise my progress. My faith in 'Captain', 'Professor' Meistermann was shattered. Needless to say, my parents had definite plans for my future, and becoming a professional pianist was not one of them. They did, however, find me another teacher, and thus my tutelage under 'Professor' Meistermann reached its somewhat ignominious end.

But let me return to that December night of 1939 in Łódż. Suddenly, at about 11 p.m., the peace was shattered by loud banging on the front door, accompanied by shouts in German: '*Tür öffnen!* [Open the door!]'. Four strapping, grim-faced, steel-helmeted German policemen, rifles over their shoulders, burst in. Snowflakes, just starting to melt, covered their green overcoats which reached almost to their ankles. They practically goose-stepped through the hall and into our small lounge which was dimly lit by concealed lamps. It served as a living room and, before we had to surrender our radio, this was where we used to gather in the evenings to listen to the news, to discuss the day's events and to inspire one another with hope – a commodity now in short supply.

The officer in charge appeared to be checking our names against a list he was holding. He then barked orders at us in German. Father translated them into Polish.

'Get dressed, pack one rucksack each, leave all your valuables behind and follow us.' And then, 'Get a move on! Hurry!'

Father's question 'Where are you taking us?' remained unanswered.

Mother turned to me: 'Put your warmest clothes on, remember your fur-lined coat, and don't forget your woollen scarf . . .' With her maternal concern she treated me again as her little boy. I glanced at my splendid grand piano in the drawing room, the silent witness of our abduction. 'Sonata Pathétique', still open, as I had left it, at the beginning of the last movement, reminded me of what I was playing only minutes before. The heavily lined silk curtains at the windows and the oriental carpets on the floor gave the room a feeling of peace and comfort, which now belonged to the past. More conventional guests used to sit in this room on the deep sofas upholstered in burgundy brocade. Tea used to be served here on small mahogany tables with dainty legs. But this was not how our uninvited visitors expected to be entertained.

Wide sliding doors led from the drawing room to the dining room, a large walnut table standing in its centre.

'Put all your money and valuables here!' barked one of them, pointing at the table. 'You can take 25 złotys each (about £1 in those days) with you. That's all!'

A narrow passage led past the door of the bathroom to the main bedroom, which had another bathroom en suite and a dressing room. One of the Germans kept a close watch on my parents, who were dithering, trying to decide which of their many possessions they would pack into the two rucksacks, all they had been allowed to take with them. Another one followed me to my bedroom where I was trying to sort out my belongings with some assistance from Nacia. '*Schnell, schnell*! [Get a move on!]' he kept urging me. Our maid stood there mute, gripped by fear, trying to make herself invisible, as if not wanting to add to the confusion.

Eventually she came to life. 'I shall get you some food,' she whispered and rushed to the kitchen. She made a few sandwiches and wrapped them up in a hurry. An avalanche of thoughts crashed through my mind: 'What will they do with us? Where will they take us? To prison? To a concentration camp? To a place of execution?' As they were leading us out I silently bade goodbye to my beloved home. 'Shall I ever see you again?'

Silent and stone-faced, the Germans followed us downstairs into the street. One led the procession, one walked behind, and there was one on each side of us, three pathetic-looking figures with small rucksacks on our backs. Mother and Father walked in front of me. The only sound that could be heard was that of fresh snow crunching under our shoes and under their boots. From Świętokrzyska Street we turned right into the dimly lit Sienkiewicza Street heading south. The town was completely deserted. We passed the German Evangelic church and other buildings that we knew so well, and on reaching Główna Street we turned left. There was still not a single word from our guards, no explanation of what was to happen to us.

Closer to our destination, half a mile or so from our home, we came across one or two other groups resembling ours. Policemen were escorting their victims. Finally, we got to a vast school hall, filling up with men, women and children. We could recognise some, and it soon became clear what all of them had in common. Jews and non-Jews alike, they represented the elite of the local community – doctors, lawyers, prominent industrialists and businessmen. In almost complete silence we sat on the chairs lining the walls, watching new arrivals. Oblivious of what the future held for us, we feared the worst. Time was dragging on. More arrivals, more new faces.

Very late at night a German voice, coming through megaphones, instructed us to get ready, and under a large escort we were marched outside. I have never seen a sight like this. As far as I could see there stood empty street trams, one behind the other. We were told to get into the carriages, and a slow but orderly process of loading the human cargo commenced. On the front and back platform of each carriage stood uniformed guards. Fully packed with people, the trams started on their journey into the unknown, making their way slowly through the empty streets, the wheels screeching against the rails around the bends. Inside, there was ghostly silence; everybody seemed to be lost in his or her own thoughts. It was strange watching a tram move from one end of town to another, without taking notice of a single stop. The procession halted only when the driver of the first tram had to move the rail points with his rod to change direction. At the approach to every junction I waited anxiously to see which way the tram would go. Ever since we'd left home, the dreadful thought of being taken to the infamous concentration camp located in Radogoszcz hung over me like a chimera. The few people who came out of there alive had some ghastly stories to tell about the treatment they had endured. One could conclude that, given the choice, they would rather die than remain there.

As the time went on – our journey took more than half an hour – it was becoming increasingly clear that we were indeed heading north towards the depressing, working-class suburb of Radogoszcz. Would we stop there, or would we go beyond?

I was still lost in my thoughts when the trams stopped in front of a factory gate guarded by heavily armed men in green uniforms. The place looked just like any other textile mill for which Łódż was famous, but although most of the windows were lit, there was no smoke coming out of the chimney, and no sound of machinery in motion could be heard. There were other buildings to be seen behind it in the same ground. The gate was guarded by more heavily armed men in green uniforms and there were more policemen around. I had no doubt that we were looking at the Radogoszcz concentration camp.

To the accompaniment of the guards' loud screams the trams quickly disgorged their cargo and we were all shepherded inside. We had to walk up a wide stone staircase and through a large door into a huge open area, the now empty old factory floor. Iron pulleys above our heads revealed the former nature of the place, which in the pre-war days must have been used for spinning or weaving. There were no machines to be seen, but the few weak electric bulbs threw their dim light on the countless rows of closely packed straw mattresses stretching from one end of the floor to the other. There was not a stick of furniture, not a single stool or bench to sit on. The place must have been prepared for us in advance. People looked baffled and bewildered. Tired by the tension and the journey I soon fell asleep close to my parents, who had hardly spoken a word all evening.

I woke up in bright daylight. For a while I wondered where I was, but the sight of my parents and other people sitting or lying on their straw mattresses brought me down to earth. There was little movement around us: some food was brought in and German policemen kept coming in and going out, visibly amused as they kept staring at us. I felt like a caged animal in the zoo looking out at visitors. But animals don't have to worry about thieves, while here, German guards-turned-robbers strolled around and, choosing their victims at random, would order them to stand up and rob them of anything they fancied. One came up to me, ordered me to empty my pockets and took away my most treasured possession, a blue Waterman pen with a gold nib – real gold – a present which had served me well for many years at home and at school. I felt as if I'd lost an old friend.

In the afternoon, a small group of Germans came to inspect us, and one of them straying behind turned round and caught my eye. He stopped, stared at my face and then his eyes turned with incredulity to my yellow armband. Obviously, he could not reconcile my Aryan appearance, my light-blond, straight hair, blue eyes and small non-hooked nose, with the stereotype of a Jew propagated by the Nazis, and thus with his image of the subhuman race. '*Jude*? [Jew?]' he asked, and on hearing my confirmation he grabbed me by the shoulder and propelled me outside onto the staircase, while at the same time summoning his mates to follow him. He paraded me in front of them. They must have been equally impressed with what they saw, as they went on gaping at me with disbelief even after I rejoined my parents.

The day dragged on and we had no idea what our captors intended to do with us. Scared and tired, we were waiting for the rest of the story to unfold. Late that evening we were told to get ready for departure. Roughly shepherded into the street once again, we boarded a long column of trams. The guessing game started all over again. Each time the tram changed direction I speculated on the destination. Before long we arrived at the Kaliska Railway Station on the outskirts of the city. A wide staircase led from the street to two elevated platforms with a large building between them, housing the waiting-rooms and station offices.

I have always been fascinated by railways and railway stations. To me they invariably meant the start of an adventure, the black shining monsters of locomotives chugging along, spewing out steam and visibly enjoying their boundless power. My eyes would follow the tracks into the distance, my imagination taking me to exciting new places never visited before.

But this was a different kind of adventure. Escorted on each side by armed policemen, we were taken first to the top of the staircase and then on to the right-hand platform, from which trains would normally travel east. As soon as the crowd filled the whole length of the platform, with the three of us trying to stay close together, a shrill command sounded from one end of the platform to the other: '*Männer rechts, Frauen links!* [Men to the right, women to the left!]' This was repeated by the guards and echoed by the walls of the building. There could be no mistake as to what this meant. In the dim light, amongst screams of distress, men were being separated from women. Sobbing wives and mothers tried to cling to their husbands and sons, but to no avail. In an instant Mother vanished in the crowd of other women, shoved out of our reach by the policemen.

A long line of covered wagons stood along the platform, their doors several feet above it. I had never travelled in a cattle wagon before. Getting inside without steps involved a considerable effort, and was particularly difficult for older people, so we helped one another. As soon as the carriage was full, the doors were slammed shut. There was not much space inside and it was practically impossible to lie down without encroaching on somebody else's space. Father and I were both anxious about Mother, but could do nothing about it. We had no idea where she might be. I tried hard to discard the thought that I might never see her again and the look of distress and tears on her face as she was being separated from us haunted me.

An hour went by, perhaps more. We were standing when, suddenly, with a violent jerk that threw us all back against our fellow passengers, the train started on its way. More jerks followed, with hisses of steam, and the carriages shook and jangled against one another as the train gathered speed on its way to destination . . . unknown. There were only four tiny windows in the wagon, one in each corner, and I tried to make my way to one, looking for clues as to where we were and in which direction we were going, but others had the same idea before me. It soon became clear that we were heading towards Piotrków Trybunalski and then further south. It was a strange experience to be transported like cattle: the ride was rough and bumpy, the train seemed to be in no hurry, stopping frequently, often in the middle of nowhere, in freezing cold weather and in total darkness. Without anything to hold on to, keeping upright was a problem, while the hard boards of the floor didn't look all that inviting, even if one could find enough room to sit down.

We started talking to one another, sharing the anxiety for our mothers, wives and daughters. The feeling of relief that followed our departure from Radogoszcz soon gave way to an even greater fear that we were being sent to a concentration camp in Germany and it looked as if we might indeed be heading there. The forced separation from our womenfolk was a bad omen and although nobody would utter the names of the dreaded destinations, they must have been on all our minds.

Exhausted by anxiety, people dozed off one by one. Half frozen, I wrapped my fur-lined coat tighter around my body. Trying to sleep, like the others, in an uncomfortable position, I kept waking up, trying again and again to get out of my mind the stubborn thought of where we might finally end our journey. The night seemed to last forever. At dawn, someone looking out of the window shouted: 'We are heading east towards Cracow, away from the German border!'

What a relief!

The train stopped again, but this time it was for good and close to the station at Cracow. It took ages but at long last the doors were opened and we were allowed out. To our indescribable relief we found that the women had been travelling in separate carriages behind us and emerged now out of the train to join us. With great joy we all hugged each other, father, mother and son.

This was Cracow, the third largest Polish city. Straddling the Vistula River, it has been the heart of Polish identity and culture for ten centuries. From 1038 till 1609 its famous castle of Wawel was the seat of Polish kings and queens and its tradition of learning, starting with its world-renowned Jagellonian University, stretched back 600 years. Now Cracow acquired the dubious honour of having been declared the capital of the newly formed German dependency, the

General Gouvernement, and thus the seat of its Governor, Hans Frank. This was a rump cut from what was before the war central Poland and it comprised Warsaw in the north, Cracow in the south-west, and Lublin in the east. The western part of Poland, including Poznań and my native town Łódź, renamed Litzmannstadt, had been incorporated into Germany proper.

In a small crowd of refugees we stood now on the railway platform, several hundred yards away from the main station building, waiting to hear what was to become of us. German policemen, like sheepdogs, herded us into a vast empty shed, one of the many outbuildings adjoining the station. After the nightmare journey, once indoors, we felt relieved and reasonably warm. At long last a voice on the loudspeaker announced: 'You are now free to go wherever you like, as long as you do not attempt to go back to Germany.' And of course Germany now included Łódź.

Though ostensibly free, in spite of the announcement I still felt held on a leash. What could I do with that new found freedom, I kept asking myself. Most people rushed out to form queues in front of the few telephone boxes around the station, Father amongst them. Before long he came back with a broad smile on his face.

He turned to Mother, 'Listen, Guta, do you remember Mr Dornbusz?' She did. He was one of Father's many customers; he owned a large wholesale warehouse in Cracow and used to visit Łódź frequently on buying trips. 'He offered us shelter and will be here soon to pick us up,' Father said.

In less than half an hour a *droshky* appeared. A man in his early 40s, rather short, his face half hidden under a black felt hat, jumped out and looked around until he caught sight of us in the crowd. His face beamed. Obviously labouring with flat feet, he shuffled through the deep fresh snow towards us, and when he took off his hat to greet us, his shining forehead stretched all the way back. He embraced us warmly, as if we were his closest relatives, and once we all got into the *droshky* and drove off, he could hardly wait to hear all the details of our odyssey. I could not take my eyes off the historical buildings, churches and palaces we were passing. This was not my native Łódź, that dreary industrial town, which could hardly boast of any construction more than 60 years old. As we approached the town centre I spotted with awe the shop windows decorated with small Christmas trees, sparkling lights, bright multi-coloured streamers and beautifully wrapped gift boxes. Among the crowds in the streets there were numerous uniformed Germans in their long black, olive and green overcoats, shopping. Most of them were wearing red armbands with a black swastika on a white circle. Flags with the same insignia were flying from many buildings. But there were also many other armbands to be seen. These ones were white with the blue Star of David, unlike the yellow ones we were forced to wear in Łódż, but identifying their wearers as Jews just the same.

Mr Dornbusz warned us: 'You must be on your guard all the time. You may get picked up in the streets, dragged out from a tram and even from your home. Like many others, you may suffer humiliation and physical abuse while doing forced labour.' He spoke animatedly with a Yiddish accent and at times spiced up his narrative with Yiddish words. Every now and then he would take off his hat to scratch his head.

The Dornbusz family lived on the first floor of a substantial, five-storey apartment house at 6 Sebastiana Street, a small, quiet road in a prosperous residential area of Cracow, adjoining Planty, once the old city ramparts, now, for many years, public gardens. Mr Dornbusz, leading the way, rang the doorbell and his wife, a buxom lady, taller than her husband, an apron over her floral dress, let us in. 'Mr Lando, Mrs Lando!' she greeted us with joy. 'How good to see you! Please, make yourselves at home. Now, what would you like to eat?' Close behind her appeared her three daughters: Hania, aged 18, a tall, attractive girl with brown hair; Niusia, 14, a pretty, shy girl with a serious expression, alluring black eyes and thick, straight, dark hair; and eight-year-old Rose, plump, full of life and fun. All were anxious to welcome us.

Off the entrance hall, a door on the left led to what was to become our bedroom, a narrow rectangle, just long enough to accommodate the two beds, one for my parents and one for me, lined up along the right-hand wall. A small wardrobe stood against the left-hand wall, leaving just enough space in the middle for one person to squeeze through. The narrow window at the far end of the room overlooked a nondescript courtyard, flanked on each side by two large tenement houses, many of their small balconies turned into tiny gardens.

Another door off the entrance hall, opposite our bedroom, opened into the dining room with a balcony overhanging the street. The room was sombre, with solid furniture in dark oak, and heavy dark drapes reaching down to the floor. Nobody was allowed there during the daily visits of Emil, Hania's boyfriend, who was in search of privacy. The third door opposite the main entrance to the flat led straight from the hall into a large sitting room, where most of the family would congregate in their leisure time. Niusia used to sit on a sofa standing against the far wall and spent most of her time absorbed in a novel. I would often sit next to her and, when we were alone, I tried to draw her into a conversation: 'Niusia, stop reading just for a while, we can make up our own plot, much more exciting than in your book. With real people in it.' Far from being convinced, she would push my arm away when I tried to put it around her waist to prove how I could be a real character in her novel. I wasn't put off easily, but when I persisted she would just move to the other end of the sofa and turn her face away from me.

A door on the left led from the sitting room to a combined bathroom and toilet that, being the coldest room in the apartment, also served as a pantry; there were no refrigerators in those days. On Fridays, one of the pots on the floor was usually filled with a calves-foot jelly, a local culinary speciality, cooling down for the evening meal. For some unknown reason it never had a lid over it. When we were invited to join our hosts for the traditional Friday evening meal, my parents, remembering its provenance, found no end of excuses for avoiding having to partake of it.

Every morning we had to wait our turn to gain access to the bathroom. The wait would be particularly long for Rose, the youngest of the three sisters. She would take ages. We all knew when Rose was in the bathroom as her special bathroom repertoire reverberated throughout the flat, her favourite being an ode sung to the tune of an old ballad, with her own lyrics, that went like this: 'O my gums, my gums, why do you hurt me so?' Whenever she saw Father, she would run away laughing loudly, as he tried to pinch her rosy cheek or her plump bottom, if he caught her unawares.

The other two doors off the living room led to a bedroom, now shared between the three sisters, and to their parents' bedroom. We were made to feel very much at home. One morning on waking up Father exclaimed with a broad grin: 'Back at home I slept with a broken head on a sound bed, now I sleep with a sound head on a broken bed.' No business worries kept him awake at night and he did not complain of any others.

It was a late afternoon, just before Christmas, when I went shopping to the city centre with Mother. It was getting dark as we were crossing the Market Square. The late Gothic and Renaissance *Sukiennice* (Cloth Hall) stands in its centre, stretching for more than a hundred yards, half the length of the square. Its origins go back to the days when two rows of mercers' stalls stood in the market place as far back as the thirteenth century. The Mariacki church, rebuilt in the fourteenth century, loomed over us on the left. It has a tall tower, from which every hour, on the hour, a trumpeter plays a bugle call that always ends on an interrupted note, to remind us of the day some 600 years ago, when an arrow from an invading Tartar horde pierced the trumpeter's throat as he was playing. The square was full of shoppers, many of them with swastikas on their armbands, the Huns or Tartars of today. German flags were everywhere.

It was snowing heavily. Sounds of German Christmas carols mixed with the noise of hundreds of feet trampling the snow underfoot. We turned left into Sienna Street and then right into Stolarska, a quiet, almost deserted street, in stark contrast to the festive atmosphere of the square. As I held Mother by her arm, my white armband was hidden from sight under the sleeve of her coat. Suddenly, a large canopied army truck driving towards us on the other side of the street stopped opposite us. A uniformed German got out, crossed the road and blocked our way. He must have spotted Mother's armband. He disengaged my arm from hers and, on seeing the Star of David, commanded: '*Komm mit, schnell!* [Come with me, quick!]'

Mother burst into tears. In vain she pleaded with the man in German: 'Please, do let him go, we have just been expelled from our home in Łódż, you can't imagine the ordeal; surely, we have suffered enough. He is only 16 . . . Still just a schoolboy . . . my only son . . . I couldn't bear to lose him!'

The German took no notice. I stood there hesitating. 'Into the truck, now!' he repeated in a voice leaving no room for hesitation. I had no choice. He quick-marched me across the road, dropped the tailboard of his vehicle and motioned to me to climb in. I did so with some difficulty. He lifted and secured the flap, and we drove off almost immediately. In the semi-darkness under the canopy I could just about see the silhouettes of three or four men sitting on the two long benches, one on each side of the truck. They were all Jews with the white armbands bearing the blue Star of David. Silence reigned for a while until somebody voiced the question: 'What are they going to do with us?' A few minutes went by. Suddenly, the truck came to a halt. After a short delay the tailboard came down again and another man with a white armband got in. The same uniformed German looked in and called: '*Wo is der junge Jude aus Łódż?* [Which one is the young Jew from Łódż?]' I came forward. 'Out!' he commanded. 'Run home.' I hardly believed my ears. My mother's pleas must have struck a chord in what served the German for a heart. I didn't give him a chance to change his mind. I was out and away in a flash. As soon as the truck was out of sight, I stopped, had a good look around to make sure that nobody was watching and took off my white armband – something I would not dare do again, and shoved it into my pocket. I asked a passer-by for directions to Sebastiana Street and ran home as quickly as I could. I rang the doorbell. Father opened the door. He stood there motionless, frozen for a second or two, as if he'd seen an apparition. Then he stretched his arms and embraced me warmly. Mother, close behind him, started crying.

It did not take Father long to set up a small office of his own in Mr Dornbusz's warehouse, where he used to spend every day. He established business links with Mr Sachs, the Volksdeutsch administrator in charge of our business in Łódż. In spite of severe restrictions on movement of goods enforced at German checkpoints along the frontier between the Polish lands incorporated into Germany and the *General Gouvernement*, a smuggling chain from Łódż to Cracow was quickly established. In this way merchandise, which was in short supply, reached the section of Mr Dornbusz's warehouse set at Father's disposal. Soon the shelves of the warehouse were bulging with a variety of cotton materials used for sheeting, pillowcases, mattresses and other household items. Now and again I spent some time in the warehouse where my job was to write letters, check invoices and assist in preparing the inventory.

Occasionally I watched Father work out the value of the stock in the warehouse. It was an amazing sight! He held a pencil in his hand and for every column of digits he ran the pencil from the top to the bottom of the page in about five seconds, wrote down a figure and then proceeded with the next column of digits at the same speed until all were added up.

I asked him: 'How do you manage to add all the columns on a page in less than half a minute? It would take me ten times as long.'

'You should have seen your father doing his books when he was a young man,' said Mother who happened to be sitting next to us. 'He was twice as fast!'

One Monday morning in January, Mr Dornbusz, who always got up very early, returned home unexpectedly, before Father left for his office. Our host was pale and greatly agitated. 'We had burglars last night,' he said to Father. 'Most of your stock has gone!' Father shrugged his shoulders as if nothing could surprise him any more. 'Well,' he replied with apparent indifference, 'I shall have to start again.' And he did.

Our family was incomplete without Nacia, herself Jewish, who had been left behind when we were expelled from our home. However, she joined us within a week of our arrival in Cracow and my parents found her accommodation. A few weeks before the outbreak of the war, in anticipation of the impending disaster, Father had the foresight to hide much of Mother's jewellery in a safe place. He dug a hole in an enclosed area of the cellar in my grandparents' house and buried it there. What we needed now was to find a reliable person who could be entrusted with the difficult mission of finding the exact spot where the jewels were buried, digging them out and smuggling them from Łódż to Cracow. Some job! But here Nacia's sister, who still lived in Łódż, came to our rescue. A woman of great courage, she agreed to take on the challenge, and to my parents' enormous relief appeared one day in our flat in Cracow, her mission accomplished. From then on Mother always kept many jewels on her person, sewn into her brassière. She also made a false pocket in Father's trousers where he kept the remainder. Now we had the means to live in reasonable comfort for some time, should the Dornbusz partnership come to an end.

Father loved poking fun at others and Mr Dornbusz became an easy target when he confided in him one day that an attractive young female had just moved into our apartment block. The two kept passing each other regularly on the stairs and Mr Dornbusz swore that she had turned her head once or twice in his direction. He asked Father, as a man of the world, to help him find a way of getting to know her. Father advised him: 'It's easy; next time you see her, just come up close to her and whisper into her ear "I am waiting . . ." He fell for it and tried it,' Father chuckled, 'but to his disappointment the lady ignored him completely!'

In the meantime many German officials were descending on Cracow, the capital of the *General Gouvernement*, and rooms were being requisitioned for them in private apartments. One day an officious-looking man came in to check the number of people occupying our flat and to assess the space available. He requisitioned the dining room and the new lodger turned up a day or two later. He was a German, a man of a kindly appearance in his early 50s, grey-haired, tall and slim. He spoke softly, mainly to say 'good day' or 'goodbye' and he treated us with respect. To my mind his body language indicated apology for the actions of his compatriots. We nicknamed him 'Giorgio'. During the week he went out early and came back late in the evening. Emil and Hania were relieved to have the room to themselves during the day, although their weekends, when Giorgio stayed indoors, were definitely ruined.

At this stage Father decided that I should learn English. He found a teacher, Mr Wiener, who arrived one day in our flat. There was something dignified about his appearance. In his early 50s, of medium height, slim and slightly stooping, he had silver-grey hair and a white moustache. Though it was the middle of winter he wore a light-beige cotton raincoat over his rather tired but well-pressed dark formal suit and a white shirt with a plain dark blue tie. He told us in a soft voice that he had spent many years in England, and since coming back home shortly before the war, he had been teaching English for a living. We started by having lessons three times a week. With Giorgio away during the day, and before Emil's daily visit, we had the dining room to ourselves. He brought with him a textbook that was quite unlike my old school books. A delight to use, it was richly illustrated with amusing cartoon characters; it immediately plunged the reader into daily conversations between real people. The new words became quickly engraved on my memory. Learning was fun. I liked and respected my teacher, I liked his kindly manner, his inexhaustible patience and the fact that he never raised his voice. I looked forward to every lesson. I struggled with the English pronunciation and with the apparent lack of logic in the way the English words were spelled – but I found that English grammar, when compared with the Latin and French I had learned at school, was a doddle. Hungry for knowledge, I made rapid progress.

One day in February Father returned home in great excitement. 'I have just met Mr Hirschberg, an old Masonic Lodge friend from Łódż, who let me into an important secret,' he said. 'He had bought Italian visas for his whole family and was about to get the railway tickets to travel to Milan. He gave me the name of the middleman. I can hardly believe it!' Father almost shouted. 'We can escape from this hell! We shall soon get out of this accursed place for good!'

In the week that followed, Father was out every day visiting various offices and coming back home with encouraging news. 'Not long to wait now,' he consoled us. 'Once we get to Italy, we shall live a normal life, no fear, no armbands! Can you imagine that?'

These were heady days. I scoured bookshops for Italian dictionaries and self-teaching manuals, and I even got hold of an Italian *Baedecker*, the famous guidebook. I sat for hours learning all about Italy: what its climate was like, what its cities had to offer, where we ought to eventually settle down. We compiled a list of items we had to buy for our new life, like new clothes appropriate to the climate. One by one, we acquired them and crossed them off the list. A date for departure was set and I started counting the days and hours to our journey.

Then, four days before the planned departure date, Father came home looking gloomy and dejected. It was clear that something had gone badly wrong. I recalled the same look on his face when we discovered on our way to Romania that the broken axle of our car was beyond repair.

'Italy is off,' he said. 'We have missed our chance. They've exhausted the visa quota just before ours came up for approval. Everything we've done is for nothing.'

As time went on, my parents increasingly felt that our accommodation was far from adequate. It was cramped for both personal and storage space, and by now our belongings greatly exceeded the capacity of the three rucksacks we had brought with us and of the small wardrobe at our disposal. Money was not a problem though and in February 1940 we moved to another block of flats in a different residential area. We now had a large comfortable room in an elegantly furnished apartment belonging to a Jewish doctor. The high-ceilinged room, off the main entrance hall, easily accommodated a double bed for my parents, a single bed for me, a generous-sized wardrobe, a chest of drawers, a mahogany desk, a small dining table, a couple of armchairs and three other chairs. This still left plenty of free space and we did not feel at all cramped. A thick carpet covered a highly polished parquet floor. Two large windows gave on to a quiet street, only a few minutes' walk from the riverbank.

A week or two after we moved in, our landlord asked my parents whether they would like to meet his relatives, refugees from Vienna, who arrived in Cracow some months ago. Unfortunately, in their attempt to escape the *Anschluss* – the recent annexation of Austria by Germany – and its consequences for the Jews, they had come to the wrong place.

'I am sure,' he said to Father, 'that you will find a great deal in common with them. You speak excellent German, you have been to Vienna many times. Your son might like to meet their daughter, a charming girl about his age; her name is Hanna.'

On the appointed day, as we were all sitting in the lounge, waiting for Hanna and her parents to join us for tea, and talking about nothing in particular, suddenly our host said: 'Perhaps you ought to know that one evening last October, an hour after the curfew, three German soldiers called on the porter of the house where Hanna and her parents lived, looking for Jews. Having got the information, they forced their way into their flat and raped Hanna in front of her parents.' He said it without showing any emotion, as if this was not, under the present conditions, an abnormal event. I was shocked.

As soon as I saw Hanna it was love at first sight. She was 18, a year older than me; a tall, slim, handsome girl with a lovely figure and long shapely legs. She had something of the gazelle in her, her movements were gracious and flowing, which made her even more attractive as she walked. She had lively brown eyes, a serious face, perfect except for a somewhat aquiline nose. We, the Jews, members of a newly condemned race, had acquired a new habit of categorising our fellow men and women by whether their appearance was good – 'Aryan' – or else bad – 'Jewish' – which did not bode well for the person's survival. Hanna's appearance was definitely 'bad'.

I did not know German and she was struggling with her Polish, having found the language difficult to learn. I still managed to understand the meaning of her words, helped by her changing facial expressions during the cascading flow of her thoughts.

While our parents and our hosts were absorbed in a conversation about the pre-war days, the wonderful bread and wine for which Vienna was renowned and my family's happy holidays in the Austrian skiing resort of Semmering, I listened to Hanna, enchanted by her every word. She gave me an account of her first impressions of a foreign country, the Polish school she attended, her favourite subjects and her new Polish friends. Everything she said stirred a sympathetic echo inside me. I seemed to share all her likes and dislikes. It was as if I was listening to myself talking. My eyes were riveted to hers and she was clearly enjoying looking straight into mine. It did not take us long to realise that we were about to embark on an exciting journey into an unfamiliar world, a relationship that neither of us had ever experienced.

I promised to call for her the next morning. She lived close by. We went for a long walk along the river. It was a bright, sunny but very cold day. There were large slabs of ice floating on the water surface. On both shores, wide embankments gently sloped towards the river and small, tired-looking patches of grass tried hard to free themselves from the embraces of dirty snow. In the distance, the river, some 30 metres wide, turned from its straight course towards Wawel, the famous royal castle, its grey different-shaped turrets rising from its redbrick towers. Hanna struggled hard to find the right words in her limited Polish vocabulary to share her thoughts, some of which would have been difficult to convey even with a perfect command of language. I tried hard to concentrate, but her fresh appearance in the bracing air, the closeness of her body and her sweet fragrance aroused in me new and powerful emotions that distracted me and made me feel dizzy.

Ours was a strange kind of relationship. When you are in love, you want to be alone with your sweetheart at least some of the time. One of the problems brought about by the war was that your living space was constantly encroached upon. It was almost impossible to be in a room on your own for any length of time. You were sharing your space with your family, your friends, or strangers and, invariably, with more than one person at a time. Escaping outdoors brought little relief. You could not hide for long under the cover of darkness, having to be indoors before the curfew, soon after the sun had set. During our long walks and endless discussions, however interesting the subject, I could not devote to it my undivided attention. My eyes wandered around, scanning the long and short distance to spot the usual danger: the Germans looking for a victim with a Star of David armband. I had to select a walking route not because I liked it, but because it might be safer than another alternative. And yet we were never safe. We think, rightly so, that our surroundings intensify or suppress our feelings. As this was my first experience of love I could make no comparisons, but I felt that I was not getting my fair share of it. I felt very protective of Hanna, and though I never talked to her about her terrible ordeal, I knew that it must have made her particularly apprehensive of the dangers confronting us.

We had to choose quiet streets, remote corners of public gardens, paths along the river, deserted corners under the bridges. On rare occasions, with nobody around, we managed to hold each other close and allowed our lips to meet.

'You are keeping your eyes open when you kiss me,' she once observed.

'I know. I have to keep a lookout.'

She laughed. It was hard to be a lover and a sentry at the same time. At the sight of anybody coming close we would quickly resume our walk. Although her Polish was improving I knew she wanted to tell me a lot more than she was able to. Fortunately, what was most important to us needed no spoken words. When we looked into each other's eyes, when we held and pressed each other's hands, we were reassured. We loved each other.

We were allowed less than four months of happiness.

Our world had changed out of all recognition, but soon winter, as always, gave way to spring. We were often invited to dinner with Mr and Mrs Grunbaum. He used to be my father's customer and had soon become a friend. The family lived in a comfortable apartment not very far from us. We joined them every Friday for a traditional evening meal preceded by the lighting of Sabbath candles and the customary Hebrew blessings. We sat around a long dinner table, large enough for 16 people. The conversation would usually start with an exchange of views on the progress of the war and on the innumerable instances of German cruelty and ruthlessness. It would then turn to light-hearted topics, such as the habits of Jews living in central Poland (represented by us) compared to those living in Polish Galicia (like our hosts). For over a century, until the end of the First World War, Eastern and Central Poland was ruled by the Russians, while the South, called Galicia, formed part of the Austro-Hungarian Empire. The very formal Galician manners came from their Austrian rulers. Men were addressed by their titles such as Mr Doctor, Mr Professor, Mr Director, Mr *Mecenas* (lawyer), Mr Inżynier Engineer etc – and their wives as Mrs Doctor, Mrs Professor, and so on. Only the very closest of friends and members of the family were addressed by their first name. Even the Galician table manners were different from ours and Father always turned that into a joke.

'A Galician Jew,' Father started, 'was on a visit to Warsaw. He was invited to a meal by his friends and he greatly enjoyed his soup. However, when asked whether he would like a second helping, hungry as he was, he refused. According to Galician *savoir-vivre* he would have to be asked three times before saying yes. But, to his great dismay, his host passed on to the next course. The same happened with the second and then with the third course. It wasn't until the next day, when he complained about his inhospitable friend to an acquaintance from Cracow living in Warsaw, that he learned about the misunderstanding!'

Somebody else related another apocryphal story: 'One Friday evening meal after all the members of the family and the invited guests finished their meat course, an extra piece remained on the serving plate. The host offered it to every one of the five guests in turn and, well versed in Galician etiquette as they were, they all politely declined. Suddenly there was a power cut and all the lights went out, plunging the room into darkness. Immediately a loud scream pierced the silence, and when the lights came back on, one hand reaching for the platter had four forks stuck into it!' The story was met with general merriment.

Deprived of our radios as we were, our only source of information was the heavily censored Polish daily newspaper, *Kurier Krakówski*. With experience we learned to read 'between the lines' and in time all news favourable to Germans, as it mostly was, was treated by us with scepticism. But even then we could not find anything to cheer us up.

On Sunday, 7 April 1940 we read that German warships had left their Baltic harbours. During the early hours of 9 April the troops came ashore without meeting any resistance in Norway, at Bergen, Kristiansand, Trondheim and Narvik. They also occupied Copenhagen, the Danish capital. Was this true?

On 23 April, the first night of Jewish Passover, the Grunbaums invited us to *Seder* night, a traditional meal and religious service at home that commemorates the release of Jews from Egyptian slavery in the days of the Pharaohs. Pesach, or Passover, is the oldest of Jewish festivals. Jews have observed it from the dawn of our history as nomadic shepherds in the wilderness. Originally a 'nature' festival, it evolved into a historic and national holiday, the celebration of the Exodus from Egypt, symbolising the liberation of the Jewish people. The eating of *matzos*, unleavened bread, during the eight days of the festival, was to remind us of the haste of Jews fleeing Egypt, when they had no time to wait for leavened dough to rise.

It is an ancient custom to invite friends and even strangers to the Pesach meal and our hosts were truly glad to have us with them. No other tradition could have had, at that time, a deeper meaning for us, a people again reduced to slavery, desperate to regain our freedom – and, indeed, to survive.

The service was to start earlier than usual to give us a chance to get home before the curfew. We covered the short distance to our hosts without any problems. We entered the apartment and as the door opened we were greeted with the traditional words of '*gut yom-tov* [have a happy holy day]', and other expressions of warmth flying back and forth. There was much hand-shaking all round and the kissing of ladies' hands. The delightful smell of chicken soup filtering through from the adjoining kitchen made my mouth water. With much ceremony we were shown into the dining room, which was bathed in bright light from the large crystal chandelier above the table. The smart clothes of those present, their smiling yet solemn faces, the polished silver cutlery, the sparkling crystal glasses on the table – all stressed the festive atmosphere of this special occasion. Yet the memories of happier Passovers were tangibly present. I felt that we were characters in a play: slaves, in constant fear for their lives, feigning to be free, if only for a couple of hours.

Fourteen people sat down around the long dining table, covered with a starched, white tablecloth, with festive candles in silver candlesticks at one side. Prominent on the table was a platter with three *matzos* under a white napkin. Some brave Jewish baker must have managed to bake them surreptitiously in defiance of the Germans. Placed next to the platter were two richly ornamented china plates with the symbolic herbs, eggs and fruit to be shared in the course of the service. One of them contained my favourite, *haroseth*, a mixture of ground nuts and dried fruit in wine. I contemplated them full of anticipation and was not disappointed: they were delicious. We all stood up while Mrs Grunbaum lit the festive candles, whispering the blessings.

As the host poured each guest a glass of wine and we opened the small books called *Haggadah* placed in front of us, the service began. In one of his works the German poet Heine had this to say about *Haggadah*: 'The master of the house sits at the table and reads from a queer book called *Haggadah*. Its content is a marvellous mixture of age-old legends, miracles of the Exodus from Egypt, curious discussions, prayers and festive songs.' My book was richly illustrated with biblical scenes; there were ancient cities basking in the sun and happy families celebrating the *Seder* night. At the start of the service the custom was for the youngest person present to ask in Hebrew about the meaning of the ceremony. As I recited the lines, asking how this night was different from all other nights, I couldn't help going back in my mind to the *Seder* nights at home in Łódź in the recent – and yet now so remote – past. I saw Father not as a guest, not as a homeless refugee, but as the host, sitting in an armchair at the top of the table, reclining on a cushion, observing a long tradition that contrasted our comforts with the hardships suffered by our ancestors.

As our host started his answers to my question with the words: 'We were slaves to Pharaoh in Egypt . . .' I asked myself: 'And what are we now?'

It was then my turn to perform the ceremony of looking for a piece of *matzo*, called *afikomen*, hidden somewhere in the room by Mr Grunbaum. I searched behind the vases on the sideboard, one of which I almost dropped. I opened all the drawers: again, no luck. Then I had an inspiration. I walked towards the gramophone, lifted the lid and there it was, on the turntable instead of a record! As tradition demanded, I was rewarded with some pocket money. Later on in the evening we read the traditional lines from the *Haggadah* and exchanged wishes: 'Next year in Jerusalem', 'Yes, next year in Jerusalem. Such an enticing yet impossible prospect!

The meal started with fish, followed by chicken soup with *kneidls* (my favourite *matzo* dumplings) and roast chicken, and ended with stewed fruit for dessert.

Another Passover tradition is the pouring of a cup of wine for Elijah, the prophet. The door is opened so that he might enter and drink some of it. I closed my eyes. A terrifying thought flashed through my mind. What if a German came in instead? When I opened my eyes it seemed that the level of wine in the prophet's glass had gone down. 'Did I have too much to drink?' I wondered. More importantly, however, no German had come through the door.

Grace after the meal had to be cut short, to enable us to get home safely before the curfew. We still had time, though, to sing the old folk songs of the *Haggadah* at the end of the service. My favourite has always been the song that seems to go on forever about a father who sold a baby goat for two zuzim. Then along came a cat and ate the baby goat. Then came a dog that bit the cat. Then came a stick that beat the dog. Then came a fire and burned the stick. Then came water and quenched the fire. Then came an ox and drank the water. Then came the slaughterer that slaughtered the ox. Then came the Angel of Death and slew the slaughterer. Then came the Holy One and smote the Angel of Death who slew the slaughterer who slaughtered the ox that drank the water that quenched the fire that burned the stick that beat the dog that bit the cat that ate the baby goat that a father sold for two zuzim.

On this night the Passover story offered a ray of hope, of freedom, of our wishes being fulfilled one day.

According to Sir Martin Gilbert, the present-day historian, some 350 miles to the north, at the Stutthof concentration camp, the Germans marked the occasion of Passover by making all the Jews in the camp run, then drop to the ground, stand up, and run again without respite. The ones who were too slow were beaten to death with rifle butts. The days of freedom were a long way away. 'For now, the killing of Jews became a matter of laughter and mockery.'[2]

One day *Kurier Krakówski* brought us devastating news. The announcement, in big bold letters, filled the top of the front page: AT DAWN ON THE MORNING OF 10 MAY, THE GERMAN ARMY ADVANCED INTO BELGIUM AND HOLLAND.

As we learned later, the German army went into attack with twice the strength of the combined Allied forces. The Dutch and Belgian governments asked the British for help. On 15 May the Dutch capitulated. On 17 May the Germans entered Brussels; on 18 May they took Antwerp. By 21 May they reached the Channel coast at the mouth of the River Somme and thus cut the Allied armies in half.

The time was 9 a.m. on 15 June, 1940. My parents and I were sitting in our room having breakfast. I was tense and apprehensive, hungry for the latest news from the Western front; our destiny depended on what happened there. At that moment our landlord

[2] Martin Gilbert's *Second World War*, revised edition, p.57.

walked in and silently put a newspaper on the table. A massive banner headline on the front page screamed: NIEMCY ZAJELI PARYŻ [GERMANS HAVE TAKEN PARIS]. The French were about to capitulate. Mother and Father turned the colour of ash and neither uttered a word. I could not stand the silence. 'Could this be the end?' I asked. I got no reply. I came up with it myself: this must be the end of the war. But was it also the end of us?

A feeble consoling thought shot through my mind: Great Britain was still fighting, we did have some allies we could count on, the day would surely come when good would triumph over evil. Hope and despair were wrestling in my mind. Overcome with nausea, I did not finish my breakfast.

A few days later Dr Frank, the German Governor of occupied Poland, issued a new order: all Jews who had come to Cracow after the outbreak of war were to leave the city. By then, so much had happened to us that we felt no surprise, no indignation. We were just one family among some 35,000 being evicted and who now decided to make their way to Warsaw, the former capital of Poland. 'We have little choice,' my father said. 'Besides, we might be better off in a larger city, where we can be with people we know. It might give us a greater chance of survival.'

The preparations for departure did not take long. We took leave of our friends, who were genuinely sorry to see us go. It was worse for me; my heart was breaking having to part from my beloved Hanna. We spent our last afternoon together, walking as usual through the side streets of Cracow, tense and on guard. Hanna's face was wet with tears and I kept blowing my nose. We hardly spoke at all. We did not dare to ask the obvious unanswerable question: were we saying goodbye or just au revoir? Would we ever meet again? The chances of it were very small indeed. Our future looked bleak and we did not dare to even try and imagine what it held. Shocked by the speed with which the hands on our watches were marching on, we prolonged our walk for as long as we could. When I got home with only minutes to spare before the curfew, my parents greeted me with relief.

I never saw Hanna again.

The next morning we took a train to Warsaw. The journey of just a few hours passed without mishap. We left our luggage at the station and made our way to the Jewish accommodation bureau. We took a room in Żelazna Street, near the corner of Leszno Street, in the commercial district of Warsaw, closely packed with apartment blocks, offices and shops, all on top of one another. The owners of the room, a Jewish dentist and his family, were pleased to have us as their tenants. Nacia followed us a few weeks later, after my parents had found a room for her.

Both Leszno and Żelazna Streets were busy thoroughfares and it took me a long time to get used to the clickety-clack sounds of trams passing under our windows from early morning until the curfew. The view from our balcony, as far as the eye could see, was of half-empty shop windows; dusty pavements filled with crowds of milling people; ugly, soot-covered dark buildings and roofs with patches of colourless sky in between. We were lucky to have found a fairly large room, though quite a bit smaller than our last room in Cracow. Our apartment block looked dull, neglected and tired, just like the rest of the street; the narrow stairwell was hardly ever cleaned. I can only describe our room in terms of what it was not. It was not cosy, it was not quiet, and it was not friendly; if rooms can have a soul, this one was deprived of its. With the windows shut it was too hot, but you could not keep them open for the constant noise. And yet, afraid of being picked up by the Germans in the streets, I would spend most of the day indoors. The risk here was even greater than in Cracow and one had to use all one's wits to evade the German patrols.

The beauty of Warsaw was lost on me. I had little idea what the centre of the city looked like – I had never visited it. I had not been to the Old City, a jewel of a place, which I knew only from the reproductions of paintings by Canaletto. I was told that it had changed little since his time. I had not seen the Royal Castle or the splendid public parks with their lakes and waterfalls; I had missed out on the royal palaces and mansions of the old aristocracy, which I could only admire in the illustrated guidebooks our host had lent me. My Warsaw consisted of ugly tenement houses in a depressing part of town; of streets crowded with a multitude of drab, unsmiling, morose people. I missed the elegance of Cracow, I missed Hanna, my English lessons, and my friends.

My parents kept trying to find their friends and acquaintances from Łódż. And they succeeded, as every family they unearthed brought them into contact with another. To my great joy, I came across my dear school friend, Tadek Wolpert. With his mother (a dentist), his father and an elder sister, he lived not very far from us. Tadek had a freckled face, a turned-up nose and straight brown hair; he too had a 'good appearance'. At school he had always been top of the class in every subject; in chess he was virtually unbeatable. During our long discussions on philosophy we tried to reconcile man's interest in the purpose and meaning of life with what was happening to us now. Had the current events ever been predicted, I wondered. Was there a logical reason for a nation being wiped out in such a barbaric fashion? Having established our belief in the existence of God, were we facing His merciless punishment or His complete indifference? If we were punished, had we been capable of committing sins of such enormity that would deserve our present afflictions? Tadek tried hard to answer my questions, but if any of his answers were satisfying or even acceptable to me at the time, I do not recall.

4

THE WARSAW GHETTO

'A plague-infected area' was how the Germans described the Jewish residential area of the Warsaw of March 1940, we learned from our hosts soon after our arrival in June. At about the same time they ordered the *Judenrat*, the Jewish council, to erect a wall around it. Incredibly, it was the Council who had to pay for the walls. The town plan I saw revealed that all the Jews of Warsaw, about one third of its population, were to be crowded into something like 5 per cent of the city's territory. To make it even worse these were the oldest parts of the city, some of which were already a self-imposed ghetto to generations of poor Jews. While telling the Jews that the wall was intended to protect them against excesses by their Polish neighbours, the Germans told the Poles that their aim was to protect them from the epidemic of typhus.

On my first walk in Warsaw, as far as I could see, all the approaches to the Jewish quarter were displaying prominent warning signs in German and in Polish: DANGER! EPIDEMIC: ONLY THROUGH TRAFFIC PERMITTED.

Walls, some three metres high, topped by barbed wire or large fragments of broken glass, erected across and along many streets, overwhelmed me with a sense of panic and of impending doom and isolation. At night I was plagued by nightmares in which the walls were coming alive, moving closer and closer together, trying to crush me, or like a boa constrictor, to strangle me. In August 1940, when most sections of the wall were already in place, official posters announced that the city of Warsaw would be divided into three separate quarters: German, Polish and Jewish. To begin with, all Jews were ordered to leave the designated German quarter, but those living in the Polish quarter were allowed to remain there for the time being. However, Jewish refugees who, like our family, were newcomers to Warsaw were not permitted to live in the Polish quarter. These rules were to change soon. As all the Jews were now being ordered to move into the Jewish area, their gradual eviction from many streets led to a mass exodus in both directions. At that stage about 113,000 non-Jews had to move out of what was to become the ghetto and some 138,000 Jews were forced to take their place.

It is hard to visualise the displacement of such a huge number of people. I can still see the never-ending procession of figures moving through the narrow streets, distress painted all over their faces, pushing carts, prams, buggies, handcarts, trolleys and barrows filled with their personal belongings, some of them thrown in loose, obviously in a hurry, others in trunks, boxes and bundles, with mattresses and bedding piled on top. Household utensils, pots and pans were stuck in between the bigger items and rattled noisily, while loose articles of clothing filled every available gap. As the displaced Jews were not allowed to take any larger objects with them except some miserable bits of furniture, a broken chair here, a small table there, dangled forlornly from the sides of the vehicles. Children tried to keep pace with these mobile junk piles or were perched dangerously on top of them. Now and again, a frayed rope or bits of inadequate string would give, and suddenly a bundle, a pot or a parcel would roll into the road with a loud bang, followed by a distressed person running around, trying to retrieve it. Most adults were in addition laden, like some pack animals, with whatever they could carry on their backs, in their hands or suspended from their necks. The incredible squalor so far hidden in the deepest recesses of people's dwellings was now dragged out into the open for the first time, for all to see. More misery was in store for the newcomers in their new homes – if one could give such a name to the hovels awaiting them. Most rooms in this part of town were small and according to German statistics six to seven people on average had now to squeeze into each one of them, while within a year the numbers increased to nine people per room, with the density of population nearing 200,000 per square mile.

The curfew for all Jews living outside the Jewish quarter was now set back by an hour to 8 p.m. All buses, trolley cars and trams had separate carriages marked with a Star of David for Jews only. In the street Jews had to step aside and give way to German soldiers.

In September we moved from Żelazna Street to 47 Nowolipie, as another piece of wall was to be erected just opposite our house. There was some uncertainty as to whether the house itself would remain inside the ghetto. Our new home was only a few minutes' walk away and was reached by following Żelazna Street past the Leszno junction and turning first-right into Nowolipie. It was then only a couple of hundred yards to our new home on the right-hand side of the street. Close by there was a small gate in the wall separating the ghetto from the outside world. We were to live in the quietest section of the street, inhabited before the war by the better-off Jews.

Our new apartment block had the usual substantial multi-storey frontage with elaborate stone balconies and a large, plainer *oficyna* (the back part of the quadrangle) surrounded the courtyard on the remaining three sides. Unlike the overwhelming majority of the population, my parents could still afford to pay for the luxury of one large room just for the three of us. Our bed-sitter in its previous incarnation had served as the dining room in a comfortable flat owned by friends of some people we knew. In contrast with our previous home, there were no trams outside and little passing traffic. The apartment was full of books and I was allowed to borrow any I liked, so I spent a lot of time reading; it was safer to stay at home, and, anyway, there was no school and no jobs to go to. Not that time hung heavily on my hands. In fact, the problem lay in continuous interruptions. During the day neighbours kept coming in for a chat, even when my parents were out. People had very little to occupy themselves with, so they constantly sought the company of others. Being completely cut off from the outside world, all were hungry for news. Even gossip would do.

One always tried to hold on to some hope of good news, of learning something that would rekindle one's belief in eventual deliverance. The credulity of some people knew no bounds

A question on most people's mind was whether this was going to be an open or a closed ghetto. Many hoped that with so many Jews presently working in the Polish quarter and so many Poles working in the ghetto it would remain open, not like in Lódz, where the Germans had sealed off the local ghetto right from the start.

On 12 October, the day of Yom Kippur, that holiest day in the Jewish calendar, loudspeakers set up in the streets proclaimed the official decree establishing the ghetto. On the same day it was also announced that public religious worship was forbidden. Posters appeared showing the list of streets to be included in the ghetto. Of the 1,800 streets of Warsaw, the list named only 70 odd, and of those only a few were included in their entire length. For the time being it was to be an open ghetto, but we were now almost certain that it would not be so for long.

On 16 November some people we knew tried to cross to the 'other side', as areas outside the ghetto were now called, and found German and Polish police barring their way. There were 20 gates in the walls at the time and all appeared now to be sealed to anyone without a valid pass. The whole area of the ghetto was grim: there were hardly any trees, no parks, no open spaces – just grey and depressing buildings wherever you looked.

Not surprisingly, given the density of population, some of the streets, such as Karmelicka and Smocza Street, looked like enormous anthills. On the pavements and in the middle of the road one had to elbow one's way through crowds of people, many in rags, some wrapped for warmth in dirty blankets, hawking their belongings – used household objects, worn-out clothes, dog-eared books, broken furniture. Whatever the weather, the streets were lined with beggars, whole families with children and babies, leaning against the buildings or lying at the edge of the pavement, their hands feebly reaching out for alms. In the less crowded streets the most popular form of transport was rickshaws, their emaciated drivers pedalling as hard as they could to cope with their human cargoes.

And then there were smells – a smell of decay and dust in the summer, of mud and slush in the winter; the stench of poverty, unwashed bodies, of rags serving as clothing. Sometimes, early in the mornings there was also a sickly smell of corpses barely covered with newspapers, awaiting collection. But above all there was a smell of fear from which you were never free, a fear of ending up in a concentration camp or in the vast, pre-war Pawiak prison, which was within the boundaries of the ghetto and had been taken over by the Gestapo. It was situated in Pawia Street, not 15 minutes' walk from where we lived. An occasional burst of gunfire from a nearby street signalled to me that some Germans might be amusing themselves on the way to Pawiak or while visiting the ghetto on another errand.

Winters, with their frequent snow and sub-zero temperatures round the clock, brought even more hardships to the population who were largely deprived of fuel. Beggars covered themselves for warmth with rags or newspapers, but deaths from cold were getting more and more common. The appalling living conditions, disease and starvation were only the prologue to the systematic extermination of people whose only crime was to be Jewish. We had been issued with ration cards, but the nutritional value of the ration was ridiculously below survival level, roughly a tenth of what could be considered adequate. It consisted of about two pounds of bread and two ounces of sugar a week. Other foodstuffs, such as potatoes, flour or fat, were distributed from time to time in insignificant quantities.

Contemporary records show that from November 1940 till July 1942, of the 400,000 inhabitants of the ghetto some 80,000 died of hunger and disease. To quote from a note on the margin of Governor Hans Frank's diary of 24 August 1941: 'I confirm that we are sentencing 1.2 million Jews to death by hunger. It is clear that if the Jews do not die of hunger, anti-Jewish edicts will have to be intensified.' On 16 December 1941 he wrote in the same diary: 'One must deal most severely with Jews attempting to leave the ghetto. The death sentence has to be carried out with all speed. Any Jew found outside the ghetto must be unconditionally put to death.'

As far as my parents and I were concerned we had so far had enough clothes for our needs. Nevertheless one day Father took me to a shoemaker's in a tiny workshop off Nowolipie Street, filled with a wonderful smell of leather. An elderly man with thick glasses balanced precariously at the tip of his nose and an apron tied around his waist, sat at a small wooden bench placed against the wall. He motioned me into one of his two chairs and, sitting on a low stool, he checked my feet for size. He presented me with a selection of skins of different colours and various degrees of softness, from which I chose a very soft burgundy-coloured leather. The price he quoted for the shoes seemed to me astronomical, but Father did not bat an eyelid. Ten days later we went to collect them and they proved to be the most beautiful shoes I have ever had and, at the same time, so sturdy that I thought they would never wear out. But, by the time we got home one of them was pinching my toe. Thinking of the expense I kept quiet about it, but Mother quickly sensed that something was wrong. We took the shoes back to the shoemaker who stretched them for a few days on a larger last. After this treatment followed by several weeks of daily wear the new shoes gave me no bother.

My uncle Edek was released from the Radogoszcz concentration camp in the autumn of 1940 and came to Warsaw with his wife, Mala, and Krysia, their one-year-old daughter. The months in the camp had left obvious marks on him. He had lost many stones in weight, and he looked pale and dejected, years older than when I had last seen him. Holding back her tears, Mother embraced and kissed her brother. Of all the family he was her favourite and during his imprisonment hardly a day went by without her mentioning his name. Edek and Mala had managed to salvage some of their valuables. They now found a room near us in Nowolipie in a flat shared with Mala's older brother, Moniek. I liked Moniek, his cheerful chubby face, his warm heart and his jokes. He never complained, never grumbled. He adored little Krysia and used to spend hours playing with her, crawling on the floor, talking to her incessantly as if she could understand his every word.

Another surprise was the arrival in the ghetto of my old English teacher from Cracow. He still looked upright and dignified, although his dark suit, the only one I had ever seen him wear, was shinier and more crumpled, and his beige raincoat even shabbier and stained in places. I was glad to resume my English lessons.

At one stage, not having seen Moniek for several days, I asked Edek about him and was told that he was laid low by an abscess in his armpit. In the conditions of the ghetto any illness caused concern. The abscess refused to heal, the swelling increased in size and became more painful every day. Moniek became feverish and the doctor called to see him. He prescribed hot poultices and some other home-made remedies available in the ghetto. Days passed and Moniek did not improve. On the contrary, he was soon confined to bed as the high fever persisted. Mala and Edek took turns at his bedside, changing his dressings, applying poultices, nursing him as best they could. Eventually, in spite of the great risk of surgery under the surrounding conditions, the abscess had to be lanced. Two days later Moniek was dead. He was 25 years old.

Luckily for Edek and for our family, the valuables brought from Łódź ensured that we had enough to eat and had a comfortable roof over our heads. Buying food was now Father's and Edek's task: they knew their way around the black market. Butter, coffee and tea were available only in their substitute or ersatz form, but meat, poultry and bread would be the real thing. Although as a child I could not stand the taste of real honey (my nanny used to punish me for my wrongdoings by forcing me to drink a mixture of milk and honey) I loved the honey substitute, a sweet gold-coloured semi-liquid substance I used to spread over bread.

As New Year 1941 approached, the Jewish Council was given permission to open vocational courses for young people. There was little to choose from; the first course was to train locksmiths and have them qualified after six months. Father was overjoyed by the news.

'You mustn't waste this opportunity,' he persuaded me. 'Who knows how long this war will go on for? Neither I nor my resources will last forever, you must be able to make a living.' Father had very robust ideas about the importance of learning a trade. Twelve years before he had been very disappointed with his younger brother's persistent failure to earn a living. Eventually he bought him a ticket to emigrate to Brazil, supposed to be a country of opportunities. But before doing so he sent him on a watch-makers' course.

'Heniek,' he urged his brother, 'as soon as you get on the ship, set up a little table on the deck, spread out your watch-making tools and wait for customers; there are sure to be passengers needing their watches repaired. By the time you get to Brazil you will have a small capital to start a business.' I learned later, though, that during the week-long voyage nobody had needed any watch repairs. After getting to Rio de Janeiro he kept sending us photographs of himself as a porter, with heavy loads on his back.

I needed no persuasion. I couldn't wait to get busy again, and the prospect of acquiring qualifications of any sort appealed to me. My friend Tadek Wolpert was of the same mind. A few days later the two of us made our way to the school in Żelazna Street, inevitably risking being caught up in a *łapanka*, a regular German round-up. It was a repetition of our daily walk to school in Łódź. Then, as now, we had to play cat and mouse with German marauders and worry about being snatched from the street. But the tension and fear were much worse now than a year ago. In Łódź, and later on in Cracow, most Jews captured by the Germans, whatever their ordeal, did eventually return home. In the Warsaw ghetto the lucky ones would do a day's forced labour of the filthiest kind. The unlucky ones landed in Pawiak. Not long ago I had met a man who, though thrown into the notorious prison, had by an unusual stroke of luck been released. From him I heard harrowing accounts of inhuman tortures inflicted there on the prison's inmates, before they were shot in the prison yard or deported to concentration camps.

The school was housed in an old, rather decrepit building, and the lessons took place in large and equally neglected classrooms. Paint was peeling off the walls, plaster coming off the ceilings would crumble onto our heads. The course covered both theory and practice. At the former lessons we sat at wooden tables, listening to the teacher and copying the notes he scribbled on the blackboard with coloured chalks. This was a far cry from the richly equipped laboratories of my Łódź school, and yet it felt wonderful to be in a classroom being taught again. We learned how to make and interpret two-dimensional drawings representing three-dimensional objects. We studied metal technology, physics and elementary mechanics.

Practical tuition took place in the adjoining vast hall, furnished with long parallel benches. Each of us was assigned his own place with a vice and tools – files of all sizes and different degrees of coarseness, chisels, pliers, hacksaws, hammers and gauges. We had access also to grinders and to large drills. We learned how to bring pieces of metal to white-hot temperatures in a gas-fired furnace and how to hammer them into the required shapes. At the end of the course I knew how to make a mortise lock, a heavy-duty padlock, vices and other iron and steel appliances. I took pride in my work and found it truly creative. For the first time in my life I became aware of the joy of working with my own hands, using my imagination and newly acquired skills, and creating objects for everyday use.

One day, walking along Nowolipie Street I bumped into a girl with a familiar face. She was of my age and an attractive blonde, despite the fact that the point of her nose almost touched her upper lip. There was no mistake, it was Ada, a girl I had met three years earlier, when we were both spending our summer vacations in a holiday camp for young people in Rabka, a mountain resort in the south of Poland. I had had a crush on her. She was 13 years old at the time and was my constant companion and table-tennis partner. She was probably the first girl I ever kissed and we'd had plenty of opportunity to be on our own and to kiss and cuddle. She lived in Poznań and when the summer ended we lost contact with each other.

I stopped and called out, 'Ada?' She looked at me with amazement.

'Jerzy?' she replied, smiling broadly. We were both delighted to meet again.

'Where do you live?' I asked. 'At Nowolipie 49,' she said. It was incredible – she lived next door.

When I went to visit her the next day she was in bed with glandular fever. The bed took up nearly half her tiny room, leaving space only for a small wardrobe and a chair on which I would sit every evening holding her hand. She had always had a pale complexion, but now her cheeks were the colour of her pillowcase. She kept asking me to read to her from her favourite books, sentimental stories of romance and love. 'Read it again,' she would plead, when a sentence or paragraph appealed to her. Some colour would come back to her cheeks as she listened to the more intimate details of amorous adventures. She hoped we could recapture the excitement of our Rabka holidays, but I was becoming increasingly bored with the monotony of our literary diet. I was losing interest in

Ada too, but did not want to upset her by telling her how I felt. By the time she recovered I found enough excuses to avoid her company and our relationship came to an end.

We lived in Nowolipie Street until January 1941 when we moved again, to a parallel street, just ten minutes' walk away, with a rather similar name, Nowolipki. Here, at number 14, we found a comfortable room in a large apartment on the second floor of the building that still bore the hallmarks of its recent prosperity as the home of wealthy professionals and businessmen. The seven-room flat belonged to Dr Leinkram who retained one large bedroom for himself and his wife and an adjoining smaller room for his daughter, Bronka, a young woman of 23. Apart from ours, three more bedrooms were rented to refugee tenants. All were allowed the use of the dining room, which one had to cross on the way to the shared bathroom and kitchen. Ours was a large, bright and airy front room facing south, so that in good weather it basked in sunshine for most of the day.

Our immediate neighbours were Mrs Seideman – a middle-aged war widow, a tall elegant lady who lived in one of the smaller rooms in the flat – and a couple of refugees from Germany, Mr and Mrs Hirsch. He was about 50, a big, stocky man, who had been forced to leave behind a prosperous business in Berlin. His wife, grey-haired, a year or so younger, was a corpulent, softly spoken lady. Their command of Polish was limited, but most people in the flat could speak German. Soon after we moved in, the Hirsches asked us to tea. Their room adjoined ours, but the connecting door was permanently locked. It was a bright day and we were enjoying the early spring sunshine flooding the room through the closed windows. While our hostess was getting the drinks ready, Mother talked to Mr Hirsch.

'When did you come to Warsaw?' she asked.

'Six months ago.'

'Were you forced to leave?'

'I was, but Berta, my wife, was not.'

'Why not?'

'She was born Protestant and her family has strong links with the Nazi Party. In spite of great pressure from them, she converted to Judaism and decided to marry me some 15 years ago. Ever since, and especially since Hitler came to power, they have been desperate to get her away from me.'

'Does she keep in touch with them?'

'She doesn't, but they do with her.' He pointed to a pile of papers on a small mahogany desk. 'She keeps getting letters urging her to leave me and go back to Berlin, where they would welcome her with open arms. But she refuses.'

I know that they did stay together to the bitter end, being eventually deported together.

Facing our room across the entrance hall was a library converted into a bedroom-cum-living room. The dark walnut shelves extending along the entire wall on the right-hand side of the entrance door were packed from floor to ceiling with books and medical journals. The room was occupied by a middle-aged journalist and writer – a friendly, outgoing man – along with his wife and their son, Albert. Albert, in his early 20s, of medium build, pensive but not melancholy, seemed shy and taciturn. Most of the time he gave the impression of not knowing what to do with himself.

Small amounts of news reached us from the outside world, but it was greatly sought after. There was only one official newspaper available in the ghetto, a German propaganda rag called *Gazeta Żydowska – The Jewish Gazette*. Again we employed our skills of reading between the lines, which we had developed in Cracow. Luckily we also had access to some unofficial information. Every evening after the curfew, which varied between 7 and 8 p.m., the occupants of the flat would gather round a long table in the dining room, waiting for Dr Leinkram to appear. Sitting down, he would pull out of his pocket a sheet of paper. We have never found out where these sheets came from. Each day he would get the typescript of the latest news broadcast from the BBC World Service from a secret source. This became the most important event of our day and we absorbed his every word avidly. By revealing the German propaganda fed to us by the official newspapers for what it was, this news gave us hope. We filled the inevitable gaps, using our imagination. The persistent lack of reference to our own plight was, however, heart-breaking. Each time, we sought even the slightest hint that the Allies knew of our desperate plight, and of the barbaric treatment meted out to us by our common enemy – but always in vain.

In January 1941 Dr Leinkram read to us that in a single day 1,500 civilians had been killed in bombing raids over Britain. In February we heard that the British had captured 20,000 Italian soldiers in North Africa, pushing Mussolini's forces westwards, very much to Hitler's annoyance. But in the Atlantic, German U-boats were inflicting heavy losses on British merchant shipping, posing a serious threat to the British war effort. Every evening the news session was followed by a lively discussion. Every person present gave his or her interpretation of the recent news, but we all tried to draw as much hope from them as possible. At one stage we even went into discussions of the writings of Nostradamus, the most widely read seer of the Renaissance, whose book *Centuries*, published in the middle of the sixteenth century, appeared one day on our dining table. We had difficulty in deciding which of his prophecies had already come true and which were still to be fulfilled, and of these, which referred to our own plight. Hoping to penetrate the obscurity of his writing, we tried to foresee how the war would end and to deduce our own chances of survival. As far as we were concerned, the outcome of the war was never in doubt: we had to believe that Germany would be defeated. But boundless faith was needed to expect that we would be there to see its death throes.

Sitting there at the table, taking part in a heated discussion, I tried to imagine myself after the war, alive, surrounded by family and children and bearing witness to our present reality. However, deep down, I had many doubts: even if I lived, would my tales find credence? Would my children have the patience to listen to them?

One morning in the spring of 1941, during breakfast, Edek, who had by now regained his self-confidence and poise, walked into the room. Although he was dressed in his old tweed overcoat, he looked rather different. The coat was held with a leather belt, he wore a police armband, a cap with a star badge and brightly polished black boots. With the long rubber truncheon in his hand he was, unmistakably, a member of the Jewish police force. The force was formed at the same time as the ghetto and had attracted a large number of volunteers, mainly from the intelligentsia. By the end of

December 1941 well over 1,000 men were serving in it and there was a long waiting list of applicants.

Tall, upright and handsome, Edek appeared to have acquired an aura of authority. He took off his belt and overcoat, put them on the bed and sat down at the table. He took an identity card with an impressive-looking stamp out of his coat pocket and passed it around. 'Do you know why I joined?' he asked, sounding slightly on the defensive. Without waiting for a reply he went on: 'I went through hell in the Radogoszcz camp, but this ought to make me safe!'

'What did it cost you?' Father asked.

'Not a *grosh*,' he answered. 'I volunteered, went for an interview and they took me on.'

I suspected that he liked the idea of wielding power and that he also needed something to keep him busy.

'What are your duties?' I asked, looking admiringly at his shiny boots.

'Our main job is patrolling the ghetto gates to stop smuggling, checking people's identities and guarding approaches to the walls. We shall be directing traffic, supervising sanitation, dealing with small-time crime. We may even be solving disputes between people.'

'To whom are the police responsible?' Father wished to know. Edek went into an involved explanation that did not make much sense to me. As it turned out later, the lines of communication between the Jewish police, the Polish police, the Jewish Council and the Germans were never properly defined and remained fluid. From my own observations, the police at first were regarded with respect by their fellow Jews. Rather than hand petty criminals to the Polish police for harsh treatment, they themselves administered some kind of justice. They even had, Edek told me, their own small prison in Gęsia Street, not far from our house, where they kept people, mainly smugglers, and half of them children, in abysmal conditions. As time went on, the Jewish police fell into disrepute for their corruption – they became the most enthusiastic recipients of bribes from the very people whose excesses they were supposed to control – and for their blind obedience to the Germans.

Life in the crowded ghetto with very little to do was taking a heavy toll on Father's equanimity. Not surprisingly, something was happening to him, as it was to all of us. For some reason he took to nagging me, picking on me, calling me names and constantly grumbling about me to Mother.

'How could I ever leave you?' he would say to her, 'to be cared for by this cretin of a son? He'll never be able to earn a living even for himself!'

This kind of abuse went on daily and I had no choice but to get used to it, even though at times I would half-heartedly answer back. Mother's reaction was twofold. On the one hand she attempted to defend me (though usually in vain) and on the other she must have tried to take into account the stress Father had to endure, a man previously so active and now totally frustrated. Mother's own impatience would show at times. When Father turned up very late for lunch one day she suspected that he had met with Ewa Blumental, whom my parents had known in Lódz. She burst out:

'Where have you been? I know, you don't need to tell me! You've been whoring again! Whiling your time away with Ewa, that despicable red-cheeked creature with her bust like two balloons and her low-slung bottom practically brushing the ground!'

Sometimes at night I would take my revenge. Woken up by rustling and creaking sounds from the direction of my parents' bed I would shout: 'Dad, leave Mother alone! I can't sleep with that noise going on!' They had enough of a sense of humour left to laugh it off.

There were other funny moments. One bright day in early May my uncle came to see us. With feigned surprise he looked at Father sitting at the table. 'Jakub,' he said to him, 'turn your face towards the light, closer to the window, so that I can have a better look at you.' Father obliged. 'I really don't know what's happened to you,' my uncle went on in a serious tone. 'You have this peculiar blemish on the left-hand side of your nose, and it's never been there before.' Mother and I approached to have a closer look at my father's nose and it did not look any different to us. He was as amused as we were. 'It's grown as quickly as a mushroom!' Edek continued. 'For all our sakes I hope it's not catching,' and we howled with laughter. We obviously needed something to laugh about.

Uncle Edek dropped in to see me one day and said casually:

'What has come over you? Every time I come here, you are out on the balcony staring into the distance, yet always in the same direction. What is there to look at?'

I blushed, but decided to confide in him. 'Come out here,' I said, and nodding towards my left I added, 'look at her, isn't she pretty?'

'She is that all right,' he agreed, when I pointed out to him the attractive brunette of my own age on the balcony of the adjoining building, some ten yards away. Only her head was visible above the ledge; the rest of her body was hidden from view by the balcony's stone pillars. She was looking at me with the same intensity that I was looking at her.

'When did all this start?' Edek was curious.

'Some two weeks ago, on one of the first warm spring days,' I answered.

'And how often do you exchange these smouldering looks?' he continued.

'Every day, weather permitting.'

'You can't go on like this forever, looking won't get you very far. Let me sort this out for you.'

He went out and a few minutes later emerged on the girl's balcony. I saw him talking to her and when she smiled, Uncle beckoned me to come downstairs. Breathlessly I ran into the street, and a minute later there he was with the girl in tow. Then, tactfully, he withdrew. I now had a chance to look at her closely. Beneath her pretty face there was an exceptionally short body of a rather unappealing shape, far from what I had imagined. We exchanged names and then I was stuck – finding it difficult to choose a subject of mutual interest. I felt awkward, there were more pauses than words. We walked round the block before I found an excuse for going home. For the next few weeks, I avoided the balcony, whatever the weather.

What struck me when I first saw Bronka, Dr Leinkram's only daughter, were her very thick glasses; she was obviously short-sighted. She had a curvaceous but well-proportioned figure and her hips swayed slightly as she walked. She was not a beauty, but she was intelligent, well-read, witty and amusing – really interesting to talk to. Her husband, a reserve officer, had been called up at the outbreak of the war, and if he was still alive, which I thought was doubtful, must be a POW somewhere in the Soviet Union. I had a feeling that Bronka was interested in me. We kept meeting in the corridor or in the dining room and she would smile at me and keep the conversation going beyond the customary exchange of greetings. One late afternoon, as we were both trying to squeeze past each other between the wall and the chairs in the dining room, she stopped for a few seconds. I could feel her breasts pressing against me and her fragrance made me feel dizzy. I brushed her cheek with my mouth and she did not turn away. Not a word was said. From then on, whenever we met on our own, we would come close together as if drawn by a magnet and stay in silent contact for a while. In the evenings, political discussions raging all around us, we kept our eyes glued on one another. One day, when there was nobody around, she asked me if I would like to spend an afternoon just with her. I hoped that my eagerness didn't show when I said yes! Next evening she slipped me a piece of paper with an address and time written on it. I could hardly wait for the moment.

It was an apartment on the second floor of a large building in Gęsia Street. I knocked on the door and an elderly woman let me in. Silently she led me into a small, sparsely furnished room with an iron bed, a small cupboard, a bedside table and chair. White lace curtains fluttered around a small window. It was very warm. Bronka was sitting on the bed in her familiar brown checked skirt and brown cardigan over a white blouse. She looked more attractive without her glasses. I smelled the familiar perfume.

'Have you ever made love?' she asked.

'No,' I replied truthfully.

'And would you like to now?'

My mouth went dry. I did not answer. I sat down on the bed, put my arm around her and drew her towards me.

'No, not yet,' she pushed me away. 'First take off your clothes.' I pinched myself to make sure I was not dreaming. This was a scene straight out of an erotic novel, out of my dreams, the moment I had been imagining for years. With shaky hands I took off my jacket and shirt, slipped off my shoes and pulled down my trousers. She was slowly undressing, taking off her cardigan, her blouse, her bra, her skirt, her pink knickers and slip and then stood naked in front of me.

When it was over, I was overcome with sadness. I felt like crying. She noticed and asked, 'What's the matter?'

'Nothing,' I replied, trying to hide my feelings. I suddenly resented Bronka. I could not understand how the inexplicable longing and desire I felt one minute could have changed to indifference and revulsion the next. I got dressed and found it difficult to carry on a meaningful conversation with her. I kept looking at my watch.

'We have to be back before the curfew,' I said, wishing I was home already. In the evening, when we all gathered to hear the daily news, I turned my face away whenever she looked at me. She knew that I was avoiding her and that our romance was over before it had really begun.

On June 22, 1941 Dr Leinkram announced that that morning German armed forces had invaded the Soviet Union – their former ally – without any warning. German bombers attacked seven Russian cities and countless air bases, and the German army began its advance along a 900-mile front. We could not contain our joy. New hopes were raised: hadn't we now gained a powerful ally, bringing closer the defeat of our now common enemy?

Two days later Edek appeared with more news. 'We can expect Russian air raids any day now,' he said. 'The ghetto is to create its own fire service staffed with volunteers, who will receive official identity cards and special armbands. Perhaps Jerzy should join. It might be a good idea, don't you think?'

'And what good would that do?' Father asked.

'The volunteers ought to be safe in the streets, the Germans will not bother them.'

'So what's the catch?'

'There is an enrolment charge, though I don't know yet how high.'

I decided to join. Father paid the charges and I received an armband and an official identity card. But there was a catch. To my great disappointment, the card bore only the Jewish police stamp on it. It read: 'I, Jerzy Lando, certify being a member of the ghetto

Voluntary Fire Service'. There was no German stamp, no photograph, no official signature. I never had the opportunity of testing its effectiveness. When it soon became clear that the rapid advance of the Germans deep into Russian territory and the virtual destruction of their air force prevented them from launching air attacks, I gave up the armband and did not bother to carry the identity card. The scheme was one of the many German tricks intended to create illusions and raise false hopes.

From now on, the daily news read by Dr Leinkram was depressing. On the battlefield the Soviets suffered one setback after another. Within days the Germans reached Dvinsk, some 200 miles inside the Soviet border, then captured Lvov and Riga, and by 27 July they were encircling Smolensk, and took 100,000 Russians prisoner. On 19 September the German army entered Kiev. By the end of September they cut off Crimea from the rest of Russia and by early November they laid siege to Leningrad.

By the summer of 1941 the conditions in the ghetto – the overcrowding, the general privation and poor sanitary standards – led to a serious outbreak of typhus that went on unabated until the spring of 1942. According to official statistics, in the winter of 1941–2 200 people died daily. Typhus is spread by lice and the incubation period is 9 to 14 days. The onset of the disease is marked by a high temperature, accompanied by severe headaches and prostration, a feeling of utter physical exhaustion. After three days a rash appears, the patient descends into stupor and keeps slipping into a coma. Most patients die. Like the lice which carry it, typhus respects no social barriers. We all dreaded the disease.

My English teacher used to come twice a week to give me lessons. No longer did he even try to look smart; that old raincoat which he wore all the year round had more holes and patches from one week to the next. The clothes underneath it looked shabby, worn out and tired. They hung on him as on a scarecrow; he was visibly losing weight. His face was getting increasingly pale, more drawn and wrinkled. Every time he came for a lesson Mother offered him a meal. One day I noticed a whitish speck of an insect on his jacket lapel. I wasn't absolutely sure what it was, but I panicked. Mother was sitting at the other end of the room and as discreetly as I could

I beckoned to her, urging her to have a look. She had no doubt – it was a body louse. Mother didn't betray her anxiety, but explained to my teacher that we could no longer afford the lessons and that, to her great regret, this would have to be my last one.

Soon after we moved house, in the spring of 1941, I heard the sound of a violin playing. The sound was coming through our windows, so I looked out. The musician in the street was a handsome, well-built man in his early 30s with thick blond hair, and he was wearing a light-beige raincoat. Standing next to him was a pretty little boy, some four years old, blond with blue eyes. They were leaning against a black wooden fence. The man would play the same few tunes every day from dawn to dusk and sometimes passers-by would drop a coin or two into his cardboard box. As the months went by his appearance kept changing. He was now hunched, leaner and dishevelled; the fair stubble on his face showed that he had given up regular shaving. His shoes first lost their shine and later their shape. By autumn his raincoat reappeared and when winter came, it turned shabby and dirty. His music changed too – it grew quiet and subdued, his melodies more melancholy. On cold winter days both the man's and the child's faces would change from pink to white and then to blue. The man's fingers, visible through his torn gloves, increasingly crooked and swollen, eventually assumed almost grotesque shapes, while his bare shins, swollen by hunger, peeped through the holes of his ragged trousers.

Winter snow no longer brought a sense of wonder. The ghetto was not transformed suddenly into a magic land, where what had been grey and dirty was suddenly pristine white, and where harsh sounds were muffled. The snow, as soon as it came down, turned into slush, mud, and with a further drop of temperature, into treacherous ice. Thousands of people were said to be dying of cold. One morning in late January 1942, surprised by no music reaching me from across the road, I looked out of the window; there was no violin player and there was no child. I never saw them again.

Towards the end of November the news reaching us from the outside world turned more cheerful again. The British had finally broken the German siege of Tobruk and the German army was now in retreat in North Africa. The Germans had also suffered their first serious setback on the Eastern front, having had to give up Rostov-on-Don, thus halting their advance towards Caucasus. Their continued attempts to occupy Moscow were thwarted. On 8 December came the news of the Japanese air force's attack on American warships in Pearl Harbor, bringing the Americans into the war. A few days later Germany declared war on the USA. This brought us more hope. In the second part of December, Rommel's German army in North Africa suffered more heavy losses and on the Eastern front German forces continued their retreat. The end of war seemed closer; it could not last long and our side was sure to win.

In the meantime, the occupants continued to tighten the screw. On 25 December 1941 posters in German and Polish appeared on the walls with the following announcement:

> DECREE CONCERNING FUR ARTICLES. ALL FUR COATS, FUR CAPES, FUR COLLARS AS WELL AS ALL OTHER FUR ARTICLES OF ANY SORT, WHETHER RAW MATERIALS, FINISHED OR SEMI-MANUFACTURED GOODS, ARE TO BE HANDED IN BY 28 DECEMBER 1941. JEWS FOUND IN POSSESSION OF THE ABOVE ARTICLES WILL BE SHOT.

There followed addresses of the collection points.

The decree was issued in the middle of a severe winter, which started early with temperatures of 15 to 20 degrees centigrade below freezing point. On the morning of 27 December I went with Father to the Grzybowska Street depot to hand in Mother's fur coat as well as Father's, and my own fur-lined overcoat. We joined a long queue of people.

'This will hit the poor very hard,' Father remarked, as we were waiting. 'They have little to eat and no fuel to heat their homes with. Most of their winter clothes are nothing but a patchwork of bits of old fur.'

'How on earth can the Germans justify such mass robbery?' I protested bitterly.

'What their newspapers say,' Father replied, 'is that it would not be right for German soldiers to freeze on the Russian front while Jews walk around in furs. The Germans were so convinced that they would defeat Russia before the onset of winter that they did not bother to equip their armies for winter conditions.'

We waited in the queue for nearly two hours before finally reaching the official who handed us receipts for our fur coats.

Even in the ghetto, my thirst for knowledge had to be assuaged. Once my friend Tadek and I had completed our first course and received certificates of proficiency (a source of pride for us), we were given the chance of going on to the follow-up course of mechanical engineering. There, I learned how to operate a lathe and Tadek worked on the largest machine in our school, a giant mechanical drill, reaching all the way up to the ceiling. The machine and Tadek, the tallest in the class, looked as if they were made for one another. After a month or two, though, I got bored with the course; it wasn't stretching me enough. And I did not like the look of my hands, covered with dirt and oil which were hard to remove; at the end of every day I had to scrub my hands till they hurt, and even then I couldn't get rid of the grease under my fingernails. Consequently, as soon as I heard that a six-month commercial course was about to start in nearby Leszno Street, I applied. There we learned bookkeeping, shorthand, typing and office routine, subjects that appealed to me much more than using machine tools. At the end of the course I could type quite fast with all ten fingers and take down shorthand dictation at a reasonable speed. I was fascinated by the principles of double-entry accounting. The knowledge I acquired came in handy sooner than I expected in a true business environment, but at this point my enthusiasm for figure work started to wane.

During and after the course I devoted a lot of my spare time to studying languages. I tried to improve my school French and greatly profited from the advice of our neighbour from across the entrance hall, the journalist. 'Get yourself a French magazine,' he said, 'or a French book and just read it. Try to guess the meaning of the words that you don't understand, and only when you really cannot make any sense of the text, look them up in a dictionary.'

I was also determined to learn German, but there wasn't anyone to teach me. Our host, Dr Leinkram, owned two massive volumes of a well-known self-teaching method, the *Langenscheidt*, written for

German speakers learning English. The initial lesson plunged me into the first instalment of Dickens' *A Christmas Carol*, which struck me as a gem of English literature. Each lesson consisted of a half-page extract from the book, a list of the new words encountered together with their translation, a section on grammar plus some examples of daily conversation, such as 'Where is the nearest bus stop?' and 'How much do you charge for a room?' I used the manual in a manner for which I do not believe it was intended by the authors: I was learning German, while improving my English, and made rapid progress in both.

In the ghetto, almost hermetically sealed as it was from the outside world, any rumour would spread like the proverbial bush fire. There were 'good rumours' (meaning good for Jews) and 'bad rumours', and the general tendency was to believe the former and reject the latter. Some of these originated in the daily bulletins, but most spread from mouth to mouth, coming from uncertain sources.

In early 1942 a particularly worrying rumour had it that Jews who had been ostensibly deported from the vicinity of Łódż to forced labour camps were disappearing without trace in the palace at Chełmno-on-the-Ner, some 60 miles away, which had been taken over by the SS. Then a further newsletter carried a short report by three men who had escaped from there and who had witnessed the mass-killings of Jews and gypsies in lorries converted into gas chambers. Chełmno was, then, a death camp. There was no room for doubt any more. The men passed the information to the *Judenrat*, the Jewish Council, in Grabów and one of them managed to reach the Warsaw ghetto and lodge the report with the Jewish Council there.

The advent of spring could have been easily overlooked in the ghetto. No buds heralded its coming and no tender shoots of green appeared. There were no flowers to be seen. In an area where there was hardly a tree and where an empty patch of land was a rarity, there was no smell of spring in the air. The warmer weather brought out more destitute people from their miserable dwellings into the narrow streets, clogging them up and making any kind of traffic impossible. As time went on, and in spite of the exceedingly high mortality rates, the population of the ghetto kept growing as more and more people arrived in the walled-in area. In the spring of 1942 they included Jews from the adjoining towns and villages, gypsies and Jews from Romania, Bulgaria, Hungary, and later from Germany and Czechoslovakia. More and more people of all ages were begging in the streets.

I do not remember how I first met Mirka Baron. And when I did meet her I was not immediately aware of the importance she was going to play in my life. Every story needs a heroine and she soon stepped into that role. This was a girl who could smile and giggle even when there was nothing to laugh about. She arrived in the ghetto from her native Włocławek, a small town north-west of Warsaw, with her mother and her dentist father. They lived in a room in Dzielna Street, less than ten minutes away from us. She had a pretty face, a rather low forehead and black expressive eyes, full of sparkle. Her thick, black hair was plaited into a pigtail. She was my age, and, though rather chunky, she was graceful and her legs were shapely; she was slightly shorter than me. At the slightest hint of a joke she would burst into peals of laughter, revealing two rows of dazzling teeth behind full, sensuous lips. She liked to wear low-cut blouses and dresses that showed her ample bust to great advantage.

We fell madly in love at first sight. Unfortunately, we had little chance to be on our own: the ghetto was a chaperone's paradise. We just walked through the crowded streets, following the same route each day. Every afternoon I walked from Nowolipki to the corner of Zamenhofa Street, where I turned left and left again into Dzielna, the street where she lived. She was waiting for me. We would then walk together to the end of her street, turn left into Smocza and back to Nowolipki past my home, repeating the circle several times, until forced by the curfew to get indoors. We were absorbed in each other, oblivious of what went on around us, unaware of the starving figures lining the dirty, crowded streets. But, as in Cracow with Hanna, I never forgot the ever-present danger of getting caught. We developed an instinct for avoiding it, and could almost sense the approach of man-hunting expeditions before it was too late.

At the end of our walk I would take Mirka home and go up to the room her family occupied, where at least one of her parents was almost always present. The room, facing the courtyard shaped like a well, was dark even in daytime. Even the curtains were made of a thin, dark material. In the evenings the room was poorly lit and rather depressing. In the corner a narrow shelf housed a small Primus stove, a kettle and a few cups and plates. Mirka's father, a bald man, short and thin, always greeted me warmly and invariably offered me a cup of the usual ersatz tea. There were no more than one or two occasions when Mirka and I were in the room on our own for an hour or so and on one of these occasions she was ill in bed. Just a few times, when my parents were out, we had the opportunity to be alone in our room. Though we were desperately drawn to each other, I could count on the fingers of one hand the number of times we were able to kiss in those early days of our friendship.

Mother's sisters, Hela and Frania, were still living, together with their families, in the Łódź ghetto and we were able to send and receive occasional postcards. All the correspondence to and from the Warsaw ghetto had to be written either in German or in Polish and was strictly censored. However, it wasn't difficult to devise a kind of code, which would not be picked up by the censor. If you had a relative by the name of Yankel who had died before the war and you wished to convey the news that your brother was killed last week, you would write on the postcard that your brother had just met Yankel by accident.

It was clear that Mother's family had hardly any money left and were on the edge of starvation; the conditions in Łódź were even worse than in the Warsaw ghetto and we feared for their survival. In mid-March, in the course of one of our evening news sessions, we heard of the mass murder of the Jewish population in Lublin and later on, in April, of the liquidation of Lvov's Jewry. There were rumours that the population of the Łódź ghetto, which was now part of the German Reich, was soon to be liquidated. All this raised our concern about our family, who could be rescued only by being smuggled illegally to Warsaw by bribery, which would cost a fortune. Mother was getting desperate and, as our own financial position was steadily deteriorating, Father was at his wits' end about how to resolve it.

One day in early May Father came back from one of his walks looking rather pleased with himself. 'Do you remember,' he asked Mother, 'Szmul Margolis, my Masonic "brother" from the Łódź lodge? I met him by chance last week. Imagine – he has kept in telephone contact with Mr Dzieniakowski, you know, Jerzy's pre-war chemistry teacher.'

Mr Dzieniakowski was a Christian, now living in Warsaw. When he had been in financial difficulties before the war, Father had helped him out by lending him some money. The same man now owned a successful business, re-processing gold and other precious metals in partnership with Stasio Kleiman, a Jew from Łódź and an acquaintance of my parents. Although Dzieniakowski lived on the 'other side' and Stasio lived in the ghetto, they worked together effectively and made a small fortune between them.

'I met Margolis again today,' Father continued. 'He told Stasio about me and now Stasio would like to see me.'

And so Stasio Kleiman came to visit us and discussed financial affairs with Father. He offered to lend him several thousand 'greens', as US dollars were called, to be repaid more than 20-fold after the war, once the conditions got back to normal. My father agreed, a contract was signed and our money problems were solved. My parents could now afford the cost of smuggling Mother's family out of Łódź and supporting them.

The technicalities of this enterprise were left to Edek. He contacted two rather mysterious people, Messrs Heller and Kon, Jewish refugees from Łódź both, known as 'fixers', working under German patronage. They had powerful protectors in the Gestapo (but this did not prevent them being eventually abandoned to their fate during the mass deportations). For a substantial payment (20,000 złoty per person was the going rate) that they obviously split with their German masters, Heller and Kon made all the necessary arrangements.

Eventually, Mother's two sisters arrived with their families in Warsaw on 12 June 1942. After their experience of the Łódź ghetto they initially thought that they had come to paradise, but, as it soon turned out, their joy was short-lived. The older of the two, Frania, was a woman of striking beauty, a tall slim blonde, with no apparent trace of Jewish blood in her. She was married to her cousin, Edek Engel, who was nicknamed 'fat Edek' or 'bald Edek' to distinguish him from that other Edek Engel, Mother's brother. It would have been in bad taste to refer to him now as 'fat Edek', as, like the rest of the family, he looked emaciated, but he was still bald, so there was no problem with his other nickname! His strikingly deep bass voice also sounded unchanged.

They had a boy called Oleś, 18 months my junior, who used to be my closest childhood friend, and a sweet ten-year-old daughter, Halinka. Up to the start of the war I spent most Saturday afternoons in Oleś' company. Our favourite game was Monopoly, which first made its appearance in Poland in 1936. I hadn't seen Oleś for almost three years, though, and found him changed beyond recognition, both physically and mentally. He was listless, seemed detached, constantly in a daze, and for the first time in my life I found it difficult to get him to talk. The conditions in the Łódż ghetto must have wrought havoc with his personality.

Mother's youngest sister, Hela, slim and short, was married to Eliasz Wolczyks, a man with an amazing sense of humour. At the drop of a hat he could make anyone cry with laughter. He would abuse his gift, though. Whenever he incurred his wife's wrath (and, as he tended to approach life casually and was irresponsible in his financial affairs, this was often enough) he would crack jokes to the point when, disabled by laughter, she would forget his transgressions. He had a great artistic talent and I loved watching him draw; in five minutes flat the most lifelike shapes of men, horses and other animals would appear beneath his black ink pen.

The Wolczyks' only son and my namesake, Jerzy (known as Jerzyk), was a boy of 12, short and gawky. He seemed a slow developer and while ostensibly intelligent, he lacked concentration, was withdrawn and unable to work.

My parents found accommodation for the new arrivals not far from our apartment. Still mourning her parents' death in the Łódż ghetto, Mother regained her equanimity – and joy – now that both her sisters as well as her brother were close to us.

At the same time, Father had another unexpected encounter, with one of his pre-war customers, Bogusław Howil. He, along with his brother Henryk, was managing a large shop owned by their mother Helena, in the very centre of Warsaw at the corner of Marszałkowska Street and Aleje Jerozolimskie. The brothers came from Poznań, where their parents had been brought up as Germans. From the end of the eighteenth century, after the partition of Poland, Poznań had been incorporated into Prussia and many of its inhabitants were either ethnic Germans or else had adopted the German culture. The Howil parents now lived in Cracow and found it expedient to opt for the *Volksdeutsche* status. As such they were entitled to almost all the privileges of *Reichsdeutsche*, actual German citizens. Generally speaking, the *Volksdeutsche* were feared and distrusted by the Polish population. Henryk, the elder son, followed in his parents' footsteps, but Bogusław, or Boguś for short, obstinately remained a Pole. It was Boguś who now introduced my father to one of his own pre-war business associates, Józiek Płomnik, a man in his 30s, who with his brother-in-law, Sam Morgenstern and both their wives, lived in the Warsaw ghetto.

Sam had no children but Józiek had a one-year-old baby daughter who, like other babies, had no chance of survival in ghetto conditions. Boguś Howil volunteered to help save the child. Being a bachelor who lived on his own in Warsaw, he arranged for his parents to take the baby into their own home in Cracow. They defied the threat of the death penalty that faced all those who knowingly helped any Jew living outside the ghetto. The Howils told their friends that the new arrival was an orphan, whose parents, their distant relatives, had been shot by the Russians.

At that time many so-called *szopy*, or workshops, were springing up in the ghetto. They were being set up by Christians from 'the other side', usually in partnership with local Jews. Considerable skills and cheap labour were easily available in the ghetto and, as such enterprises could claim to be supporting the German economy, starved of everyday necessities, the authorities did not object to their creation. The Poles trading with Jews could obtain passes for access to the ghetto. Thus the Howil brothers formed a business venture with Józiek Płomnik and his brother-in-law. They invited Father to join them as a partner; he was able to offer them his considerable business know-how and some additional finance from the loan he had just negotiated. Suitable premises were found – a fairly large apartment at the back of one of the shabbier houses in Nowolipki, a few hundred yards east from where we lived. They bought a number of sewing machines and other equipment and started producing leather goods for the Howils' retail outlet. Using the skills I acquired on my commercial course, I was employed as their bookkeeper and secretary.

Sam Morgenstern, one of Father's new business partners, introduced us to an acquaintance of his, a Mr Tylbor, a short, fat, balding man who spoke Polish with such a strong Yiddish accent that at times I found it difficult to understand him. A widower, he had a beautiful 19-year-old daughter, Marysia, who looked like a typical Aryan – a petite blue-eyed blonde with the face of an angel. In addition she was vivacious and intelligent. I do not know how Marysia had first met Leon Wołowski, who was soon to play a major role in my story, but it happened in the late spring of 1942 and most probably on a tram ride, as Leon was a tram inspector and his job might have taken him on occasions into the ghetto. He was a Catholic, a stocky, well-built man in his forties, of a rather rough appearance. He was married, had two small children and spoke with a working-class accent. A man of a solemn disposition and rather fond of vodka, he was depressing in company. He fell in love with Marysia and soon after their first meeting he put a proposition to Mr Tylbor and his daughter. 'Marysia has no chance of surviving if she stays in the ghetto,' he said. 'If you agree, I am ready to find her somewhere to live outside, where I can look after her and where she will be safe.' The implied condition seemed a small price to pay for an almost assured survival, and she accepted.

In the meantime our news sessions with Dr Leinkram became disheartening again. Since June 1942, in the southern sector of the Eastern front, the Germans were pushing the Red Army back once more and expected an imminent victory. In the second part of July they were well on their way to Stalingrad and on the verge of retaking Rostov-on-Don. Once more they seemed unstoppable. There was nothing to suggest that the Red Army might again recover the lost territories. We learned at the same time that the Western Allies lost 124 merchant ships in the North Atlantic, the highest monthly total of the war, and that the Japanese were victorious in their fight against the British in the Far East.

As usual – and to our great disappointment – no news referred to our plight. The world appeared to have forgotten us.

5

THE FINAL SOLUTION

On Wednesday 22 July I left home in the morning, as usual, on my way to work. As always, the streets were crowded. But here and there the crowds were bigger, people were standing, looking at the walls. I pushed my way through and I suddenly stopped, feeling as if I'd been struck by lightning. On the walls official posters announced in large, fat letters: BY THE ORDER OF GERMAN AUTHORITIES ALL JEWS LIVING IN WARSAW, IRRESPECTIVE OF SEX AND AGE, WILL BE EVACUATED TO THE EAST.

There followed a list of people exempt from deportation: Jews employed by the authorities or by German enterprises; members of the *Judenrat*, the Jewish Council, and those who worked for it; members of the Jewish police force; staffs of hospitals and of the sanitation squads, with their wives and children.

The notice continued:

ALL JEWS FIT FOR WORK WHO HAVE NOT YET BEEN INTEGRATED INTO THE LABOUR PROCESS NEED NOT BE INCLUDED IN THE DEPORTATION BUT WILL BE CONCENTRATED IN BARRACKS WITHIN THE GHETTO AND PUT TO WORK. JEWS, PATIENTS IN HOSPITALS ON THE FIRST DAY OF EVACUATION AND NOT IN CONDITION TO BE MOVED, ARE EXEMPT ON THE PRESENTATION OF THE APPROPRIATE MEDICAL CERTIFICATE.

THE EVACUEE ALLOWANCE PER PERSON SHALL BE UP TO 15 KG OF PERSONAL BELONGINGS. ANYTHING IN EXCESS OF THE STIPULATED WEIGHT WILL BE CONFISCATED. GOLD, JEWELLERY AND CASH ARE ALLOWED. TAKING ENOUGH

FOOD FOR THREE DAYS IS RECOMMENDED. THE
EVACUATION WILL START ON 22 JULY AT 11 A.M.

The declaration was signed by the *Judenrat* clearly under the
dictation of its German masters.

There was no one available for guidance or for comments. The
wording gave many people a false hope of exemption. The reference
to hospital patients suggested that Jews would be treated humanely
and there was no hint whatsoever that they would be sent to their
deaths. As I soon discovered, the Germans deliberately kept on
throwing such hints of false hope to the Jews, so that right to the
very end they would not know the fate that awaited them. This was
their perfidious way of stunning the victim before slaughter, so that
it would offer no resistance.

In addition, they had an uncanny gift of making every single Jew
believe that whatever fate was bestowed on others, he or she alone
would survive.

The next day Edek brought even more alarming news. 'I have just
heard,' he said, 'that a high-ranking German officer accompanied by
some aides came to the headquarters of the *Judenrat* yesterday
morning. Their demand was simple: a minimum daily contingent of
6,000 people are to be delivered for deportation to the east, until
eventually all Jews, irrespective of sex and age, will be deported.'

'Though they did mention some exemptions,' he added as an
afterthought.

It all sounded implausible. Where the hell in the east are they
setting up those workshops for Jews, I wondered. They had been
gradually emptying the other ghettos – and with all those thousands
of new arrivals we were talking about something like 350,000 Jews
here, in the Warsaw ghetto alone.

People I talked to were convinced at first that no more than a
quarter of the population would be affected by deportations and that
they would be those for whom there seemed little hope of survival
in the overcrowded, starved and typhus-ridden city. They
themselves reported for transportation, hoping for a better future
elsewhere. Others, who did not work and believed that having a
productive job would protect them from deportation, desperately

tried to find jobs or at least get certificates stating that they were employed. At first the Gestapo accepted such documents at face value when they were presented to them for accreditation, and this fact further deceived people into believing that only the poorest would be deported.

During the first phase, lasting eight days, the responsibility for the evacuation was placed on the shoulders of Jewish police. Edek explained that initially the German SS were involved only in the planning of the *Aktion* – as they referred to the process of deportation – and, like a dragon whose voracious hunger has to be regularly sated, they named the daily quota of people to be delivered by the Jewish police.

Father made sure that our family and the workers were issued with certificates of employment. He also insisted that all his employees regularly reported to our workshop and stayed there all day. We were making leather goods for the business owned by Mrs Helena Howil and her two sons and thus, admittedly by some stretch of imagination, were assisting the German war effort. I managed to persuade Father to let Mirka and her parents join our workforce. I did not emphasise Mirka's father's profession, nor his experience of putting stitches into patients' gums after extractions as a factor in his favour, even though he would be expected to stitch together pieces of leather.

On the last day of July the atmosphere in the ghetto visibly changed. As I soon realised, the day marked the beginning of the second phase of the *Aktion* that was to last for a fortnight. The SS now took over from the Jewish police full charge of the deportations, and a large number of German gendarmerie, Ukrainian, Latvian and Lithuanian soldiers, descended on the almost deserted streets. For weeks to come they would follow a systematic procedure of laying siege to the buildings and streets to empty them of their inhabitants. After coming back home from work I heard a neighbour describe what had happened to him:

'We were all ordered to come out into the street and were herded together into a long queue. We were surrounded by armed men and after two tense hours of queuing I reached a spot where a number of German officers were inspecting every person passing in front of them. Quite often they took no notice of certificates that were shown to them. I think that in the main they only allowed people they took a fancy to to go free.'

'What do you expect?' commented Edek. 'There are the waiting railway wagons to be filled and if there are empty spaces left, no bit of paper is going to save you.'

What we wanted to know, what terrified us, was the fate of our people packed into those trains and taken – who knows where? We too might find ourselves among them at any time. There were a few deportees who had managed to escape from the trains before they reached their destination and who subsequently returned to Warsaw. They reported terrible overcrowding and many deaths from suffocation. We still knew nothing of the ultimate destination, but rumours were already filtering through from Eastern Poland that the so-called *Einsatztruppen*, the German Special Combat Troops, were systematically murdering the remaining Jews who had not been expelled to the Warsaw ghetto.

All this somehow did not square up with the 'labour camps in the east' to which the Warsaw Jews were supposed to be going.

On 3 August Father and his partners decided that it would be safer for the entire workforce to move to the building where the workshop was located. Although we hoped that our workshop would guarantee everybody's safety, we had no illusion that we were in any way protected from being dragged out into the street and taken into the unknown. With the population of the ghetto shrinking, many apartments now stood empty. Our employees soon found out that it was a major task to make the abandoned lodgings, which had been left in a state of total chaos, fit for habitation. Mirka and I found a small shabby room in the basement with a cooking stove and primitive sanitary facilities, and we made it into our home. Paint was peeling off the stained walls and we had to put up with the scruffy furniture: a rusty iron bedstead with a straw mattress, a small table with a broken leg and a couple of folding chairs threatening to collapse under one's weight. Being together on our own made us unaware of our surroundings though, and here, after finishing work, we talked and ate and slept, trying to forget that our days might be numbered.

Amongst the inhabitants of the building was a sad, lonely man in his 30s. He invited me once to his tiny flat. Its only room looked unusual, with wooden shelves all round its walls. On them, in orderly rows, stood jars and dark glass bottles in assorted sizes and shapes, filled with various liquids, crystals and powders. He confirmed my guess – that he was a pharmacist.

An idea flashed through my mind: 'Would you happen to have some arsenic powder?'

He looked at me with suspicion. 'You are not thinking of taking your life, are you?' he asked.

'Oh no, nothing is further from my mind,' said I, with a straight face. 'Rats plague me down there in the basement. I must get rid of them.'

He wasn't really convinced. 'You may not realise it at your age,' he said, as if he had not heard my reply, 'but life has so much to offer. It is the most precious gift from Heaven. I wish I had the words to convince you. Nobody has the right to cut it short. Don't ever give up hope!'

In our present predicament, how could I share his views? I'd had little chance so far to experience the wonders of life. To my mind suicide was a better alternative to a slow death by suffocation on the way to an unknown destination, almost certainly my final one. There were no rats in the basement and I needed no poison to get rid of them.

'All right,' he said after some hesitation. 'I'll give you some arsenic now and if you need more you know where to find me.' He put some white powder into a small jar and carefully closed the lid. A couple of days later I managed to get a gold-plated locket on a thin chain and emptied the contents of the jar into it. From what I knew about the stuff, I had enough of it for my purpose. From then on I never parted from the locket, the chain was always round my neck. Just in case . . .

I was working as usual, but my mind was elsewhere. I feared that there was no escape, that our turn for the *Selektion* would come sooner or later and the dice of my life or death would be cast. And what happened after you were selected? The same thing must have been on everyone's mind in the workshop, but we all kept our thoughts to ourselves. My feelings kept swinging like a pendulum between hope and fear. It was not so much death itself which I feared, more the agony which might precede it. Meanwhile we led an unreal existence, pretending that all was normal. But we did not have to wait long.

Shortly after we moved into the workshop building, one hot bright summer day at the beginning of August, we suddenly heard loud screams coming from outside, followed by orders issued in German – '*Alle Raus*! [Everybody out!]' – then a gunshot, then another. I put on my jacket, grabbed my small suitcase which I'd pre-packed for such an occasion, and looked out through the open window. There they were: the Germans in their green police uniforms, Ukrainians and Lithuanians in black, a dozen or more automatic weapons pointing towards the windows. '*Schnell, Schnell* [Hurry, hurry],' they kept yelling.

'Come with me,' called Father, and Mother and I followed him outside. The forecourt was quickly filling with people, numb with fear, silent, not daring to open their mouths. Some carried bundles, others were empty-handed. Small children, sobbing, clung to their mothers' skirts. A few uniformed men ran into the building, searching for those trying to hide. An officer stood motionless near the street gate and from time to time barked an order to his men. He was obviously in charge of the operation and Father, with us closely behind him, went up to talk to him. He addressed him in fluent German, showed him documents testifying that we were working for the German war effort. He might have been talking to the wall, the man totally ignored him. Pushed and shoved by the surrounding police, we were roughly shepherded into the street. In the chaos that ensued, Mother hanging on to me, both of us trying to follow Father, we soon lost contact with the rest of our family and friends. We now stood in a huge queue in Nowolipki, facing the corner of Nalewki.

Now I know what this dreaded *Aktion* or *Selektion* is like, I thought to myself. But what would follow? We formed a long column, some six people wide, hundreds and hundreds of men, women and children, advancing slowly in the middle of the road, under the watchful eye of the Germans and their henchmen, marching up and down the pavements on either side of us, their automatic guns at the ready. From where we were I could not see the end of the column. In the intense summer heat the old and the sick dragged their feet with evident difficulty. There were people clad in rags; some men wore shirts and trousers or suits and ties. There were women in their summer frocks; some were bareheaded, others wore hats or caps. More provident people had extra garments hanging over their arms; some carried briefcases, suitcases, bundles or bags. We walked at a snail's pace in a ghost city in an eerie silence broken only by the shouts of guards. We were players in a monstrous lottery game, our lives as the stakes. I looked around. Not a single familiar face in sight.

I could not rid myself of the vision of Father, Mother and myself separated from one another, waiting in front of an overcrowded railway wagon and of us being pushed inside like sardines into a tin. I imagined a revolting stench of a human mass imprisoned for long hours in sweltering heat in a confined space, without anything to eat or drink. I could hear the clatter of wheels. And then I heard the sound of the car doors being opened. I saw people that survived the journey coming out. But what awaited us at the other end was beyond my imagination. My fingers kept touching the small locket hanging round my neck to reassure myself that it was still there. If I decided on this course of action, would I first offer some poison to Mother, if she was close by? Would there be enough for both of us?

It took us more than an hour to reach the Nalewki crossroads. From a distance of some 50 yards I could clearly see a small group of Gestapo officers standing in the middle of the road, examining each family group as they were made to stop in front of them. After a brief glance one of the officers would decide their fate, pointing them to the left or to the right. Every family with children was made to join the left-hand queue, which was moving away from us and gradually disappearing northward into Nalewki Street. The right-hand queue, that of people whose lives were spared, was slowly dispersing in the opposite direction.

Which way would they make us go? Right or left? I tried to weigh up our prospects by comparing our appearance to those who had been spared, but it was impossible to establish what the criteria of the selection were. In any case, for most of the time I could see the lucky ones only in the distance, from the side or from the back.

I prayed ardently to God as I had never prayed before: 'Hear me! Hear me! Please let us be saved!'

All of a sudden, there was Father a few yards ahead of us, upright, dignified and self-assured. He stood close to one of the officers and, as he addressed him in German, he was pointing his finger at us. The officer, whose grim expression never changed, stared for a while at Mother and then looked straight into my eyes. After what seemed like an eternity he raised his arm and pointed to the right. He allowed Father to join us.

We were safe!

The overwhelming feeling of relief was repeatedly broken by spasms of anxiety. Who would we find on returning home? I held Mother's arm tightly, trying to reassure her without words. I did not know what to say and she too evidently ran out of words. We hurried back to the workshop. One by one people were drifting in, their eyes anxiously searching for their loved ones. My eyes too were on the door.

The numbers of people returning rapidly dwindled to a trickle and, just as it seemed to have stopped, Mirka appeared in the door, her face wet with tears, followed by her father. Her mother was missing. My aunt Frania, 'bald Edek', and their children Oleś and Halinka did not return; it was Halinka's young age that sealed their fate. Mother's youngest sister, Hela, stood there in hysterics next to her husband Eliasz, but their son Jerzyk was not with them. More than half the people I knew were missing, but our old housekeeper, Nacia, Mr Tylbor, Marysia's father, the Płomniks and the Morgensterns were with us. The pharmacist, though, was among the missing.

Uncle Edek returned with Mala and their daughter Krysia. It was his job as policeman that saved them. Greatly distressed himself, Edek was trying to calm Hela, already mourning her son, and to console Mother, who was grieving for her sister, brother-in-law and their two children. She reproached herself for bringing both her sisters' families from Łódż to the Warsaw ghetto only two months earlier.

Edek made a decision. 'I'll go to *Umschlagplatz* [the trans-shipment place],' he announced. 'Though Hades would be a more appropriate name,' he added. Undaunted by the almost impossible task of finding our missing relatives amongst the crowd of thousands, he ventured out with the faint hope of saving their lives. He came back late that evening, disconsolate, accompanied by Jerzyk alone, who had been exchanged for a watch with a Ukrainian guard. The crowds were such that he failed to find the others.

'What is the *Umschlagplatz* really like?' I asked Edek.

'It's just a large yard with a high fence around it, at the corner of Dzika and Stawki Streets. On one side there is a grim, empty multi-storey building, which used to be a hospital. The yard is next to the railway sidings and so is convenient as a loading post. Six thousand people a day are herded from there into railway wagons.

'All I could see in the dusk,' he continued, 'were masses of people in two huge rows, squatting on the ground, with armed guards pacing up and down in between them. There must have been thousands more inside the building but I wasn't allowed in.'

That was all Edek was willing to tell me about his mission and I didn't ask any further questions.

Mirka was disconsolate over the loss of her mother. She could not stop crying and there was nothing I could do to help.

What was going to happen to us? Would we ever see the end of the war? Rumours were circulating of people receiving postcards from Eastern Poland from their deported relatives, apparently reporting that they were safe, had enough to eat and were working in labour camps in decent conditions. However, I had yet to meet anybody who had actually seen such a postcard. If indeed there had been any, they must have been few in number and they must have had to be written by the deportees under duress, to their captors' dictation and distributed in the ghetto by German agents.

Some of the Jewish policemen working at the *Umschlagplatz* took to recording the number of each train's engine. It soon became clear that the engines leaving Warsaw one day were back at the sidings the following morning. This could only mean that if people were being resettled in the east, that eastern destination was only a short distance away.

In the second part of August the name Treblinka[1] was on everybody's lips. Many people I talked to believed it was the destination of the trains leaving the *Umschlagplatz*. This was apparently the place where the deportees were put to death. Some four weeks later a copy of a news-sheet issued by one of the Jewish Underground ended up in my hands. It carried an article, which described how, on their disembarkation from trains in Treblinka, the deportees from the ghetto were forced by the Germans into enormous barracks. The barracks were then locked and for about five minutes, terrible, heart-rending screams kept coming from inside. Then everything went quiet, grotesquely swollen bodies were removed from the barracks and gravediggers, previously selected from among the victims, buried them, only to be killed themselves the next day.

In the late afternoon of Saturday 5 September, megaphone announcements sent people running in panic to read the new placards, which had just appeared on the walls.

> BY ORDER OF THE CHIEF OF DEPORTATIONS DEPARTMENT, THE JEWISH COUNCIL ANNOUNCES THAT BY SUNDAY, 6 SEPTEMBER 1942, AT 10 P.M. ALL JEWS, WITHOUT EXCEPTION, WHO ARE INHABITANTS OF THE *LARGE* GHETTO SHALL ASSEMBLE FOR REGISTRATION IN THE DISTRICT DELINEATED BY THE FOLLOWING STREETS: GESIA, SMOCZA, NISKA, ZAMENHOFA, SZCZELIWA AND PLAC PARYSKI.
>
> TO ALLOW MOVEMENT OF THE JEWS IN THE NIGHT, FROM 5 TO 6 SEPTEMBER 1942, THE CURFEW SHALL BE TEMPORARILY SUSPENDED. THE ABANDONED DWELLINGS ARE TO BE UNLOCKED. THE RELOCATED JEWS SHALL TAKE WITH THEM FOOD FOR TWO DAYS AND DRINKING UTENSILS. ANYBODY DISOBEYING THIS ORDER AND REMAINING IN THE GHETTO OUTSIDE THE ABOVE MENTIONED AREA AFTER THE SPECIFIED TIME WILL BE SHOT.

The new Jewish quarter adjoined the *Umschlagplatz*.

We packed our rucksacks and small suitcases and joined the crowd

---

[1] See Prologue (towards the end).

of people making their way along Zamenhofa towards Niska, where Jewish policemen were directing the relocated people to their new lodgings. This was the poorest quarter of the ghetto, most apartments consisting of a small room and a kitchen. Our family and the remnants of our workforce kept closely together and managed to procure adjoining units in one building. My parents and I occupied the only room and Edek, Mala and three-year-old Krysia slept in the kitchen of one of the flats. Aunt Hela, Eliasz, their son Jerzyk, Nacia, Mirka and her father settled next door. The place was filthy. It smelt of sewage and dirt. Unwashed pots, plates and cups were strewn all over the sink and the one rickety table. What looked like dirty rags lay scattered on the floor. Our predecessors must have been made to leave at a moment's notice, giving me an uncanny feeling that they were still around. Perhaps they'd just gone out looking for food and would shortly return to claim back their home.

It was late and we were all tired. The choice was to sleep either on a primitive iron bedstead with a bug-ridden straw mattress or on the dirty floor, but we were too weary even to mind. Krysia was the first to fall asleep. She was a sweet three year old, who rarely cried and though she was an only child, was quite exceptionally unspoilt. Now, lying there quietly, her eyes closed, her thick dark hair tied with a red ribbon, she reminded me of a little cherub.

The silence was suddenly broken by Mala's outburst. 'What shall we do with her?' she cried with tears in her eyes. 'No family with a young child passes the *Selektion*.' She covered her face with her hands, shaking. A few days earlier the size of the Jewish police force had been drastically reduced and Edek had lost his job, and with it his family's privileged status.

'We shall give her sleeping pills,' Edek said, 'and once she is asleep I shall conceal her in my rucksack. She won't wake up for a few hours. By then, God willing, the *Selektion* will be over.'

We were awakened in the morning by screams and shouts ordering us to come outside. Edek quickly dissolved several sleeping pills in a glass of water, added a spoonful of sugar and managed to pour the contents down the unwilling Krysia's throat. In a few minutes she was fast asleep and tucked into Edek's rucksack. In the meantime the yelling outside became more insistent. By the time we got downstairs, a vast crowd was already assembled in a wide, never-ending column, with more and more people coming out of the houses and joining it. Like tributaries after heavy rains, they seemed to be flowing into the swelling river of the procession advancing slowly down the street. Troops of heavily armed Germans and Ukrainians, their automatic guns at the ready, surrounded us on all sides. Our little group tried hard to stay together.

I could not take my eyes off Edek's bulky rucksack. Hours were passing. Would she cry or wouldn't she? I could not think of anything else; even the concern for my own fate had temporarily receded. Would she remain still or would she move around at the *Selektion* point? I could now clearly see a German walking round the assembled crowd, lifting his truncheon and hitting first one rucksack, then another, totally at random, presumably probing for any live cargo. Would he choose Edek's rucksack? Would Krysia cry out? How were Edek and Mala coping with the tension? All their three lives depended on some tiny pills, the effect of which could wear off any moment now.

At last we reached the *Selektion* point, manned by German officers. Our luck held. Krysia did not wake up. The German took a close look at Edek, at his wife and at us and then waved us through. Once again we had been spared. The Wolczyks, Nacia, Mirka and her father had also escaped selection. For the time being.

By the end of the afternoon the remnant of our group huddled together in a large, dimly lit dormitory, with hundreds of bunks standing four high, one above the other, like shelves in an ill-maintained warehouse. These were supposed to be our beds. I found a place on one of the bunks close to a wall and held Mirka in my arms.

Walter C. Töebbens was a German businessman who owned a network of *szopy*. According to Yisrael Gutman, author of *The Jews of Warsaw*, he first gained control and then ownership of most of the Jewish workshops and factories in the ghetto operating under the auspices of the *Judenrat*. His orders came from the *Wehrmacht*, the German armed forces, and he supervised the production which was undertaken with Jewish labour and with Jewish-owned tools. At the peak deportation time he employed as many as 12,000 people, though many of them were 'ghost' workers, people who in a desperate attempt to save their lives sought certificates of employment. The following morning we found out that our dormitory was part of the largest of Töebbens' enterprises, a huge factory in Leszno, located almost opposite the building where I had learnt my secretarial skills.

We were taken to the factory and marshalled into a vast hall on the second floor, filled with sewing machines. Dozens of men and women were sitting on workbenches or bent over the machines, busy sewing and joining pieces of material together, making army rucksacks. Although the windows facing Leszno were wide open, the hall was very hot. Guards, whips in hand, moved stealthily round the hall. Now and then the swish of a whip would be followed by a scream of pain.

Before I even managed to get my bearings, a man, presumably the foreman, motioned to me. 'Come,' he said curtly and led me to a workbench where he proceeded to show me how to stitch pieces of leather together. It took me almost an hour to get the knack of it, and after that I just went on sewing. Other than the hum, whirr and clatter of the machines, an occasional shout and the recurrent swish of a whip, the hall was quiet. There was no talking during work; nobody would have dared. With just a few breaks we worked till late in the evening, when we were shepherded back into the dormitory. Our remuneration was some meagre food, but no money.

Days passed, each an exact replica of the one before. Work, sleep, work, sleep, became our daily routine. The thought that we were genuinely employed by a German enterprise, working for the German armed forces, sustained us; it fed our hope that we were safe.

Not that this lasted long, perhaps not more than a week or ten days. One morning the screams of '*Raus, raus*! [Everybody out!]' reached us again from the street below. Soon the forecourt of the factory filled with a mass of workers and there were armed men all around. As I was standing with my parents at the side of the forecourt, I saw a small group of Germans some ten yards away. One of them was carrying a thick bundle of white cards which had numbers stamped on them. Within minutes he was surrounded by a throng of people and started handing out the cards indiscriminately, without any rhyme or reason, purely at random. But as the news spread that these were the *Lebensnummern*, the 'cards of life', the forest of the outstretched arms around the man reached hundreds. As the pile of cards got visibly thinner and as the crowd realised that the man was the only 'life giver', the confusion grew. When realisation dawned that some members of the same family got the cards while others did not, the pushing and shoving, the shouting and wailing, stoked by the panic, created absolute chaos out of the confusion. The bundle of cards had now been reduced to only a few and I was momentarily deafened by the cries of despair. I too pushed and shoved, elbowed my way to the man and succeeded. I got my card. I was lucky.

Someone shouted: 'It'll save your life!' This was my hope too.

I looked for Mother but she was nowhere to be seen. In the utter confusion I was not aware of people around me. All I wanted was to find her. And then I spotted her.

'Have you got a card?' I called.

'No,' she replied. She looked shattered. I gave her my card.

Nacia was standing close by, baffled, uncertain what to do. She held a 'life card' in her hand. Suddenly, a man appeared from nowhere, snatched it from her and ran as fast as he could. Before I could follow, he managed to vanish in the crowd. Nacia was desolate.

Next we were all herded into a long queue moving slowly to the selection point, manned by still another group of uniformed Germans. We had to pass in front of them, presenting the white cards. Those with cards were sent back to the factory, but all those without, as far as I could see, were being directed to another queue leading away from the factory in the direction of Żelazna Street. This was the queue of the condemned.

I had no card and thus no right to life. I walked slowly towards the selectors, resigned to the fact that my luck had finally run out. This time there could be no hope of escape. Then something strange happened. I came level with the officer, empty-handed. He looked at me closely. Was it my wishful thinking, or did his impenetrable expression seem to soften, perhaps just a little? For the briefest of moments he seemed to hesitate and then to my absolute amazement, he pointed towards the factory.

When I got there, my parents were there, so were Hela with her family, and Mirka and her father. But we never saw Nacia again.

We knew from Edek and his colleagues that every day the Jewish police had to deliver 6,000 souls to the *Umschlagplatz* for deportation. Of the 350,000 inhabitants of the ghetto at the start of the *Aktion*, more than 280,000 must have by now disappeared. A visible confirmation of this fact was provided by the number of empty apartments and by the absence of crowds in the streets. It was obvious that only a small fraction of the original population had been left in the ghetto.

My parents and I thus had no difficulty in finding an apartment close to the Töebbens factory. One evening in late September, as we sat down to a meal, Father seemed to be particularly tense. Several times he opened his mouth as if to say something, but whatever it was, he found it very difficult to articulate. 'I don't believe,' he said hesitantly, 'that we have much chance of coming out of here alive. Certainly not if we stay in the ghetto. Here we can only expect death.' He stopped and mopped his eyebrow. 'To give ourselves a chance,' he continued a moment later, 'however small it may be, we have to escape to the "other side". There we may – just may – survive. No more than that. Yet our chances there must be greater than they are here. Surely . . . ' he stopped in mid-sentence and looked askance at Mother and me.

'But how can we get out?' asked Mother. 'And how would we survive there?'

'I have been giving it a lot of thought in the last few days. We'll have to escape one at a time. Out there, we shall live separate lives. It would be far too risky to stay together. If one of us aroused any suspicion, all of us would be put at risk.'

'You, Jerzy,' Father continued, 'have the best appearance. Nobody will take you for a Jew. You will go first. We shall follow later. My looks are the worst and my accent [he had a very slight Yiddish accent] does not help. I will have to remain in hiding. You, Guta, don't look too Jewish and with false papers, once settled, you may be able to lead a fairly normal life.'

The idea of escaping from the ghetto had crossed my mind on numerous occasions, but the obstacles, the difficulties involved, seemed insurmountable. From 15 October 1941 the Germans had imposed an automatic death penalty on all Jews found outside the ghetto without a special permit, and on any person 'who knowingly offers shelter to such Jews'. Once outside I would be like a leper, putting at risk the life of anybody prepared to shelter me. I would have to obtain a *Kennkarte*, a compulsory identity card. When mixing with Aryans, I would have to be consistent in everything I ever said about myself – my history, my mythical family. A vast majority of Poles were practising Catholics and almost all attended church at least once a week. If you lived under one roof with a Catholic, you had to know the words of the common prayers, the church liturgy, the prescribed form of the Mass, the wording of Grace before meals, the rituals of all the religious festivals. I had a great deal to learn. Jewish customs were different in so many ways. For instance, we celebrated our birthdays, while the Catholics celebrated 'name-days', the day of their patron saint, instead. On my name-day – and at this stage I had no idea when it was – I should try not to show surprise when friends came to see me with their best wishes or brought me little gifts.

There were other specific dangers, such as being recognised by somebody who knew me before the war, or being picked up by *szmalcownicy*, the professional blackmailers, experts in recognising Jews by their appearance, their behaviour and by their understandable nervousness when challenged. And finally, there was the unavoidable Jewish male giveaway sign, the indelible stigma: the visible mark of circumcision. A circumcised Christian in Poland was a rarity. Rumour had it that on the 'other side' there were surgeons who for an exorbitant fee would perform an excruciatingly painful plastic operation to conceal the effects of circumcision.

Father must have made some preparations beforehand, as the next day, on his return home, he pulled out of his pocket a blank birth certificate with an official stamp of the birth registry in Wilno, a remote town in north-eastern Poland, captured by the Germans early in their Russian campaign.

'What would you like to be called?' he asked, raising his eyebrows.

Many names came to my mind, but in the end I settled for Kazimierz Kowalski, a surname as common in Poland as Smith is in England, while Kazimierz was a first name I had always fancied, regretting that my parents hadn't given it to me instead of Jerzy.

'What about your denomination?' Father asked.

'Roman Catholic, of course.'

'Date of birth?'

'My own date, 31 December 1922 will do, it's certainly easy to remember.'

Father carefully filled in all the blank spaces in the document, and Mother could not suppress a smile at this kind of christening.

'I wonder where to go once I am out. Any idea?' I asked.

'Leon Wołowski gave me his address the last time I spoke to him before the liquidation started,' Father replied. 'He suggested I kept it in case we ever need his help. So here it is for a start, try going there.' He gave me a piece of paper. 'You could try Howil too. I have also written down the address of Józef Kozłowski, one of my pre-war customers. I used to know him well. He now lives in Zakopane. Stasio Kleinman had been in touch with him recently and gave me his address. I only wish I could think of anybody else.'

And then Father went on to explain his plans. 'As you know, there are a number of *placówki* in the ghetto [workshops owned by Aryan entrepreneurs and staffed by their Christian employees who come to the ghetto each day to work]. The official German pass they use doesn't give a name, only a number. Tomorrow morning the group will be one short when they come into the ghetto. After work you will leave with them.'

What Father never told me was how much my escape had cost him.

That evening was spent on preparations for my escape. Mother put together all the clothes she thought I could possibly carry with me and made sure that they were ready, washed and darned. The curfew stopped me from going out to say goodbye to Mirka and to my relatives. I slept fitfully that night. I could hardly wait for the next day, yet felt anxious at the same time. Mother had everything ready for me in the morning. It was forbidden to take anything of value out of the ghetto without an official permit and carrying a rucksack or a suitcase was out of the question; I would stand out like a sore thumb in the group of workers returning home. Although these last few days at the tail end of the summer were still reasonably warm, I put on three pairs of pants (including two long woollen ones), two vests, three shirts, a pullover and a jacket. I carried a warm overcoat over my arm. On my feet were my handmade shoes, from the best craftsman in the ghetto. In my jacket pocket I carried a wallet with enough money to last me for some time. Mother was in tears as she kissed me goodbye. 'Shall I ever see you again?' she sobbed.

Who could answer her?

Father accompanied me to a large apartment in Ogrodowa Street, in a part of the ghetto unfamiliar to me. Just before we entered the building, I turned round to make sure that there were no spying eyes about and furtively took off my Star of David armband. I handed it to Father. Never again, I vowed to myself.

Father rang the bell and a young man with an air of authority let us in. He was expecting us. 'My son – Kazimierz Kowalski,' said Father to him. And to me, 'This gentleman is in charge of the working party and he will look after you until you are on the other side.'

'Wait here,' my new acquaintance said to me and motioned Father to follow him to an adjoining room. I heard them talking but could not make out the words. This must have been an apartment that had been converted into a workshop and it resonated loudly with the hum of machinery. The two of them came back, Father embraced me and held me for a long time in his arms with a warmth I had not experienced before. He then turned his face abruptly away, and, without another word, disappeared.

I sat alone in a small, sparsely furnished room for the rest of the day, having taken off a few layers of clothing. There were some books on a shelf and I tried to read, but found it impossible to concentrate. The day was long, would it ever end?

At 5.30 p.m. the noise of machines died down. In the bathroom I replaced my extra clothes and waited to be called. A group of some 20 men was just coming down the stairs and following the man in charge's direction I merged in without anybody appearing to notice.

In total silence we walked along a deserted street. It was a short distance, but I found it difficult to move, perspiring under the weight of my warm clothes, now my only worldly possessions; they must have made me look quite fat. The Elektoralna Street gate, set in the 12-foot high walls, separating the ghetto from the 'other side', was a red-and-white striped barrier and next to it stood a sentry box with a small slit of a window. The barrier was up. Several German and Polish policemen stood or strolled on the pavement, the helmeted Germans in their green uniforms, rifles over their shoulders, the Poles in navy blue, armed with truncheons.

Past the gate, I could see trees, still green, welcoming me with outstretched branches, like arms of long-lost friends, waving to me, waiting. I could hear my heart pounding against my chest while I prayed silently to God. Would any of my companions remember that I was not amongst them this morning as they were entering the ghetto? Would they give me away to the Germans? What about this leader I had met? Could I really trust him with my life? I knew that he had been paid for his services but would he be true to his word? And even if these Poles did not betray me, would the sentries recognise me as a Jew? The guide went up to one of the German policemen and presented him with his pass. The sentry examined it carefully and waved us on. He started counting. Another policeman, ahead of us, was stopping some of the workmen from my party. He asked one man to open his small briefcase. He frisked another one to check for contraband. The Germans had declared themselves the owners of everything of value in the ghetto and they were making sure that no one would deprive them of even the smallest thing. I was just passing the last of the policemen and hoping that my ordeal was over, when '*Zurück*! [Come back!]' he yelled. As he gave me a penetrating stare I got even hotter under my extra vests and shirts. He made me unbutton my first shirt, then the next one. He then noticed the locket on the chain round my neck, and made me take it off. '*Mach es auf*!' [Open it!]' he barked. He saw the white powder inside it and, thinking presumably that it concealed something of value, told me to empty the contents into my hand. There was nothing else inside. He looked at me again, obviously perplexed. The end has come, was my only thought. The leader turned back from the front of the column. He did not say a word, but looked at the German policeman, glanced at me and tapped his forehead with his index finger, indicating the presence of an idiot. The guard must have believed him, and he waved me on as I put most of the powder back into the locket.

6

ON THE RUN

For a few minutes I stood still, trying to take in the unfamiliar scene. It was like waking up from a nightmare, yet I was not in bed, I was just outside the ghetto walls. I stood there in the street, close to Plac Bankowy, facing a world that had forgotten me and which I had almost forgotten. I was dazed by the wide expanse of blue sky, the neat, well-maintained streets, the trees . . . I felt like a blind man regaining his sight. Yet like a bird escaped from its cage, I was free, but aware of predators lurking around.

Massive public buildings enclosed a large town square. From an unpaved area close to its centre rose majestic trees, their leaves slightly tinged with yellow, signifying the onset of autumn. The air smelt fresh and exhilarating. It was good to rediscover plants, I had almost forgotten what they looked like. Birds were singing – such an unfamiliar sound. To the accompaniment of clanging bells, trams unblemished with the Star of David were passing me at frequent intervals. They were packed with people returning home from work and, unlike those behind the wall, they were respectably dressed, not walking cadavers. Their limbs were not swollen from hunger, and they had no despair painted over their faces.

I kept telling myself that there was nothing unusual in my appearance, that passers-by were paying me no attention, yet I panicked each time I thought that someone's eyes lingered on me for a few seconds too long. Could they sniff a Jew? Although for the first time in three years I was not wearing the armband of shame, the thought that my Jewishness might be stamped on my face wouldn't leave me. But in reality nobody bothered. There was no time to waste. I looked at my watch. It was past 6 p.m. and the curfew was starting in less than three hours, by which time I had to be indoors. I looked up the address of Leon Wołowski in my notebook; I hoped that he would be able to get me false identity papers and shelter me until then.

My immediate destination was Praga, a working-class suburb of Warsaw, on the other side of the River Vistula. A nun in a black habit with a wide white collar passed me. I caught up with her and asked her which tram would take me there. She pointed to the nearby stop and told me which number was going in my direction. The tram arrived a few minutes later; it was full, with many people, including some uniformed Germans, standing inside. I remained on the platform until a seat became available.

I had not been inside a tram for nearly two years and looking out of the window I saw a new world: wide avenues lined with trees, historic buildings, palaces, parks with benches beckoning the weary passer-by to take a rest. I was telling myself: be normal, behave like those around you, believe that you are who you pretended to be. But it was not easy. We crossed the River Vistula, which was at least three times wider than the same river flowing through Cracow. Out of the rear window of the tram a magnificent panorama appeared: an ancient castle crowning a steep hill, rising from the bank of the river. I asked the conductor where I should get off.

The address was only short walk from the tram stop and I found myself in front of a large, dreary tenement block. It was five storeys high and must have provided accommodation for hundreds of people. Like most Warsaw apartment blocks it consisted of a long frontage with side and back wings, enclosing a deep courtyard. I chose the far entrance on the left and walked up to the third floor. It was nearly 7 p.m. when I knocked on the door of Leon Wołowski's flat. To my utter surprise it was Marysia Tylbor who opened it. What was Leon's mistress doing in his home? She looked more beautiful than ever in a bright floral dress, her long blond hair and blue eyes belying her Jewish origin. She stood in the doorway dumbfounded, as surprised as me. She quickly recovered her composure.

'Jerzy!' she cried out – luckily not too loudly.

'Not Jerzy,' I whispered, 'but Kazik.'

Nonplussed, she called out, louder: 'Look who is here! Kazik, how wonderful to see you!' A rather plain woman in her early 40s, short, plump, with a tired face, untidy hair and thick glasses appeared behind Marysia in the narrow hallway.

'This is Kazik,' said Marysia, introducing me to Mrs Wołowska. 'Kazik lives in Cracow, he is my cousin on my mother's side, so he is not related to Leon.' I shook Mrs Wołowska's hand. It felt limp and rather damp, as she looked at me without emotion.

'You know,' Marysia went on, 'Kazik is my favourite cousin and I haven't seen him for more than a year.' I tried to work out the relationship between the two women. It was obvious that the lady of the house knew nothing of her guest's true identity, nor of the dubious relationship between her husband and Marysia.

'What a pity Leon is away. He would have loved to meet Kazik,' Marysia chattered away.

'When is he coming back?' I tried to sound unconcerned, though I was beginning to feel somewhat faint.

'I've no idea,' replied Mrs Wołowska. 'Haven't seen him since yesterday. Perhaps he's lying drunk somewhere, who knows.' I went to the toilet, took off my excess garments and folded them neatly. Would Mrs Wołowska notice how much weight I had suddenly lost? Marysia took my clothes quietly from me and put them out of sight.

'Do you mind if Kazik has supper with us?' asked Marysia.

'Not really,' answered Mrs Wołowska without enthusiasm. 'Come in and sit down,' she muttered, as she showed me into the living room.

Marysia went into the kitchen to finish preparing the meal and I looked around. The little living-cum-dining room was cluttered but spotless. It housed a small sofa and four cheap-looking chairs around an oblong wooden table. Worn-out net curtains were draped around two narrow windows. A plain cotton rug partly covered the narrow planks of the brown-stained floor. Faded family photos in simple frames stood on the dresser in the company of ceramic figurines, some with limbs missing. Above hung a large picture of the Virgin Mary holding the infant Jesus in her arms. There was a tall, white-tiled stove in the corner. On the opposite side of the hallway two more open doors led to the bedrooms, the main one and the children's room. A boy of about ten, and a girl, about eight, sat on the floor building a tower with coloured wooden blocks. 'The tower of Babel?' I asked, trying to be friendly, but got no reply.

'How old are they?' I kept the conversation going with Mrs Wołowska.

She looked a little happier and told me all about her children. When she finished I ventured into more open waters, 'What do you make of the news from Stalingrad?'

'I don't know what to make out of it,' she replied, pointing to the newspaper lying on the sofa. 'If I am to believe what I read, the Germans are about to capture the city. That might be the end of Russia, but who knows whether it would make the war shorter or longer.'

A delicious smell of frying was wafting up from the kitchen as Marysia appeared at the door, holding a tray with three plates of fried eggs and sausage, a piece of hard white cheese, a large loaf of bread and a packet of margarine. I suddenly felt hunger pains, having had hardly anything to eat all day. 'The children have already eaten,' Marysia said, taking the plates off the tray. 'Where is that bloody Wołowski?' I kept asking myself. 'What shall I do without him?'

Mrs Wołowska broached a new subject. 'Thank God, at last the Germans are really getting rid of the Jews. True justice is being done to these antichrists, the killers of our Lord Jesus.' She crossed herself piously. 'At last Poland will be free from them.' And then she addressed her new concern directly to me: 'Do you know, are they also getting rid of the Jews in the Cracow ghetto?'

I had no idea and improvised: 'They will very soon, I did hear some rumours; yes, we'll be better off without them. I don't know why the Germans are taking all this time.'

Was I overdoing it? I caught Marysia's eye and a very faint smile crept over her face. There was a small gold cross hanging from a chain around her shapely neck and I could not help thinking that the last time I saw her she had been wearing a Star of David on an armband instead.

'This is delicious,' I changed the subject, 'it's my favourite food.' I was telling the truth for the first time that evening. I was trying to eat slowly, so as not to show how famished I was. I was trembling inside every time I heard footsteps on the staircase – the walls seemed rather thin – expecting Wołowski to come through the door. Where on earth was the man? I was more worried by the minute.

'Jesus Maria!' cried Marysia, as if guessing my thoughts. 'Look at the time!' She pointed to her watch. 'Curfew in half an hour's time! We can't let you go now, it's too late to find a hotel room.' She turned to Mrs Wołowska.

'Could Kazik stay here for the night?'

A moment's silence. 'Well, I suppose so,' she replied, her face remaining as blank as before.

'Would you mind staying?' asked Marysia.

'No, no, you are right, I have left it late, haven't I? Thanks for the offer,' I tried to sound indifferent.

'Well, let's enjoy the rest of the meal.'

With a stay of sentence granted, I could relax till the morning. We continued talking about the general political situation and the likely outcome of the war, when at last Mrs Wołowska left to put the children to bed.

'How is my father?' Marysia whispered. 'When did you last see him?'

'A week ago. He survived all the selections. He was OK.'

'Leon is looking for a room for me. I am about to get an identity card. He introduced me to his wife as his bereaved cousin who'd just lost her parents. She believed him and agreed to have me stay here for a while,' Marysia explained.

'Any idea when he's coming back?'

'None, but try to see him in a few days' time if you can't get fixed up. I am so sorry that I can't give you more help. It's breaking my heart.'

She put up a camp bed in the sitting room and brought back my clothes, which she had wrapped in brown paper. She put a sheet, a pillow and a blanket on the bed.

'What time do you wake up?' I asked.

'At seven.'

'I have no alarm clock, please wake me up. I shall get ready and go.'

She bade me good night and left me alone with my thoughts. The antisemitic remarks I had just heard might be a warning of what I could face, if suspected of being a Jew. The majority of Polish Catholics hated the Jews. Why? I remembered Jerzyk Dzieniakowski, my Christian neighbour who at the age of six was my best friend. I was always envious of his Christmas trees. As soon as he started school our relationship changed. He did not want to know me. Like all the Catholics he was filled with antisemitism by his religious teacher or his priest. Wasn't it the Jews who crucified Jesus?

But I had to think of more pressing problems. I could obviously not remain here, waiting for Wołowski's homecoming. The only other address in Warsaw I could try was that of Bogusław Howil. I had met him twice and he would hardly consider me a friend. Why should he risk his life for me, a total stranger? But then, what else could I do? I thought of going to a phone box in the morning to search through the telephone directory for the names of my Christian friends from school. I was terribly tired. I fell asleep and was woken up in the morning by Marysia's voice.

After breakfast I thanked Mrs Wołowska for her hospitality, embraced Marysia and strolled out into the open world with a large parcel under my arm. It was a warm autumn day. I walked for a while, looking for a telephone box. When I saw one, it dawned on me how unlikely it was that I would find, in a city of over a million inhabitants, someone I had known from my school days, who had moved to Warsaw – and then expect him to risk his life for my sake. It was idiotic. In any case, as my friends were barely 20 years old, the directory entries would list their parents' names or initials that I didn't know. For a couple of hours, after crossing to the other side of the river, I wandered around and then started making my way towards the city centre, but with no clear idea of my final destination. The only other address, apart from Howil's, that I had in my notebook was in Zakopane. But leaving Warsaw and risking, without identity papers, a journey to Zakopane, some 250 miles south, just because I had an address there did not make any sense. I was in Marszałkowska Street, close to Aleje Jerozolimskie, when I finally made up my mind. There would be very little to lose if I went to see Boguś Howil.

A sign inscribed with '*Galanteria Skórzana*' ('Leather Goods') and

'Helena Howil' (Boguś' mother), hung above the imposing store at the corner of Marszałkowska and Aleje Jerozolimskie, probably the busiest junction in the heart of Warsaw. Its large windows were packed with suitcases, ladies' handbags, briefcases and other leather articles. German police, SS officers and soldiers in their green, olive and black uniforms stood out from the dense crowds of civilians. Warsaw was the centre of communications for men and supplies destined for the Eastern front, and the main railway station was only a few hundred yards away in Aleje Jerozolimskie. For a long while I stood outside the store, staring at the multitude of leather objects, a few of them known to me from my workshop days in the ghetto. I was still undecided. I hesitated until I saw the familiar figure of Boguś standing close to the glass partition. He was a handsome, tall, athletically built man with a round, open face, and was around 30 years old. As I entered the store, he took a look at me and his expression froze, as if he had seen an apparition. 'Jesus Maria, what are you doing here?' He tried to keep his voice down. The shop was some 15 feet wide and 80 feet deep. The left-hand wall was lined with shelves, reaching all the way up to the ceiling, all packed with merchandise. A few salesmen stood behind the long counter that extended the length of the premises; they were serving a dozen or so prospective customers, mainly women. Before I could reply, Boguś asked me to follow him to his office at the far end of the shop. This windowless room contained a small oak desk, several filing cabinets and a couple of revolving office chairs. As soon as we sat down Boguś asked me:

'How is your father?'

'He's all right, he sends his regards.'

'And your mother?'

'Surviving.' (This was meant to be taken literally.)

'Płomniks? Morgensterns?'

'I saw them a couple of times at the Töebbens' factory. They were busy sewing.'

He then got to the point.

'Why are you here?'

'I planned to see Wołowski, but he's away.' I paused to take a deep breath. 'Can I ask you to help me? I need somewhere to live. I need a

job. I have learned bookkeeping. I can type fast. I know shorthand.'
So many words to convey a simple plea: 'Please, save my life . . . '

He was silent for a minute or two. And then he said:

'I have to think about it. I'll have to speak to my brother, Henryk.'

He went out of the room and returned with a young man, short
and slim with dark hair and a friendly face. 'This is my manager,
Heniek Czapski and I trust him implicitly.' Boguś then turned to
him: 'This is Jerzy, Jakub Lando's son.' We shook hands. 'Jerzy has
just escaped from the ghetto. He needs help but Henryk and I have
to think what, if anything, we can do for him. Take him out for
lunch, he must be starving, poor fellow.'

Have I done the right thing by coming here, I wondered. It may
or may not work, but in the meanwhile a total stranger had learned
who I was. Would he keep it to himself? Or was I risking more than
I had bargained for?

I said nothing and followed him to a café five minutes' walk away.
It was in a side street, with a small bar and no more than five or six
tables, most of them empty. I could smell fried meat and cabbage
soup. We sat down at a table in the far corner. From a menu
presented by a buxom waitress, I chose cabbage soup and fried pork
cutlet. I had not eaten in a restaurant for three years and found it
strange to be served by a waitress. As we were waiting, Mr Czapski
looked around, to make sure that nobody was listening, and said
almost in a whisper: 'I met your father a couple of times when
collecting merchandise from the ghetto workshop.'

Instead of looking at my host, my eyes kept wandering off in the
direction of the front door, expecting a German policeman to walk
in to take me away. 'Our workshop does not exist any longer,' I told
him. 'Whoever is left in the ghetto, and there are not many, works
for a German enterprise of some sort. It's all like a gigantic labour
camp.' He was interested in how the Germans managed to get rid of
so many people in such a short time and I told him what I had seen.
What should have been an enjoyable occasion, a tasty meal out in
pleasant company, felt more like a nightmare. I could not
concentrate on what I was eating or what I was saying, as two trains
of thought went round in circles through my mind. Had I been lured
into a trap? What kind of decision awaited me on my return to the

store? On the way back, I was already mulling over what my next move would be after Boguś refused my plea for help.

I waited inside the store, close to the entrance, while Boguś was serving a difficult customer who could not make up her mind what bag to buy. On the counter in front of her there were at least ten bags of all sizes and colours, for every occasion. She went on inspecting them time and time again. It was taking ages. She must have seen every bag in the shop, before deciding that she did not like any of them.

'How did you enjoy the lunch?' Boguś asked me, when she finally left.

'It was delicious. Thank you.'

He led me to the far end of the store, past the entrance to the office, until we reached a door opening into a small courtyard. 'This is my little pied-à-terre,' he explained, pointing to a one-storey outhouse on the right, 'and this is where you are going to stay for the time being,' he added, opening the door for me. It was, in fact, a comfortable self-contained flat. It comprised one large bed-sitting room with no windows but with a glass skylight in the roof. There were three comfortable-looking, leather-covered armchairs around a low table. A double bed with an adjoining bedside table was facing me and a mahogany wardrobe covered with elaborate beading stood to my right. A door led to a small kitchen and to a bathroom. A few paintings, mainly of sparsely dressed women, hung on the walls. The room felt warm and cosy.

'You will work in the shop,' Boguś told me. 'Apart from my brother Henryk, Czapski and myself, nobody will know who you are. I shall sort out your salary another time, but if you need some money now, I can give you an advance.'

I was searching for the right words to thank him, but he must have seen my gratitude and relief, as he gave me a broad smile. 'Good luck!' he said. 'Make yourself at home and, when you are ready, come and see me in the shop. Here is the key to the room and another to the Aleje Jerozolimskie entrance.' I took my clothes out of the parcel Marysia had wrapped for me, put them in the wardrobe, had a good wash and went back to the shop. Boguś introduced me to some of his staff and within an hour I was serving customers. The experience I had acquired in the ghetto workshop helped.

LEFT:
The author's parents in
Krynica, 1935.

BELOW LEFT:
The author in 1934,
aged 11.

BELOW RIGHT:
The author aged 14.

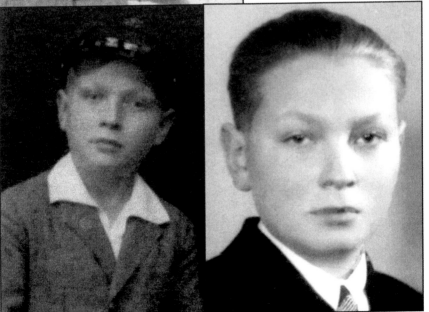

LEFT:
Edek Engel and Michał Lando (author's brother) Łódż, 1937.

BELOW:
The author's parents in Karlsbad, 1937.

LEFT:
The author's parents
in Krynica, 1937.

RIGHT:
Mala, Edek and Krysia
Engel in Tel Aviv, 1947.

ABOVE:
Jerzyk's parents, Elias and Hela
Wolczyk in Łódż 1947.

LEFT:
Jerzyk Wolczyk in Tel Aviv, 1950.

LEFT:
Michal, the author's brother, in Karlsbad, 1937.

RIGHT:
Edek Engel in Łódż, 1938.

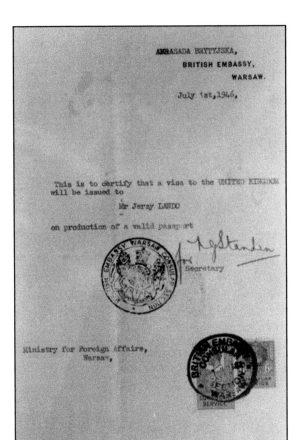

Edek Engel with his daughter Krysia, in Warsaw, 1943.

LEFT:
Edmund Holka, 1946.

RIGHT:
Boguś Howill, 1944

In the early evening I ventured into the street on my own. I did some shopping and bought newspapers. While getting ready for bed, I was overwhelmed with joy, hardly able to believe my luck. Then I looked at the newspapers: the Russians were retreating with heavy losses and it seemed that their defeat was inevitable before long. Even allowing for the distortions of the German propaganda, I saw little hope of a quick victory by the Allies. The Germans would have plenty of time to get rid of the few Jews in their care. My thoughts turned to my family. Would they have time to escape before the rest of the ghetto was liquidated? What about Mirka? How did she feel about me abandoning her without as much as a note? We did live in abnormal times, when basic principles of decent human behaviour could not always be applied. Sadly, I had to admit to myself that the instinct to survive was my primary concern. Tired as I was, falling asleep was not easy. The noise from Aleje Jerozolimskie kept me awake. There was a constant roar of lorries, no doubt army transportation going to or coming back from the Eastern front. As I tossed and turned, feeling terribly lonely, I started getting frightened. There were too many people around with good reason to suspect me of being a fugitive for my peace of mind. If I fell asleep, would a banging on the door wake me? Would there be police outside? I felt more and more tense and sleep didn't come until the light of dawn filtered through the skylight.

The next few days were uneventful. I spent some of the time in the office taking dictation from Boguś or Henryk and typing their letters. I also managed to sell a few handbags and suitcases. I was introduced to the rest of the staff and joined them when they went out for lunch. I was regaining confidence in my 'Aryan', non-Jewish, appearance. I had no means of sending any news to my parents and no news could reach me from them. Leon Wołowski might know something, but I had no time to make a journey to the suburb of Praga and there was no certainty that I would find him at home. I was getting used to my lonely nights and, instead of feeling sorry for myself, I started feeling sorry for Boguś' girlfriends, deprived of the facilities his pied-à-terre had offered them in the past. Unfortunately, my new existence was short-lived.

Four days after my arrival, in the early afternoon, as I was finishing serving a customer, Boguś called me into his office. All three of them were there, Boguś, Henryk and Heniek Czapski. They were visibly agitated. Boguś took a letter out of his pocket. 'Read it,' he said. It was typewritten and unsigned. It read:

'Mr Howil. I know that your mother is harbouring a Jewish child in her flat in Cracow. I am about to pass this information to the Gestapo in Warsaw and in Cracow, unless you hand over 100,000 złoty. The exact amount, wrapped in a newspaper, is to be placed inside the waste bin located 20 steps to the right of the main entrance to the Principal Post Office Plac Napoleona at 8 p.m. today.'

I stared at the note. I was stunned. For a while I was unable to open my mouth or move. I read it for a second time to make sure that I had not missed any reference specifically to my own presence. I gasped: 'What are you going to do?' Boguś did not reply. He opened his notebook, looked up a name and dialled a number.

'Bogusław Howil here, am I talking to Stefan Zejda?' There was a pause. 'I want you to come over to my store immediately. There is not a minute to waste.' He put down the receiver. The three of us spoke little until a tall man in his early 30s, with a military posture and a hard face, appeared at the door some 20 minutes later.

'Stefan Zejda, private detective,' Boguś introduced him and we all shook hands. 'Look at this!' He almost threw the letter at the detective and the man read it.

'Is it true?' he asked.

'Of course not,' came the reply.

'Do you suspect anybody?'

'I can't think of anybody behaving in such a dastardly way.'

The man appeared lost in thought for a couple of minutes. 'Right,' he said, in the tone of somebody who is used to issuing orders. He turned to Boguś. 'I want you to order two *droshkies* for 7.30 this evening. I want you to bring a newspaper and some old paperbacks here. We'll make a newspaper parcel the size of a stack of 100,000 złotys. You, Mr Howil, will go with your brother in the first *droshky* and you'll take the parcel with you. I shall follow you in the second *droshky* with Mr Czapski.'

I could see that my presence was not required and excused myself to go to my room, as the store was about to close. Half an hour later

I heard the sound of a horse-drawn carriage stopping outside and, as I peered through the open door, I saw the four men get out of the gate into Aleje Jerozolimskie. 'The Plac Napoleona post office,' I heard the order being given, followed by the sound of the horses' trotting receding into the distance.

I sat down in an armchair, tense and apprehensive. I did not know exactly what the plan was but it was bound to be risky. As Boguś had told the detective that the contents of the letter were untrue, their enterprise was based on a lie. They obviously intended to lay a trap of some sort, but doing so in Plac Napoleona of all places would be more than daring, it would be madness. The area, only 20 minutes' walk away, was amongst the busiest in Warsaw, with large numbers of Germans coming in and out of the main post office building, using the postal services to send parcels and collect letters from home. Nothing taking place there, particularly close to the main entrance, could escape their attention. What would happen to me if the four men failed to achieve their goal, whatever it was? They might come back escorted by police. And what if none of them came back? I would have to stay indoors till the morning. And what then? Disappear – but where to? I tried to occupy my thoughts with another subject but found it difficult.

Some time after 8 p.m. I heard the sound of horses' trotting coming to a halt outside. I held my breath. Through the half-open door I saw the gate open and two groups of three men come into the courtyard. A young man I had not seen before half walked and was half dragged by Boguś and Henryk who held him by an arm on either side. Czapski and Zejda followed them close behind, dragging another youngster between them. Czapski shut the gate and, before I had a chance of catching another glimpse, they disappeared into the cellar below the shop. I got ready for bed but found it hard to fall asleep. A terrible din was going on in the basement. I heard a regular sound of blows, each one followed by a shriek of pain. This heavy thumping and screaming went on for a long time. A knock at my door made me sit up. It was Heniek Czapski and I let him in. He looked exhausted.

'What's going on down there?' I asked. 'And tell me all that happened from the beginning.' He slumped into the armchair and asked me for a glass of water.

'Zejda gave us clear instructions before we got into the cabs. We got to the Plac Napoleona post office a few minutes before eight. Zejda asked the cabbies to wait some 30 yards away from the waste bin and to look for a sign from one of us to come closer, when we were ready to leave. We got out and melted into the crowd, keeping a few feet away from one another. At 8 p.m. precisely, Boguś approached the waste bin, opened his briefcase, took out the parcel and dropped it into the bin. He then walked away and hid in a flower shop close by. Two young fellows in their early 20s came up to the bin and one of them picked up the parcel. They did not have a chance to get very far, though, as the four of us pounced on them. Boguś and Henryk held one, Zejda and I grabbed his companion, while the two cabs drew up. "Gestapo," we whispered into the boys' ears as we dragged them into the cabs. Before they recovered their wits, they were being driven away under escort, one in each cab. Everything happened so quickly that no passer-by seemed to notice or understand what was going on. You heard the thumping from downstairs?' Czapski asked.

'I would have to be deaf not to,' I replied. 'What is it all about?'

'We keep hosepipes in the basement in case of fire. They came in handy. We made the fellows tell us all they knew, and until they did so we kept bashing them. Boguś did not even bother to take the nozzle out of his hosepipe. In fact we went on bashing them even after they revealed all.'

'What did they tell you?'

'There is another chap involved. His name is Bielany. He is the son of Boguś' next-door neighbour from Wilcza Street, one of his best friends. Boguś unwittingly confided in him how his mother had saved the life of a Jewish baby and the young Bielany overheard the conversation from an adjoining room. He and his two pals are yachting enthusiasts and it occurred to them that if they used their wits, they could buy a yacht, which otherwise they could never afford. Nothing simpler than a little blackmail, they thought. You can come and have a look,' he said. I followed him into the basement. I could not bear the sight in front of my eyes. The two men were stripped to the waist, their skin covered with black and blue stripes, making them look like zebras. They were wriggling about on the floor in agony.

In the morning, before letting them go, Boguś called the young

Bielany on the phone. 'Come over straight away,' he said. 'I am about to give away a slightly shop-soiled travelling set and you may as well take advantage of the bargain price.' In less than half an hour the youngster Bielany appeared, but before he was shown any bargain, Boguś and Henryk grabbed hold of him and forced him to go into the basement where the other two boys were locked up. Boguś then called Mr Bielany, the father. 'Your son is here with me in the shop,' he said. 'Something happened, I cannot tell you what on the phone, and he wants to see you urgently.'

Mr Bielany turned up quickly, anxious to hear the reason for such an urgent appeal. When he heard the story, he was appalled by what had happened and could not apologise enough for his son's disgraceful behaviour. He did not raise any objections when Boguś told him that his son was going to be severely punished. The boy got the same treatment as his friends and before the three were allowed to go home, Boguś told them without mincing his words 'One word about this to anybody and all three of you are dead. Understood?'

Later that morning Boguś asked me into his office. He was on his own. 'We were lucky last night,' he said, 'but I have to be careful. My mother has already made arrangements to find another home for the Płomniks' little girl, away from her flat. I now fear that it might not be safe for you to stay here any longer. Make a note of my parents' Cracow address. They live at Karmelicka 49. Mother knows many people in Cracow who might be able to help you, some in the Underground. All I can suggest is that you should try to meet her and see what she can do for you.'

'When ought I leave?' I asked.

'As soon as possible, today would be best.'

I thanked Boguś for all he had done for me, found out the time of trains leaving for Cracow and started getting ready. I put my belongings into a small suitcase that Boguś had given me. My dream had come to an abrupt end.

The evening train to Cracow was due to leave just after 9 p.m. I made my way to the railway station in Aleje Jerozolimskie, half a mile from Howil's store. Hundreds of people were milling around the vast main hall. There were throngs of soldiers in full combat gear, with rifles, helmets and bulging rucksacks, on their way to or from the front. I was assailed by a mixture of sounds: countless footsteps resonating against the concrete floor merged into the buzz of conversations, loud announcements of trains arriving and leaving, cries of news-vendors, the heavy breathing of engines and the clatter of wheels. An aromatic cocktail, made up of engine oil, steam and smoke, wafted in from the platforms. Long queues of people formed in front of the booking office windows and snack bars. But what are all those SS men and police doing here, I wondered. Checking papers, no doubt, that could be the only answer. If they stopped me, what could I show them? I had no *Kennkarte*, the identity card with a photograph, which most people had been issued with. All I could produce was a false birth certificate, which was an obvious forgery to an experienced eye. My imagination, thus given plenty to chew over, easily presented me with a sequence of events leading to my departure from the land of living.

After waiting in the queue for a while, I bought a single, third-class ticket to Cracow. Clutching my small suitcase, I made my way to the platform to board the train. As it was early, I managed to get a seat on a wooden bench next to the window. A fat man sat next to me and as soon as he settled down, he pulled a large slice of bread and a piece of sausage out of a small basket and started munching.

'Would you like some?' he asked generously.

'No, thank you.' I gave a short reply, trying to avoid being drawn into a conversation.

The compartment soon filled with people until all eight seats had been taken. Nobody was talking or taking any interest in me. I felt relieved when the train moved off, without anybody coming into the compartment to check papers. It was a very slow train, stopping frequently, but the only people coming in or out wore uniforms. Outside it was dark; behind the dark silhouettes of telegraph poles, buildings and trees rushing by I could glimpse a multitude of stars shining in the clear sky. I dozed off and was woken up by the compartment door sliding open. A uniformed man stood in the doorway. My heart sank. 'Tickets, please!' he called. I relaxed with relief and soon went back to sleep. When I woke up, the sun was just rising, a red ball on the distant horizon. I suddenly felt excited by the view I'd almost forgotten of an open, incredibly flat countryside, green fields, white birch tree forests and dusty roads disappearing in the distance.

The train arrived in Cracow early in the morning. The last time I'd seen the Cracow railway station was nearly three years previously, when I arrived in a cattle wagon after being deported from my native Łódż. This time, though, I enjoyed the luxury of leaving the station through the passengers' entrance and not through the loading bay. I stopped for breakfast in a nearby café that seemed to be popular with travellers. I was not in a hurry, as I didn't want to disturb Mrs Howil too early in the morning. After asking the waiter for directions to Karmelicka Street I started making my way slowly into the town centre. I strolled around aimlessly till 9 a.m.

I reached my destination, a four-storey block of flats in a smart residential area, walked up a wide staircase adorned with a graceful balustrade to the second floor and rang the bell. A rather short old lady with grey hair and a twinkle in her eye showed no evident surprise and greeted me warmly in a deep, slightly hoarse voice. 'You must be Kazik, I guess. Do come in, I know a lot about you.' She called out, 'Apek?' and a stout man in his 60s, with a short neck and a serious face came in, dressed in a silk dressing gown. 'This is Apolinary, my husband. Let me introduce Kazik to you.' We shook hands. 'Come in and have breakfast,' she offered.

'Thank you, but I had some this morning,' I replied.

From a spacious hall with a grandfather clock in the corner, a door led to a long salon, elegantly furnished with upholstered mahogany armchairs and a matching sofa. Richly coloured rugs were scattered on the highly polished parquet floor. In the centre of the room stood a pillar-based table with a marble top. A crystal candelabra hung above it. The side table close to the window was covered with a variety of tasteful china objects.

I noticed a black upright piano standing against the wall and my spirits instantly lifted. The change in my expression did not escape my hostess's attention.

'Do you play piano?'

'I used to,' I replied.

'You must play something for us, then!'

I sat down and played a bravura piece by Weber. I was surprised that three years after I had last touched the keys I could still play tolerably well. My hosts were delighted.

Helena Howil knew my parents from pre-war days and wanted me to describe to her in detail the events of the last few months. She also asked me about my education and what training I had received after leaving school. After listening attentively she excused herself, went out of the room and left me alone with her husband. Mr Howil wanted to hear all I knew about the recent blackmail. 'I would have never suspected a boy from such a good family to behave so despicably!' he said.

Mrs Howil reappeared after a while. 'I phoned a few people and made some arrangements for you,' she said. 'As you can guess, it would be folly for you to stay here, but my friend Mrs Szczepanek has a spare room in her apartment, which she will be happy to let for a reasonable rent. *Inżynier* [a professional title] Zamojski, another friend of mine, owns a chemical laboratory. They are always short of staff and he believes that he could employ you as a trainee. I told them that you were a distant cousin of mine.'

I could not thank her enough. 'And there is another thing,' she added. 'I arranged for you to meet Mr Rapacki this evening. He is involved with the *Armia Krajowa*, the Underground Home Army, you know, our underground resistance. You'll have to get a passport photograph first, but leave it with him and you will have a *Kennkarte* ready in a few days.'

I wrote their addresses down in my notebook. 'You can leave your suitcase here for today,' she concluded, as I was getting ready to leave.

I first went to see *Inżynier* Zamojski. His chemical laboratory, in a one-storey modern building standing in its own grounds, employed some 20 people. He was a smartly dressed man in his mid-30s. He asked me many questions, being particularly interested in my knowledge of chemistry, which did not extend beyond the high-school curriculum. At the end of the interview he offered me a job as a trainee at a starting salary that would cover the cost of my food and rent and suggested that I should begin the following morning. On the way to Mrs Szczepanek, I had a passport photograph taken which would be ready next day. I also stopped in a couple of bookshops to buy some German language and shorthand manuals, a

large Polish–German dictionary and a German shorthand
dictionary. I was delighted with the accommodation I was offered, a
sunny, simply but comfortably furnished, bedroom in a quiet
suburban street. Here I would spend most evenings and weekends,
learning German shorthand and improving my knowledge of the
language. In the late afternoon I went to collect my suitcase from the
Howils and was asked to stay to supper. Later, at Mrs Howil's
request, I played more of my piano repertoire for her and her
husband. I had to promise to come back again three days later.

The next morning I was shown around the laboratory. Long
wooden benches stretched along the full width of the spacious floor;
an acrid smell pervaded everything. Glass flasks of various shapes
and sizes glinted in the pale blue flames of Bunsen burners. Amid
countless funnels, burettes and test tubes stood precision scales. I
was assigned a place in the laboratory as well as a space on a long
desk in the adjoining general office, shared by a dozen people. A
man slightly older than myself, called Marian, was sitting next to me.
He seemed keen to befriend me and in the days that followed, when
not busy writing notes, he kept bombarding me with questions:

'Where were you born?'

'What school did you go to?'

'What happened to you when the Soviets invaded and captured
Wilno?'

'Did you get a *matura*?'

'Did you work in the industry after leaving school?'

'Have you any brothers or sisters?'

'What happened to your family and where are they?'

'When did you come to Cracow and why did you decide to settle
down here?'

I tried to be as polite as I could be and improvised answers to his
questions, some of which he might repeat a few days later, as we
were having lunch or when we were at work. I tried hard to be
consistent in my answers and present a profile of a well-educated
young man from a middle-class background, trying to make his way
in life having lost contact with most of his family.

After collecting my passport photograph I took it to Mr Rapacki
who lived in a rather dingy flat not far from the town centre. He was

a man of few words. He took the photograph and copied the details of my false birth certificate and asked me to come back three days later.

One Sunday I took a walk to find the house where Hanna had lived. I did not bother to knock on the door of her apartment, as no Jews could have remained in Cracow after their expulsion to the ghetto in nearby Kazimierz. From her house I retraced my steps along the route we used to follow during our endless walks two and a half years earlier. The sounds and smells of the river and the familiar sight of Planty brought back old memories. Hanna's voice reverberated in my ears and I mused on how many goodbyes I went through in such a short time.

I could hardly wait to get hold of my *Kennkarte* and when I went back to collect it Mr Rapacki invited me to his study, a room full of bric-à-brac. He sat at his desk and motioned me to sit down in the chair next to him. He took out of a drawer an identity card, bearing my photograph stamped with the official seal, the German eagle above a swastika.

'There are no records of your *Kennkarte* in the issuing office,' he said, 'but it looks genuine in all other aspects. Sign it here.' He pointed to a line below the photo. I took a pen out of my pocket and signed: 'K. Kowalski'. Then I realised that my pen was filled with green ink, which I felt sure was the wrong colour, although I did not know why. It should have been black or dark blue, I fretted. The thought spoiled my excitement but all I said was: 'How can I possibly thank you? How much do I owe you for it?'

'Nothing, nothing at all,' he replied.

The next morning, before work, I went to the janitor (who was also the administrator) of the apartment block to register my domicile, as required by law. It was his duty to keep a register of tenants, available for inspection by the German authorities. The register was a large bound book, in which the details of all the inhabitants of the building were entered. It also gave dates of when they'd moved in and out. He stamped the last page of my *Kennkarte*, which was reserved for changes of address, with his official seal, not at all concerned with the colour of my signature. Enhanced with one genuine entry the document appeared to me in a new guise, like a real thing. My confidence got a boost.

In the evenings I quite often visited the Howils and shared supper with them. Having declared themselves *Volksdeutsche*, they had special privileges not extended to Poles. They had a radio set that no Pole was allowed to own. I listened avidly to the news that for the first time since the beginning of the war offered real hope of a German defeat. The Germans, it appeared, were unable, in spite of inflicting heavy casualties, to overcome Russian resistance at the gates of Stalingrad, and as far as the other theatres of war were concerned, even their distorted propaganda could not conceal the reverses suffered by their army in North Africa. After supper, the Howils invariably asked me to play the piano for them and their occasional guests, to whom I was introduced as their distant cousin.

I would travel by tram to and from work and, encountering so many uniformed Germans, I could not always suppress my fear. They were everywhere and in every guise, the *Wehrmacht* and police in uniforms of two different shades of green; the *Luftwaffe* men dressed in grey and the black-clad members of the SS, skull and crossbones on their lapels. One morning, as I stood on the platform of a tram, close to the driver, I suddenly felt an urgent need to pray, simply begging God not to let me be found out. Though my new *Kennkarte* increased my confidence, I was still aware of the Jewish emblem fatally marked on my body that could lead to a cruel investigation followed by execution. I wondered why, in the face of never-ending persecution, countless generations of my forefathers kept making it easy for their enemies to single them out so easily. Nature itself provides camouflage to protect most of its creatures, so why did they defy it by obeying an ancient commandment?

Some four weeks after I had left Warsaw, on one of my evening visits, Mrs Howil appeared distressed as soon as I walked in.

'Kazik,' she said, 'I have some bad news to tell you. Your boss came to see me today. He told me that some of his employees are convinced that you are Jewish. He asked me to tell him the truth, as he does not wish for his sake or yours to get involved in something that might lead to police intervention. I tried hard to assure him that he was wrong, but after the recent panic over the Płomniks' child, I wonder whether we dare take any more chances. What happens if somebody informs on you and the police decide to follow it up?'

I felt the blood draining from my face. 'Of course,' I mumbled. 'I understand. It must be too risky for me to stay in Cracow. You've helped me a lot. You took enormous chances. Thank you for all you and your husband have done for me. I shall never forget it.' I bade them farewell and went back to my lodgings, trying hard to work out a new plan of action.

By the following morning my mind was made up. The last address Father gave me was that of Józef Kozłowski who had moved to Zakopane earlier in the war. I would have to meet him in person and ask him for help. I had to leave Cracow immediately and, totally dependent as I was on the assistance of others, I couldn't think of anyone else. The idea of going to Zakopane must have appealed to me for another, more emotional reason too: nostalgia. Zakopane, in the Tatra Mountains, 50 miles south of Cracow and some 2,500 feet above sea level, was, until the outbreak of the war, the most popular mountain resort in Poland. I loved my summer vacations walking in the mountains there and, since I was seven years old, I had spent all my winter holiday breaks there too. Skiing was hard work in those days, as until 1937 there were no mountain lifts, and skiers, unless they hired a sledge, had to walk to the top of the pistes, before being able to enjoy the downhill runs. The happiest moments of my life had been spent in Zakopane.

I explained to my landlady that I had just received an urgent message from my father and had to rejoin him without delay. I packed my meagre belongings, paid the bill and went to the railway station with my new *Kennkarte* in my breast pocket to wait for the next train to Zakopane. The route was familiar to me, but I found it no less exciting than on previous occasions in that other world, when I was a child. Soon after our departure the countryside started changing. A flat, endless expanse of green fields interspersed with leafy woods gave way to an undulating panorama of low and gentle hills that soon grew steeper and higher. The areas of woodland grew larger and changed their character, soon being host only to pine trees. Wide rivers gave way to fast-flowing, narrow streams. Beyond Nowy Targ, about half an hour from my journey's end, the landscape changed again. The train climbed slowly, winding its way up, passing through tunnels and across viaducts, revealing constantly changing views. At times only a small section of sky was visible as the rest was obscured by an endless expanse of meadows above the tree line. Higher up, patches of snow, looking abandoned, glistened between naked granite rocks. Past the next bend, deep valleys covered with large patches of trees stretched all the way down to where, in the far distance, the sun's rays were reflected in the mirror of streams. Men now boarding the train wore round hats adorned with a white feather. They were *górale* (highlanders). They spoke with a specific, strange-sounding, local dialect.

I arrived in Zakopane past midday on a sunny early November day. Unlike four years ago, when I had last seen the small town in busy mid-season, there was little traffic now, the silence being only occasionally broken by the clatter of a steel-shod horse drawing a *fiaker* (a hackney carriage, or country cart), most of them carrying German soldiers. Cabbies wore their traditional highlander outfits: that round hat and an embroidered waistcoat over a white shirt. Lost in thought, I took no notice of the posters at the station. I was soon to discover what they were warning against.

I walked up Kuprówki, the main street, which was almost deserted. On both its sides stood Alpine-style houses constructed of wood, with steep roofs; across their width stretched balconies full of ornate carvings. There was a shop on every ground floor. Their display windows, which used to be packed with climbing and camping gear in the summer, and skiing equipment in the winter, were almost empty.

I checked the address in my notebook, asked a passer-by for directions, and after ten minutes' walk turned left into a secluded street on the southern outskirts of the village. In front of me stood the wide mass of Giewont, an almost vertical granite mountain in the shape of a sleeping giant lying on his back, with a steel cross marking the highest point where his nose should be. Its lower half was obscured by a chain of gentler, smaller mountains covered with thick pine forests, separated from one another by three picturesque valleys. I approached one of the attractive villas, which stood some distance apart with nothing to obstruct their mountain views. Dark-brown beams and richly carved wooden balconies stood out against the white walls. I walked up a few steps, crossed a verandah and knocked on the main door. A servant wearing a white apron over a black smock let me in.

'Could I see Mr Kozłowski?' I asked.

'He is out,' she replied, 'but I am expecting him at 5 p.m.'

I looked at my watch. It was just after two. 'I will come back,' I said. 'My name is Kowalski. He doesn't know me. Could I leave my suitcase till I return?'

'Yes,' she replied.

I turned back in the direction of Giewont and followed Kuprówki until, after a gentle ascent, I found myself in a forest at the foot of a mountain outside the village. In the silence broken only by the magic whisper of the mountain stream, I continued into the Kościelisko valley amongst the towering pine trees. The path was well signposted and my boots, made to measure in the ghetto, coped well with the rough ground covered with loose stones. The rocky face of Giewont grew larger as I approached it; it was overwhelming in its majesty. I was in an enchanted land, and it was the same as when I had left it four years ago.

But I was not the same. Being witness to what I would have never believed to be possible – the unprecedented cruelty of man to man, the demise of humanity as I had known it – could not but leave me a changed person.

Soon, more practical thoughts returned. What next? Wasn't I a fool, about to entrust my life to a man I had never met before? Did I, a complete stranger, have a right to ask him for help at the risk of his own life? The only way to calm my thoughts was to persuade myself that in my circumstances I had to follow my instinct rather than my reason.

Suddenly, a man appeared in the far distance. He wore a uniform and shouted something in my direction. He spoke in German but I could not make out the meaning of his words. I decided to change direction. I avoided the temptation to run away, as I thought that it might make him suspicious. I started walking away from him but the sound of his voice did not seem to be fading. I hastened along at a faster pace, pretending that I could not hear him. My heart pounded with fear and with the extra effort of getting away from my pursuer. I changed direction again and followed a narrow footpath into the woods. After a while I heard no more sounds. I looked around but there was nobody to be seen. I was not quite sure where I was and there was no one to ask. I was getting nervous, as it was getting late, but soon I found myself on a road that looked familiar. Then houses with lit windows appeared in the distance and I regained my bearings.

I got back to my destination, rang the bell and a smartly dressed man in his early 30s, tall and good-looking, opened the door. He led me to a large ground-floor room which was spacious and tastefully furnished as an office. There was a large mahogany desk in the corner, another desk with a couple of typewriters on it in front of sliding glass doors to the balcony, some typists' chairs and several filing cabinets and chests of drawers. A low glass-top table stood in the middle of the room in between two leather armchairs. He asked me to sit in one and he sat down in the other, facing me.

'Mr Kowalski, I presume,' he said, 'What brings you here?'

'My true name is Jerzy Lando,' I replied. 'My father is Jakub Lando. He suggested I should come and see you. I escaped from the Warsaw ghetto a few weeks ago and I am trying to find a job.'

As I was rolling out my lines his expression grew increasingly serious. 'What happened to your parents?' He sounded anxious.

'I have not heard from them since I left the ghetto, but I understand that the liquidation halted not long after my departure.'

He wanted to hear all about our life in the ghetto and how I managed to escape. I was careful not to mention names of people who had helped me, as I was not sure how far I could trust him. He listened to me with evident interest and his face looked warm and friendly. When I finished, he stayed silent for what seemed to be a very long time, before speaking again.

'Let me tell you my own story. About a year ago I fell deeply in love with a 20-year-old Jewish girl. She had warmth, she had character and she had beauty. She brought me happiness such as I had never known before.' He took a handkerchief out of his pocket, held it close to his face and continued. 'Three months ago, just before her parents were deported, I persuaded her to move to Zakopane and share my home. With my help she assumed the identity of a Christian and I believed that no one else knew that she was Jewish. She worked here. Three weeks ago in the night, several uniformed SS men woke us up, knocking on the door. They asked for her by her real name. They ignored my pleas and took her away. I am in the building materials industry and through my dealing with authorities I made many friends amongst German officials. Thanks to their influence, two weeks ago I received a note from her from a concentration camp telling me that she was well, but in spite of all their efforts they could help no further. I have every reason to believe that she is no longer alive . . . ' He broke off in mid sentence, unable to continue.

There was another silence and then, as if he'd woken up from a dream, he asked me in a matter-of-fact voice: 'What would you say you were good at?'

'I speak fluent German,' I replied. 'I can take shorthand dictation in German and Polish. I can type accurately and fast. I am a trained bookkeeper.'

He looked pleased. 'I need to send out a couple of urgent letters and I have nobody to type them for me.'

I sat in the chair next to the desk and he dictated two fairly long letters, one in German and another in Polish for me to type. This isn't an interview for a job but for a life, I thought, but did not feel nervous. I handed him the two typewritten letters and tried to gauge his reaction from the expression on his face as he read them.

'Very good,' he said. 'You must understand that I cannot take the risk of employing you in my office, even though I would have liked to. But I do have another job in mind for you.'

I held my breath. 'I own a quarry in Nowy Sącz, some 30 miles to the north-east, where a newly appointed manager needs a deputy. If you want the job I shall ask him to make the necessary arrangements and find you lodgings.'

I certainly did want the job! I thanked him profusely.

'Until all is arranged – and it may take a few days,' he added, 'I'd like you to help me with my work here, but remember to stay indoors! Without a residential permit, no Pole is allowed to visit Zakopane, a resort exclusively reserved for the benefit of Germans on leave or recuperating, and for the German armed forces in particular.'

I suddenly remembered the posters I didn't bother to read at the Zakopane railway station. They must have carried the warning and the man who tried to stop me earlier in the day must have been an official suspecting that I was a civilian tourist flouting the law.

I couldn't believe how lucky I'd been.

7

NOWY SACZ

Two days later, and after a two-hour train journey, I arrived in Nowy
Sącz, a small town of some 30,000 inhabitants, at the foot of the
Carpathian Mountains. I found the office of my new employer in a
two-storey house in one of the side streets. A stocky man opened the
door. His rough appearance suggested that he might be cut out for
crushing rocks himself, but the tone of his voice revealed someone
used to having his orders obeyed. If you want to cross my path, you
do it at your own risk, his facial expression warned. He was my new
boss. He did not bother to ask me anything concerning my past and I
assumed that having spent his life in the company of quarry workers,
coming from various, possibly suspect, backgrounds, he was not in
the habit of asking personal questions. He was just getting his supper
ready and after introducing himself as Jan Zamczyk, he asked me to
join him. He spoke little. 'You will start tomorrow,' he said. 'You will
stay here tonight and at seven in the morning we shall leave for the
quarry in Mszalnica.' He described my duties that included working
out men's wages and keeping track of their provisions. I was to
compile production records for the management and for the
authorities and to take care of correspondence and filing. 'As for your
accommodation,' he said, 'there is a spare room in my house and you
can have your meals with my family, if you wish.' He told me how
much I should earn and, without waiting for my comments, added: 'If
you prefer to stay in Nowy Sącz at weekends, you can use the room
where you will sleep tonight.' He then took me to an upstairs office,
where I found a camp bed, and left. While trying to go to sleep, I
reflected on the fate that had thrown me into such unfamiliar
surroundings and into this less than congenial company.

The next morning after breakfast we walked to the nearby railway station. The short train journey took us through hilly country. The morning dew still glistened on the leaves and grass. There was no one else in the compartment.

'Don't get involved with the men's problems,' he advised me. 'Always refer them to me.' I became aware of the rhythmic clatter of wheels during the long pause in our conversation. Mr Zamczyk finally interrupted the silence.

'How long have you known Mr Kozłowski, my boss?'

'I met him only three days ago for the first time,' I replied.

The train journey took 20 minutes. We got off at the second stop, Mszalnica, from where a short walk brought us to a hamlet of a dozen houses standing amongst apple trees, their few remaining leaves a deep orange-yellow. To my right, a rough country track led the eye through a slight morning mist towards a line of hills. A forest stretched from the top of the tallest peak to end abruptly half way down the mountain, where it looked like a giant might have sawn off a vast slice of earth, uncovering a vertical rock face. At its foot a carpet of loose stones stretched over a wide area. This was the quarry.

A jovial buxom woman in a simple floral frock let us into the house and with a warm smile introduced herself as Mrs Zamczyk. My arrival was of no surprise to her and she looked pleased to see me. Next to her stood her daughter, a plump, cheerful country girl, about my age.

'Call me Basia,' she said.

'Show Mr Kowalski upstairs,' Mrs Zamczyk asked her and I followed her to a room with a sloping ceiling and a dormer window, offering an extensive view of the hills in the distance. The room was simply furnished, with a bed, a small round table, a couple of chairs, a wardrobe and just enough hanging space for a coat and a suit. The cream walls were freshly painted; the wooden floor was bare and there were no curtains.

'We've been here for only two weeks,' Basia explained, looking straight into my eyes. 'I like this place a lot, don't you?' As she was going out, she bent down to pick something up from the floor and I noticed the soft curves in her body. She was naturally voluptuous and I was sure she knew it.

When we were outside again, Mr Zamczyk led me up a long steep slope to an open-cast quarry some ten minutes away. As we approached it, we were greeted by the buzzing noise of drills coming from the ledges on the rock face, where people were working. Some men swung their mallets and sledgehammers against lumps of rock, while others loaded wheelbarrows with stone chippings and crushed stone. In a cloud of dust, wagons suspended from a long steel line travelled from the top of the quarry down to the nearby railway siding and back, after disgorging their cargoes. Now and then the deafening sound of an explosion was followed by the rumble of falling rocks, the echoes reverberating across the valley. How would these tough-looking men, I wondered, respond to my instructions when Mr Zamczyk was away?

We went inside a modest wooden hut that served as an office. An ancient-looking typewriter and a few paper trays stood on the desk. My boss showed me around the office and I was soon busy rearranging files and getting to know my job.

Mrs Zamczyk did all she could to make me feel at home, keeping my room clean, asking me what my favourite dishes were, taking care of my washing and occasionally even darning my socks. Our first evening meal was plain but ample. I sat next to Basia and suddenly felt her thigh press against mine under the table. It was no accident, and it stayed there. As the days went by, I was becoming aware of Basia's attention. Whenever she saw me on my own, she spoke to me. She was a simple girl with little education and the subjects of conversation rarely went beyond the weather, the work in the quarry and her household duties. Living just with her parents in a small community, she was probably hungry for the company of her peers.

I was busy preparing my third week's payroll since starting work, when I noticed that the employees' list Mr Zamczyk had handed me included the names of two people who had not signed their timesheets for the last two weeks. 'There is a mistake,' I said. 'Two men are entered here who, I am sure, are no longer employed.'

'Don't worry,' he replied. 'This is done in our industry all the time. Managers don't get paid as much as they should be and the only way to supplement our income is to draw cash and rations for fictitious employees. You will get your share too. We must use our common sense and not overdo it. But two piddling employees? It's nothing.'

I recalled the conversation we had on the train the day after we met. After Zamczyk found out that I hardly knew Mr Kozłowski, he must have concluded that he was safe confiding in me.

I preferred to spend Sundays in Nowy Sącz to avoid making excuses for not accompanying the Zamczyks to church, but when I came back from town one Sunday earlier than usual, Basia was at home alone.

'My parents won't be back till late this evening,' she said, coming up very close, her breasts almost touching me. 'Would you like to kiss me?'

I did so without the slightest hesitation, but I suddenly remembered that I had to keep the secret of being circumcised away from her. Hungry for love after months without female company, I freed myself unwillingly from her embrace. I had to find an excuse.

'Basia,' I said gently, still short of breath, 'I am very fond of you, but I live under your parents' roof and feel responsible for you. I cannot trust myself for what will happen if we carry on like this and we may regret it later. Let's just stay good friends for the time being.' It sounded hollow and she was hurt.

On further reflection, I suspected that Basia's parents might have been involved in a matchmaking plot. They showed me more consideration than my position as the firm's employee would merit and I wondered how I could put an end to their hopes, without endangering my present existence. As the days passed, I realised how precarious my position had become. Mr Zamczyk regarded me as his future son-in-law and co-conspirator, and his daughter saw me as her future husband. Mr Kozłowski, having taken huge risks for my sake, would not want to see me fiddling his books. I was caught in a trap from which I saw no easy escape.

I kept out of Basia's way and I also told Mr Zamczyk that I was not happy to claim provisions for absent employees. The atmosphere in the house and in the office had now visibly cooled. I became convinced that my days in the quarry were numbered. A few days later I accompanied Mr Zamczyk on his visit to Nowy Sącz for a meeting with Mr Kozłowski. Mr Zamczyk saw him first, while I was completing the management reports in an adjoining office. When I saw Mr Kozłowski later that morning, he appeared indifferent and distant. He must not have been pleased with whatever he had heard from Mr Zamczyk. He said nothing on the subject, but I was now even more certain that I had to find another job. I knew I had to go. But where?

I looked through the pages of a local newspaper and an advertisement caught my eye. Organisation Todd, a German paramilitary organisation, engaged in construction projects in the East, were seeking interpreters in the areas adjoining the pre-war borders between Poland and Russia. In addition to a modest salary, accommodation and board would be provided – a highly desirable prospect in those days. This, I reckoned, could be the safest place for me, as few people would suspect the organisation's employee of being Jewish. I could now produce my *Kennkarte*, and though it was false, it had two genuine official stamps, confirming my addresses in Cracow and Nowy Sącz, where I was registered at the office address. I sent out an application with a short CV and got a reply a week later. I was requested to attend an interview in Rzeszów, some 50 miles east of Nowy Sącz, on a Monday in December 1942 at 9 a.m. I asked Mr Zamczyk to let me miss one day under the pretext of meeting a relative.

I stayed in the Nowy Sącz office over the weekend. It was freezing hard when I boarded an early train heading east. The trains were not heated and even my constant excitement at seeing the splendour of the hilly countryside under a blanket of snow did not compensate for the unbearable cold. I kept recalling the last time I travelled in this area in August 1939, returning from my first independent vacation, a carefree teenager. Could it really have been only three years ago?

By the time I got to Rzeszów, a small sleepy town, I was frozen stiff. The interview room would not be open for another half hour and the only place where I could find shelter from the cold was a church, where, frozen to the bone, I joined a few early worshippers. Even a Jew, in great need of divine intervention, could find it a good place to pray.

The interview took long enough to let me thaw out. In a large hall of a low brick building I was introduced to a panel of three men, who put to me a number of questions in Polish and German and then gave me a written text to translate. Finally they told me to expect their decision in a week's time.

The following day, amongst the mail brought to the quarry, I found a letter from the local *Arbeitsamt* (labour office), addressed to me. Its formal appearance with its swastika stamp made me feel uneasy, but all it asked was that I call on them as soon as possible. I chose to go the next afternoon. I showed Mr Zamczyk the letter and asked him for a few hours off. This was the last time I saw him.

The *Arbeitsamt* was housed in a public building in the centre of Nowy Sącz. On showing the reception the letter, I was directed to a first-floor office shared by a German official and his secretary. Without any preamble the official burst out:

'I must remind you that any job you ever take has to be endorsed by this office. I have no details of you ever applying for a work permit. You have very clearly ignored our regulations.' He looked peeved. 'What qualifications do you have?' he went on. As soon as he heard that I was fluent in German, he switched the conversation to German. He filled out a form and left the room.

He came back five minutes later. 'I cannot grant you a permit to work in the quarry,' he said. 'I have to direct you to a more important position. I haven't been able to find anyone so far with the right qualifications.'

I felt like jumping for joy at the prospect of being introduced by the *Arbeitsamt* to a new employer, saving me the effort of finding one. My enthusiasm evaporated, though, at what followed.

'I shall refer you,' he continued, 'to the Headquarters of *Sicherheit Polizei* [the Security Police – that to me meant the Gestapo], where they have an urgent need for a male interpreter and shorthand typist, something you have told me you are qualified for.'

I was gripped with panic as he made a phone call to confirm that I was on my way. He scribbled something on a piece of paper and put it into an envelope, which he addressed and handed to me. 'They are expecting you now,' he concluded. The ground was sinking under my feet. What irony! Of all the jobs that were going around I, a Jew on the run, was assigned one in the Gestapo!

'I would really prefer to decline your offer,' I pleaded. 'I have a position of responsibility in a business supplying vital building materials for the German war effort. I had not realised that I had to get your prior permission, but now that I know, and am here, couldn't you issue me a permit to go back to my job?' He would not listen. When he left the room for the second time, I turned to his secretary.

'You are Polish, aren't you?' I asked.

'Yes,' she replied.

'I beg you to help me. How on earth can I, a Pole, take this kind of a job?' I asked. 'I would be ostracised by my family, by all who know me. I shall have no friends left.'

'I am afraid there is nothing I can do for you. I know how you feel, but I have no influence over my boss. He never changes his mind. You'll just have to do what he tells you,' she replied.

My world was on the verge of collapse. Against heavy odds, I had survived the liquidation of the ghetto; against further odds I had succeeded in escaping from it and successfully assumed a new identity. I had a *Kennkarte* with two genuine address stamps on it. Facing the possibility of losing one job, I found myself free to try and find another. I lived in a part of Poland where there was hardly any chance of meeting someone who had known me as a Jew. And now all this was about to end. I was confronted with two equally ghastly alternatives: take the job I was being sent to – or disobey the order, seek shelter in another part of Poland and start all over again. I would need a new identity, though, and by now I was well aware of the difficulties involved. There was also the immediate risk of being followed and apprehended by the police. Yet perhaps there was a further alternative: could I wriggle out of my predicament by persuading my prospective employers that I was not the right man for the job? In this case I would have to attend an interview. Would I be able to get through it without being found out? I had got used to my false identity, but of all the people I'd had dealings with, *Sicherheit Polizei* must surely be the most difficult to deceive. What would happen if they assigned me to the job in spite of what I told them? How long would I be able to pull the wool over their eyes, working with them six days a week? What sort of life could I lead in a place the very name of which inspires nothing but fear and hatred?

There was not much time left. I had less than half an hour to make up my mind about turning up for the interview. I made my decision. I would keep the appointment. When I left the *Arbeitsamt* it was freezing cold on a winter afternoon. The fresh snow on the pavements was ankle deep. As I walked out of the town centre in the direction of the suburbs, I met few passers-by and hardly any traffic. Judging by the types and the sizes of the villas around me, I was now in the most affluent area of Nowy Sącz. Snow was now coming down heavily. Large flakes were landing on my face and eyes and I had to wipe them off every now and again. My destination proved to be a large white villa, with the notorious nameplate and emblem on its wall. It looked like all its neighbours, except that when I got close, I noticed that its porch had a barred hatch window placed well above eye level. Having rung the bell I had to raise my head in order to see the face behind the bars. A man in police uniform opened the window and took my letter. A heavy front door, more like that of a steel safe than a house, opened, squeaking ominously. '*Kommen Sie herein* [Come in],' called the voice. As the door slammed shut behind me, I was overcome by nausea. I suddenly realised that I was walking into a lion's den and that I may never come out alive.

Although he was not quite a gorilla, the man that stood in front of me certainly looked like one. More than six feet tall and of athletic build, he wore an SS uniform with a skull and crossbones badge on his lapel. He showed me to a small room on the left off the entrance hall, which was bare but for one chair, and asked me to sit down. After he left, I looked through the barred window. It was almost dark. I tried to get prepared for the interview. I was guessing the questions I may be asked and trying to think of the answers. The prospect of producing my identity card frightened me. Admittedly, it had two genuine endorsements of domicile, but it was, after all, a fake. And that green ink I used for signing it! Would one normally sign an identity card with *green* ink? This *was* probably irrelevant but it still would not leave my mind. What was relevant was the fact that one telephone call to the Civil Registry in Cracow would confirm that they had no record of ever having issued it. Why had I not thought it through before coming here? Who was I to fool the police? What would they do next? Would they shoot me on the spot or pack me off to a concentration camp after extracting from me, by torture, the names of people who had helped me? It was my own foolishness that been my undoing.

My hand reached for the small locket, filled with the white arsenic powder, to make sure that it was still hanging from my neck. At the crucial moment would I have time enough to swallow it? I looked again out of the window at the vast expanse of snow and at the lights of the nearby houses and prayed. Like in a silent movie, a never-ending succession of scenes from my life flashed in front of my eyes and I recalled people saying that this is what happens when one is about to die.

The gorilla appeared in the doorway and told me to follow him. We turned left and then immediately right into a dark long corridor, at the end of which a door led into a spacious corner room with heavy oak furniture, dark brown carpets and curtains drawn over the windows. The decor itself was oppressive. In the far right-hand corner of the room, behind a massive wooden desk, an SS officer sat upright in a leather armchair, framed by two windows on the two adjoining walls. His uniform was immaculately pressed, he wore military decorations and the familiar skull and crossbones on his lapels. As he got up, I saw he was tall and slim. His face was serious and during the whole of our conversation his expression never changed. Speaking in German, he invited me to sit down in a chair facing him. The gorilla stood behind me.

'What is your name?' he asked.

'Kazimierz Kowalski,' I replied.

'Where were you born?'

'In Wilno.'

'How old are you?'

'Nineteen.'

'Did you serve in the Polish forces?'

'No.'

It was a strange question. He must have realised that I was only 16 at the outbreak of the war.

'How good is your typing?'

'I type quite fast, considering that I use only two fingers,' I lied.

'There must be some misunderstanding, this is not the information I got.'

He exchanged a few words with the gorilla. He spoke fast and I did not quite catch what he said. The gorilla led me back to the room with the barred window, where he left me on my own again.

I tried to think fast. My first guess was that they would now be making enquiries about me. Surely, they would not employ anybody without security checks. The officer was even concerned about my possible association with the Polish forces. I checked the time. Ten minutes had gone by since the end of the interview. By now, I concluded, they must have had enough time to confirm that a Kazimierz Kowalski born in Wilno did *not* exist. My only hope rested on the belief that the SS chief would not want to employ a secretary that could not type properly, however good his German, and that he would not waste his time with security checks. As minutes that seemed like hours passed, my mind became a battlefield, where conflicting thoughts were locked in a deadly combat.

Before long, I heard the sound of heavy footsteps and saw the gorilla at the door. He led me back to the large office. His superior sat behind his desk as before and spoke to me briefly. 'I want you to go back to the *Arbeitsamt* right now. The man that sent you here is waiting to see you.' This was too good to be true. Was I really free? I suspected a trap, and thought the gorilla would lead me straight to a cell to await execution. But I was wrong. As we reached the end of the corridor, the heavy steel door opened and seconds later I stood on the street outside. My courage – or was it recklessness? – had paid off. I had succeeded in talking myself out of my predicament. I hurried back to the *Arbeitsamt* but as soon as I entered his office I saw how furious the official was. 'You told them a lie!' he yelled. 'Did you think you could make a fool of me? I know what you are up to, but you won't get away with it!' I stood there terrified. 'You'll report to the *Sicherheit Polizei* at nine tomorrow morning. Understood? And no tricks this time!' he concluded, still fuming.

On that dark winter evening, in heavy snow, I walked, dejected, slowly to the Nowy Sącz office to spend the night there. I was not hungry; my appetite had gone. I sat down for a while, my head buzzing with ideas. Like a chess player, I was looking at the chessboard of life, playing against an imaginary opponent. For every move I made I had to predict his response and then my own, and so on and so on. Unhappy about the first outcome, I would go back to my first move, change it and weigh up the consequences. But I was getting nowhere, I was just getting tired. I decided to go to sleep and to put off the decision until the next day, when I was rested. I got the camp bed ready but found that I could not fall asleep for a very long time. I kept waking up, weighing up the alternatives. Of one thing I was certain: if I did not turn up at 9 a.m. for the appointment, they would start looking for me. For all I knew, somebody may have been already standing outside in the street shadowing me.

Morning was fast approaching. The time for hesitation was over and I finally made up my mind. Whatever the consequences, I would not go back to the lion's den. I decided I would go back to Warsaw instead, and start a new life there. On my way I would stop in Cracow and seek out Mrs Howil to find out news about my family and to get some advice.

But first I had to collect my belongings from the Zamczyks' house and then catch the Cracow train that was due to leave Mszalnica at 9 a.m, the time I was due to attend the second interview at the police headquarters. The unavoidable risk was, of course, that the police might pursue me on my way to Warsaw, but my diversion to Cracow might possibly put them off my scent.

I rose at 6 a.m. and got ready. Looking back now and again to check that I was not being followed, I almost ran to the railway station. Mszalnica, my home, where my train was due to arrive at 7.30 a.m. was the second stop. I got into the carriage and shared the compartment with some peasants, who certainly did not look like policemen in disguise. As we were approaching Kamionka Wielka, the first stop, it suddenly occurred to me that the police might already be waiting for me at Mszalnica. There was no time to consider the logic of my thinking. As the stationmaster was about to blow his whistle and the train was about to move on, I jumped off. How silly I am, I thought immediately. In the first place, there was no reason why the police would know before 9 a.m, the time of the interview, that I did not intend to turn up, unless they saw me board the train in Nowy Sącz. Secondly, if the police decided to wait for me at the Mszalnica station I had no way of avoiding them, as I had to catch a train to Cracow from there anyway. Under the stress I was getting completely mixed up. I was not thinking clearly.

It was now too late to wait for the next train to get me to my destination on time and I had to embark on a three-mile walk instead, and still take a risk on getting there too late. It must have been snowing heavily overnight and the going was slow. The stars in the sky went out and dawn was soon breaking. The world looked pure and innocent in its white attire, but I was hardly aware of it. With my feet sinking in the snow, I struggled hard to keep the pace, glancing at my watch every few minutes. I kept turning my head back but saw nobody behind me. I was completely on my own, both physically and mentally.

It was some time after eight when, exhausted, I reached home, the home that was not going to be mine for much longer. To my relief, nobody was waiting for me and everything appeared normal. Mr Zamczyk was at work and Basia was not around either. I explained to Mrs Zamczyk that I had to go away for a few days on an urgent family business and that I would need to take all my belongings with me. I did not tell her where I was going. I declined her invitation to breakfast and packed everything within minutes. I was the only person on the platform when I got there five minutes before the departure of the train.

As the train was gathering speed I kept repeating to myself 'Goodbye Mszalnica' – but I felt no regrets.

8

A NEW IDENTITY

From the Cracow railway station I went straight to Mrs Howil's flat. It was lunchtime. Mrs Howil opened the door and, without showing any surprise, embraced me warmly. Her husband joined us and was equally pleased to see me. As soon as I sat down, the service doorbell rang. I held my breath, but there was no need to worry; the two visitors were delivering a giant Christmas tree.

'I am so glad to see you again,' Mrs Howil started, 'I have much to tell you about your family.' In the cordial atmosphere, it dawned on me that my loneliness, helplessness and obsession with preserving my own life had stopped me from giving much thought to the plight of my relatives and of my beloved Mirka. Now, I could not wait to hear the news.

'Your father and mother escaped from the ghetto a month ago,' Mrs Howil continued. 'Wołowski helped them,' she went on. 'They lead quite separate lives on the Aryan side. Boguś saw your father recently. He is OK and expects to get false identity papers soon. Wolczyks and Engels are also safe outside the ghetto.'

I worried about Father's Jewish nose, his occasional grammatical lapses that might give him away and wondered how he would survive. As for Mother, she was not a typical Aryan either but her chances were much brighter.

'Did Boguś tell you anything about Mirka Baron?' Mirka did look Jewish.

'I haven't heard that name mentioned.'

She changed the subject. 'What brings you here and what have you been up to since we last saw you?' I had plenty to tell her and she listened with great interest to every detail of my story. When I got to my encounter with the *Sicherheit Polizei*, she burst out: 'You must have been mad! You should have never gone there; it's a miracle that you came out alive!' I tried to justify my actions but she would not be convinced. 'Don't worry, Kazik. Wołowski is bound to get you a new identity and you'll feel safer in Warsaw, where it is easier to get lost in a crowd. Here is your mother's address. Stay with us tonight and you can leave in the morning.'

'What happened to Płomnik's baby?' I asked.

'We see her regularly. She is still with our friends, but we shall bring her back shortly.'

In the evening I was asked to play one of the Howils' favourites, Beethoven's rondo 'Rage Over a Lost Penny', on the piano. After dinner Mr Howil put on the radio. As a *Volksdeutsche* he was allowed to own one but not to listen to the 'enemy' broadcasts. In spite of it he tuned to the news from London at a very low volume and we had to move close to the speakers to hear it. More than 150,000 Germans and their allies under General Paulus were encircled in a small area adjoining Stalingrad known as *Kessel*, with no hope of escape. British troops had been victorious at El Alamein. The fortunes of war had at last swung against our foes, but there was still no way of telling how long the war would last. Would we be there when it ended, I wondered. In the morning I thanked my hosts profusely and made my way to the station to board the train to Warsaw.

As soon as I got to Warsaw I hurried to the address Mrs Howil had given me, in a large apartment block in Złota Street, close to the junction with Marszałkowska Street, only ten minutes away from the station. An attractive but tired-looking woman in her early 30s opened the door. She seemed apprehensive. 'Mrs Howil gave me your address, so that I can see my mother, Mrs Lando,' I babbled out quickly, trying to reassure her. She let me in. Mother must have heard my voice from the adjoining room and she rushed into the entrance hall and threw her arms around me, covering my face with a shower of kisses. She had not changed much since I last saw her. I noticed tears in her eyes, but she wiped them away quickly. She introduced me to her landlady, who had just let me in, and led me into her room. Hela, Mother's youngest sister, stood there, her face beaming. She kissed me warmly and we all sat down. We all started talking together; questions and answers flew back and forth all at once, so that it took some time for all of us to find out what we had been through since we last saw one another. I don't know how exactly Mother and her sister had got out of the ghetto, except that it happened in mid October, four weeks after I left. My father, with Eliasz Wolczyks, Hela's husband, and their son Jerzyk followed two or three weeks later, when an apartment that Mr Wołowski had found and adapted for them was ready.

'Have you heard anything about Mirka?' I asked anxiously.

'No, I haven't seen her for a long time,' said Mother.

Mother described to me how, without concealing their true identities, Mr Wołowski introduced her and her sister to a young Ukrainian couple he was friendly with – with whom she was now staying.

'They charge quite a lot for having us here, but I know that they are taking great risks,' she said. 'Hela and I sleep in this room. There's not much space here, but we manage. Our hosts have an 11-year-old daughter, a sweet little girl, and they share the other bedroom with her. We are allowed to use the room next door.' She pointed to a lounge, simply furnished, with a table at one side. 'This is where we eat. We can also use their kitchen. It's a small flat, but we feel comfortable here.'

'How do you manage shopping?' I asked.

'We do go out. I don't think we look Jewish enough to raise suspicion. We also go to visit your father and Eliasz from time to time.' She showed me her *Kennkarte* proudly.

'How did you get it?'

'As you probably know already, every apartment building has an administrator, a person responsible for keeping the register of its inhabitants. When a new tenant moves in, he stamps his *Kennkarte* if he has one (Warsaw is somewhat behind the other districts in issuing them) with an official stamp and writes down the personal details in the register.'

'I know all this,' I interrupted. 'I had mine stamped twice.'

'When they move out or disappear, he is supposed to record the fact. Mr Wołowski is in charge of the register in the tenement block in Praga, the one where you spent your first night out of the ghetto. He issues the confirmations of domicile that are needed for getting a new *Kennkarte* and puts his signature on the back of the applicant's photograph as a confirmation of identity for presentation to the authorities. Now and again – against the rules, of course – and provided he has an incentive, he will issue a confirmation in the name of someone who has just died or moved out of town, obviously not having reported the earlier disappearance. It's not that difficult if you know the right person. That's all there is to it,' she concluded.

Mother's landlord returned home in the evening. He was a powerfully built man, with dark blond hair and piercing blue eyes, which had not even a hint of a smile about them. He spoke with a strong accent, betraying his Ukrainian origin. As he shook hands with me, he took a good look at my face and called out with surprise: 'I'd never believe you were Jewish. You certainly don't look it, lucky you! Your mother went through hell worrying, she thought she might never see you again. Look at her face now!'

'I can't say how I feel,' Mother ventured, 'but I would be most grateful if Kazik could stay here just for a while till he finds somewhere to live. He could sleep on the floor in our room, if you have a spare mattress.'

'He doesn't have to, I shall fetch a camp bed from the cellar and he can sleep in the living room. He will be more comfortable there.' I could sense Mother sigh with relief.

Next morning I went to see Father. Mother told me that Leon Wołowski, given financial assistance by Father and by his ex-partner Sam Morgenstern, had found them an apartment to which they had moved as soon as they escaped from the ghetto. I made my way to a large, grey block of flats in a quiet street off Sienna Street at the address Mother gave me. I rang the bell of the ground-floor flat, and again it was Marysia Tylbor who opened the door. I could not help thinking how Aryan she looked. I also thought that the strange relationship between her, a beautiful, intelligent 18 year old and Leon, a middle-aged ticket inspector, must have needed a world disaster to create and maintain. Marysia embraced me warmly.

'Do I still call you Kazik?' she smiled.

'Yes, but not for long, make the best of it!' I replied.

She led me through a large kitchen to a spacious, virtually empty room and called out: 'All clear!' I looked in amazement as the plain wall opposite the window appeared to split at the side and a large panel swung open to allow a procession to come out. Here were Father, Mr Tylbor, Marysia's father, Eliasz Wolczyks, Hela's husband, and his son Jerzyk, and finally Sam Morgenstern and his wife. They were all smiling as if they were playing a joke on me, but Father, his face a picture of happiness, ran towards me and held me tight in his arms. He was beyond himself with joy.

'I can't believe it!' he exclaimed in a loud whisper. 'Many a time have I doubted if I would ever see you again; and yet you are here, and we are both alive!'

Marysia showed me round the flat, which consisted of four large rooms, a kitchen and a bathroom. There were no lamps, only naked electric bulbs. All the windows had heavy nets as well as printed cotton curtains; the wooden floors were bare. One of the rooms stood empty, another had no furniture except for two beds.

'This is officially the guest room,' Marysia explained.

The next room was very sparsely furnished with a dining table, a few chairs and a sideboard, to serve as a sitting-cum-dining room. Finally, there was the main bedroom used by Leon and Marysia.

'Where do the others sleep?' I asked. 'All I can see are two beds.'

'They keep four mattresses in the hiding cupboard and take them out at night. They take their turns and sleep either in the bed or on the mattress on the floor. As you noticed when you came in, at the sound of a doorbell they all disappear into the false cupboard. In case of an alarm at night, they would have to grab their mattresses and take them back to the hideout. The two who are sleeping in beds have to make them up in record time so that no trace of their presence is left. The apartment has to look empty except for Leon and myself. We have regular rehearsals.'

Then she turned to another subject. 'Things have changed since I last saw you,' she said. 'Leon has left his wife and children – he provides for them, of course, but as far as our neighbours are concerned, we are husband and wife. We chose a ground-floor flat as a precaution against the neighbours below hearing too many footsteps in a flat ostensibly occupied by just the two of us. You might have noticed that we all talk in whispers. When Leon is out we must make sure that no noise reaches the wrong ears.'

When we rejoined the others, Marysia stopped near the door.

'Let me make the introductions. This is my cousin, Kazik Kowalski,' she announced. 'It doesn't matter if you don't remember his name; it might be changing quite soon. And,' she said to me pointing first to Father and then to Sam Morgenstern, 'this is Jan Malinowski, or "Pan Jan" for short, and that is Franciszek Wołowski, a distant cousin of Leon's.'

Marysia hadn't yet finished when (the newly renamed) Franciszek interrupted her in mid-flow: 'I can only add that we are all bored stiff and must be a very uninteresting lot. Since we got here a month ago, none of us has had the nerve to venture outside. We dare not trust our appearance.'

When I found myself alone with Father, I had to answer all his questions about my recent adventures and then he came up with a new idea.

'You ought to go and see Mr Holka,' he said. 'He is an old customer of mine. A week before I left the ghetto I met a mutual friend who gave me his address. His business is at 14 Młocińska Street, close to the *Umschlagplatz*. He might have a job for you. In the meantime, you'll have to get a new *Kennkarte*. Just in case. You won't feel safe until you have a new name. Leon will find you a new identity.'

Father looked well, he had put on some weight but complained of the lack of fresh air. Before the war he used to spend nearly two months every year in the mountains or at the seaside. Practically every spring or summer weekend he would drive to the country to inhale *frische Luft* (fresh air, his favourite expression).

'I can't stand being with Mr Tylbor all the time,' he complained. 'He is such a simple fellow, can't even speak proper Polish. As for Sam, he keeps forever repeating the same old stories. I am sick of the lot of them. At least Eliasz keeps us in stitches with his jokes.'

Father, a man of the world, had little in common with the rest of his new company; he found it oppressive. 'I also get upset,' he went on, 'when Leon Wołowski comes home drunk and rows with Marysia. You'd have to be deaf not to overhear it.'

Leon came back in the late afternoon. He was wearing his ticket inspector's cap and uniform, and his nose looked red. He shook hands with me with such enthusiasm that I had to struggle to free my hand from his, and having exchanged a few words with Father, he went straight to the point: 'How would the name Stefan Wojtyła appeal to you?'

'It's certainly unusual, I've never heard such a surname before, but I am not fussy,' I replied, 'as long as I can get a *Kennkarte* without waiting too long.'

'It won't be long. Stefan Wojtyła moved out of town a month ago to join his family in the South. He won't be coming back to Warsaw and, according to my register, he still lives in my block of flats in Praga. You need to get a couple of passport photographs, so that I can sign them when I bring you a proof of domicile the day after tomorrow. Then all you need to do is to take them to the town hall, and within about a fortnight you will get an official *Kennkarte*.'

Two weeks later I went to the town hall to collect my new *Kennkarte*, which this time I signed in black ink. Most importantly it was a document that had a duplicate in the issuing office. I became known as Stefan Wojtyła, a most unusual Polish name.[1] I have often wondered who the real Stefan Wojtyła was and what fate had befallen him.

Shortly after seeing Father, in January 1943, I went to see Mr Edmund Holka. From a tram stop in Okopowa Street, close to the Powązki cemetery in the Stawki area of Warsaw I took a short walk to Młocińska Street. I might have been in the country, as I passed only one-storey buildings and sheds standing on their own plots of land. Some of them, squalid and neglected, evidently served as workshops. In these rural surroundings I found it hard to believe that I was only a few hundred yards away from the ghetto borders and almost next to the infamous *Umschlagplatz*, from where hundreds of thousands of Jews were recently transported to Treblinka. Fourteen Młocińska Street was a sprawling single-storey corner building with an adjoining hangar-like structure. A narrow, shabby entrance door led to a lobby serving as a waiting-room, large enough to accommodate two chairs and a table. Another door on the

[1] Pope John Paul II's real name was Jan Wojtyła. Could Stefan have been a distant relation of his?

left allowed access to a small office. I knocked on a window and a young man came out to greet me.

'Could I see Mr Edmund Holka?' I asked.

'Your name?'

'I am Stefan Wojtyła. Mr Jakub Lando suggested I should come and see him.'

The young man went back to the office and a tall, slim gentleman of aristocratic appearance, in his early 50s, with grey hair and bright blue eyes, came out.

'I am Edmund Holka.[2] What can I do for you?' Without waiting for a reply he ushered me to the office, most of it taken up by a massive oak desk. On one side, close to the only window sat a swarthy man who spoke with a strong foreign, Hungarian-like accent, and also the young man who had let me in. There were two empty chairs and I was asked to take a seat.

'Do you mind leaving us on our own for a few minutes?' Mr Holka asked, turning towards his companions, and when we were alone, he was ready to hear me.

'You can speak now. That was my son Janusz and my very close friend and partner, Fritz.'

'My real name is Jerzy Lando,' I said almost in a whisper, 'but I managed to get a *Kennkarte* in the name of Stefan Wojtyła. Here it is.' I pulled it out of my pocket, as if I did not think that he would believe me without seeing it. 'My father is safe and sends his best regards.' My words must have sounded hackneyed on such an occasion. 'I escaped from the ghetto in October. I can speak and write German, I finished a secretarial course and I've got good experience working as a clerk and bookkeeper. I need a job.'

He looked straight into my eyes and replied after a short hesitation, 'Yes, I can offer you a job. We need a cashier and a reliable clerk right now. You must promise me, though, that nobody except myself will know your real name. You can start tomorrow if you wish, when I shall sort out your salary, but let me take you around the place first and show you what we do here.'

'You are very kind.' I resorted to another platitude. At the same time I could hardly believe my luck. Was I dreaming?

He led me back into the entrance lobby from where a door

---

[2] For more information about Edmund Holka see the Epilogue.

opened to a vast high-ceilinged hall, some 200 feet long by 100 feet wide. A massive pile of old clothes or rags took up more than a third of its surface and stretched some 15 feet up, almost to the ceiling, leaving only enough space for a dozen or so people, mainly women, to sit on top of the heap, sorting out its contents. There were thousands of items in that heap: pants, skirts, shirts, underwear, overcoats of every type and description.

'We are the largest firm of waste merchants in Warsaw,' explained Mr Holka. 'We receive tons of old clothing and some waste metals from various German sources and sort them for recycling in German factories.'

I did not need much imagination to work out where all this clothing was coming from. Most of it must have been ripped apart on purpose, I presumed, in search for valuables, and was only fit for reprocessing. The workers sorted the clothes according to the type of fibre they were made of and then bundled them into separate stacks, ready for shipment. I soon found out that some of the garments arrived in a wearable condition and that we were allowed to put those out on sale to individual callers. We had to account for what we shipped and for what we sold by weight. In the course of my work I saw wagonloads arriving at the railway siding on an embankment just across the road.

I enjoyed the working atmosphere. Mr Holka and his son Janusz – neither of them looked like rag merchants – treated me as a member of their family. Both men were very much alike: tall, upright, good-looking and well spoken. Mr Edmund Holka, the father, was addressed by everybody as *Pan Prezes* (Mr Chairman). Fritz and Mr Holka spoke German like natives. Fritz was clearly the expert and all technical queries were referred to him. Next to the office there was a self-contained two-room flat and a kitchen for the caretaker, who lived there with his wife, who was a shrunken worn-out woman in her 50s, and a pretty daughter of my age. The two women prepared our lunches, which were simple but tasty. Some kissing and cuddling went on in the kitchen on the rare occasions when I and the young girl found ourselves on our own.

I had a lot to do, preparing productivity and stock reports for the German authorities and accounting for the cash sales. At the end of each day I had to reconcile the money in the safe with the balance shown in the books, a task that would keep me in suspense until the job was finished. All too often I had less money in the safe than I was supposed to have, but even when the opposite was the case, my joy was short-lived. In a cashier's experience what appears at first as a surplus usually turns out to be a shortage. I would keep counting and recounting the banknotes until I got the total right; many a time I felt duty bound to make up the shortage with my own money. Once, when *Pan Prezes* caught me doing so, he was amused and insisted on using his own money to cover the shortage instead.

I saw many visitors coming and going; some of them appeared quite frequently and stayed in the building for longer visits. There was also the rather mysterious if unpredictable presence of a *Pan Inżynier*, (the professional engineer), who flitted in and out of the premises, presumably doing some work, but whose exact job was never clearly defined. I wondered at times whether it was a cover for some clandestine activity. Taller even than any of the Holkas, powerfully built, with thick blond hair, light-blue eyes and a small moustache, he had the unmistakable bearing of a career officer. He was around quite a lot, but he could not have any regular employment either at Holka's or elsewhere, as he never seemed to stay in one place for very long. He would at times disappear for days on end. He would frequently get into private conversation behind closed doors with Mr Edmund Holka or his son. At the end of the day, he would make sure that all the doors were shut, get a sheet of paper out of his pocket and, when all was quiet, he would read the latest underground bulletin to us, including the news from the BBC World Service. This was the highlight of the day. One of the first bulletins described how Stalingrad turned out to be the greatest disaster for the German armed forces. The most important information from my point of view was the reliable confirmation of the rumours about the destination of Jews deported from the Warsaw ghetto. They were true. The daily contingent went up from 5,800 people a day starting late July to 10,000 people a day from 1 September. The deportations had ceased abruptly on 10 September, a few days before my escape.

Before the end of August the Polish Underground had found out that regular passenger trains were not allowed to stop at the Treblinka station. They also had eyewitness reports that trains carrying the deportees stopped in a camp in the depths, of a nearby forest. On arrival, the victims were ordered to hand over all their valuables and then told to undress and go to the 'baths'. Large posters informed them that after the bath they would receive fresh clothing and would be assigned to work groups. The so-called baths were in reality gas chambers. The bodies of men, women and children were carried into mass graves dug by two giant mechanical excavators working non-stop day and night. The trains were filled for their return journey with the bundles of clothes. Three wagonloads of human hair were by accident discovered by some Polish railway workers at a railway junction in Warsaw. Chemical analysis of samples that had been smuggled out revealed the presence of a mixture of hydrogen and cyanide gases. At some stage the Germans reportedly replaced poison gas with water vapour, thus making their victims die of suffocation rather than poisoning.[3]

In the days when I stayed with Mother at the Ukrainian couple's flat, I kept looking at the accommodation vacant columns of the daily newspaper. One advertisement caught my eye and led me to a modern residential development close to Plac Narutowicza. From the tram stop I followed Borska Street, till I turned right into Kaliska Street and then left into Tadevsza Jotejki Street, a quiet backwater bordering on a park. It was only about five minutes' walk from the stop. Number 4 was a modern four-storey building, with two three-room apartments on each floor. Each flat had in addition a small servant's room off the kitchen. At the door of the second-floor flat a diminutive lady in her late 40s with silver-grey hair greeted me.

The room to let was on the right of the entrance hall. It was bright, had plenty of space and overlooked the park. It was spotlessly clean. All the furniture was painted glossy white: a bed along the left-hand wall, a bedside table next to it, a generous-sized wardrobe, a desk and two chairs. The parquet shone like a polished mirror, and a multi-coloured woven rug added to the warm atmosphere of the room. A large cross hung above the bed. I fell in love with the room as soon as I saw it. Charming and well-spoken, the landlady showered me with no end of questions: what kind of work was I

[3] See *Armia Podziemna* by General T. Bor-Komorowski.

doing? What was my family background? Where was I born? What school did I go to? Where did I live at present? The first and last questions were easy to answer: I worked at Holka's and lived in Praga, where Wołowski was the house administrator. For the rest, I used my imagination, trying hard to store all I said in my memory for future reference. This was the first time my landlady was letting a room, and taking a stranger from the street into her home made her cautious; hence her inquisitiveness about me. I avoided being too specific when talking about my childhood and my schooldays just in case she had some knowledge of where I claimed to have been brought up. I was very conscious of dealing with a highly intelligent and observant person and I tried to present myself as a shy young man, reticent to talk about himself.

My answers must have satisfied her, as she agreed to take me as a lodger. I moved in the next day. In the evenings, when I came home, my bed was made up and brightly coloured cotton curtains were drawn over the windows. I felt awkward being unable to display any family photos. I considered buying some leftovers from a photographer, but the risk of my landlady having seen the people in question before was too great.

She had an 11-year-old son. Her husband was a colonel in the Polish army, presumably taken prisoner by the Russians in the autumn of 1939. She believed, after the recent discoveries of mass graves around Katyń in Russia, that alongside thousands of other Polish officers taken prisoner by the Russians, he was murdered in cold blood by the NKVD,[4] a crime for which Russians refused to admit responsibility.[5]

I felt very happy with my accommodation and if I had anything to complain about, it was her constant need to chat, lonely as she must have been. I found it a strain to remember everything I had told her about myself, when some same subject resurfaced at a later date. While I hoped to stay put in her flat, I knew that a single slip would be enough to give me away and necessitate another move. To avoid suspicion I pretended on some Sundays to be going to church in another part of town, but I was not sure how I was going to explain convincingly the lack of any letters from relatives, even on my name-day.

Some time in March or April Leon brought Father news about

[4] NKVD: acronym for Russian Security People's Commissariat for Internal Affairs-Security Organisation.
[5] For 50 years, as I later found out.

Edek, whose escape from the ghetto he had recently organised. To Leon's amazement, Edek, Mala and Krysia were now staying in one of Warsaw's better hotels, Hotel Polski in Dluga Street. Edek told Leon about a new scheme announced by the Germans that he'd heard about through a friend. Palestinian nationals or those who had close relatives in Palestine would be treated as foreign nationals and allowed to stay in a hotel in Warsaw, free to move around, until they were transferred to an internationally supervised camp. They would remain there until the end of the war or until exchanged for Germans interned by the allies. Edek did not hesitate. He considered himself exceptionally lucky. His father-in-law, Mr Alt, had emigrated to Palestine shortly before the outbreak of the war. Edek went to the Gestapo headquarters with the necessary documents, was treated with utmost respect and was invited to move to the hotel with his family and their belongings.

'Edek told me to tell you,' continued Leon, 'that Honduras Consul in Warsaw sells Honduras citizenships for around 50,000 złotys apiece through some middleman. Germans will guarantee complete safety and bloody good living conditions to Honduras citizens. They are going to live in another Warsaw hotel, just as posh as Hotel Polski, while waiting to be shipped to what sounds to me like decent camps in neutral countries.'

'Edek was over the moon,' Leon went on. 'He said that many Jews are taking the chance and coming out of hiding. They are allowed to move around Warsaw, including the ghetto, as much as they like and are told to spread the good news to all their friends, to tell them how they too can survive the war. He wants you to hurry and not to miss your chance; he believes that there are only a limited number of passports to be had.

'Some of these lucky people were actually there, in the lounge of this hotel. Edek pointed out to me a young, dapper fellow, sitting at the bar, busy talking with three other Jewish-looking men. They were joking and laughing. Edek asked me to tell you,' Leon continued, 'that you, Jakub, ought to meet this man, that he will take good care of your family.' Here Leon stopped and seemed to ponder something in his mind.

'But to tell you the truth . . .' he continued after a short break, 'I don't entirely like the sound of it. These terrified people may be clutching at straws; they will believe anybody who will promise to save them from death. It looks like a spider entertaining flies . . . I could be wrong, of course, so I didn't say anything about my doubts to Edek. It would only worry him. So here we are. I told you everything Edek wanted me to tell you – and more,' Leon concluded.

The next day Mother came to see Father who, after hearing Leon's report, was convinced that he had to go ahead and buy the Honduras citizenship. But none of his arguments made any impression on Mother. 'You can go if you like but I won't. Nor will Jerzy!' she declared in desperation when he kept on insisting. 'A blind man can see that this is a trap to lure more Jews out of hiding. It may be different for Edek, he has genuine papers, but fancy buying Honduras citizenship! Through *German agents*! You must have lost all your senses.'

That was the end of the scheme as far as she was concerned.

I had some reservations about visiting Edek at the hotel. I had a lurking suspicion that people meeting the 'Palestinians' might be followed by the police on suspicion of being Jewish. And yet I loved him and was determined to see him. I also had another motive. As my closest confidant, he knew about my love affair with Mirka and I was hoping that he might know something about her present whereabouts. I took a chance. I phoned him and arranged to meet him in a café. We sat down in a corner, out of other people's earshot and I ordered a drink. Edek was most disappointed with Father's decision, but realised that once Mother said 'no', the subject was closed.

'Have you heard anything about Mirka?' I asked anxiously.

'Yes, in the last few weeks I've seen her and her father quite a few times. I've got their address. It was quite obvious that after you left she fell into some kind of depression. And then I started hearing gossip. She became known as a "good time girl". She would apparently sleep with anybody who asked her – yes, literally anybody. She's got quite a reputation.'

'Are you sure?' I felt devastated.

'Absolutely, I heard it from so many people that there is no doubt in my mind. It's a tragedy, such a lovely girl!' From the look on my face Edek must have guessed that I could not bear to hear any more and he changed the subject. For weeks to come, the vision of Mirka did not leave me alone. I was overcome by guilt. I was sure that the change in her was a direct reaction to having been abandoned by the man she loved.

And so, once more I was settling down to a more normal life, though danger always lay in wait around every corner. Any outing – even going to and from work, shopping, or visiting my family, carried a risk. It was bad enough being a Jew always running the risk of exposure, but in addition I had to share the dangers faced by all Poles. Mass round-ups, rare in the first years of the occupation, were constantly on the increase. Hitherto carried out mainly by the SS or the German police, they were now conducted on such a massive scale that even the *Wehrmacht*, the ordinary German army units, had also been brought into action. To take the intended victims by surprise, plain-clothes agents also increasingly took part in the operations. These victims included both men and women, in particular the younger ones. The round-ups could happen anywhere, in the streets, restaurants, cafés, or railway station waiting-rooms. People were dragged out from buses, trams and trains. There were larger round-ups at night, when everybody had to be indoors, and systematic house-by-house, flat-by-flat searches were conducted. Hardly a day went by without a round-up in at least one part of the city. Those caught were herded into *budy* (covered trucks) and taken under escort to the nearest Gestapo station for an initial screening. Those classed for any reason as suspect were detained for further interrogation, while the remainder, depending on the purpose of the particular operation, were despatched either as slave labour to Germany or to concentration camps. According to the bulletins of the Underground, on four consecutive days in January 1943 alone, some 35,000 Poles, mainly men, were apprehended – most of them sent to concentration camps.

Just before I left the ghetto, the deportations had ceased, but everyone suspected that it was only a matter of time until they resumed. The vast majority of its inhabitants could do nothing but hope that the end of the war would come in time to save their lives. In the meantime, with help from the Polish Underground movement, some newly formed defence units armed themselves with hand

172   **SAVED BY MY FACE**

weapons, for which only a limited amount of ammunition was available.

On 18 April 1943 my uncle Edek was still enjoying his new-found freedom in a Warsaw hotel, expecting an imminent transfer to an internationally supervised camp, when he decided that the time had come to retrieve a bundle of gold dollars he had buried for safekeeping somewhere in the ghetto. He planned a very short visit, using the pass he had received from the Gestapo allowing him to cross the ghetto border whenever he liked. His wife, Mala, had a premonition that a disaster was about to happen and tried in vain to stop him, but it was not in Edek's nature to change his mind once he had made it up.

Mala was right. Unexpectedly, the day after his departure, on 19 April, SS troops entered the ghetto in order to carry out the final liquidation and deport all that remained of the Jewish population. This time, though, they were met by gunfire, at first close to the entrances at Stawki and Leszno. Crowds of onlookers filled many streets along the walls to get a glimpse of what was going on inside the ghetto. They saw and heard shots being fired from the nearby windows and fresh waves of the German gendarmerie appearing on the scene. The defence, chaotic at first, was changing gradually to what appeared to be a regular, apparently well-planned campaign with constant sounds of machinegun fire and exploding grenades. At the same time, most of the traffic outside the ghetto carried on as usual and from the areas unaffected by fighting, Jews were still being taken away. However, on the next day, 20 April, according to some of our employees arriving late at work, trams destined for Żolibórz had to stop at Plac Krasiński and passengers, to their great annoyance, had to get out and walk to where they could catch an alternative form of transport. That night the sky was brightly lit by isolated streaks of pink flames. At night, more houses inside the ghetto were engulfed in flames. Adjoining buildings were catching fire and black smoke drifted into the sky, its foul stench reaching the areas outside the ghetto. By Thursday, 21 April, fires had spread over the ghetto districts of Muranów and part of Powązki and a foul smell of burning penetrated large areas of the town. A black, heavy cloud hung over Warsaw. On Good Friday, 22 April, the fifth day of the fighting, loud detonations reached districts lying even a long way from the ghetto. Each explosion must have started a new fire, as each was followed by a new column of smoke, rising into the sky. Dark smog blunted the blood-red sky and the incessant clatter of automatic weapons signalled continuing fighting inside the walls.

The end of the most lonely and tragic fight of the war was approaching. There was no hope for the defenders. As soon as the Germans recovered from the initial shock, they brought in fresh troops, Ukrainians and Latvians amongst them, and a large number of tanks. They isolated one building at a time, called for its occupiers to give themselves up and then, whether they had come out or not, they set fire to it. Proceeding systematically, as was their wont, they set fire to every single building in the ghetto, until nothing was left but smouldering ruins. Those who did not die in them were transported mainly to Treblinka to perish there.

In the meantime, there was no trace of Edek. And as the fires lit the sky and explosions ripped the air, Mala was going out of her mind.

Across the road from my office there was a small bare field, where during the lunch break on a bright day, after the long winter months, I would sit on a log and enjoy the spring sunshine. Here was my chance to get a breath of fresh air in relative safety. Next to the field there was an embankment and on the embankment a railway siding that lead to the nearby *Umschlagplatz*. I saw little railway traffic going through, other than the transportation of old clothing destined for our business.

Since I had left the ghetto I had never managed to erase from my mind the picture of Mirka, the girlfriend I had left behind. She used to appear in my daydreams looking just as she did when I first saw her, with a broad smile on her face. Her bright, dark eyes under her thick black hair and low forehead haunted me. I could picture her chatting as she did in that basement which we made into our home, while awaiting the fatal selections. And then I remembered her as she was on the night that we had spent together on a shelf in the Töebbens factory, when I held her in my arms, shy and self-conscious. This is when we had first made love after deciding that nothing but our love mattered, because the end was imminent. And since I had spoken to Edek about her, I could not stop seeing her in other men's arms – different men in different places, talking to them, smiling at them, making love to them – probably while thinking about me.

A few days before Easter, as the last stage of the liquidation had begun, traffic along the embankment restarted. One day, as I was sitting in the field, trying hard to suppress my nagging thoughts about Mirka, I heard the sound of a train approaching from my right, from the direction of the *Umschlagplatz*. A hard-working locomotive, spitting out white clouds of steam and black smoke, was pulling dozens of dark-red cattle wagons. All the doors were bolted and barbed wire protected small hatch windows on each side of the door. If Mirka did not get shot or burnt alive, she might be inside one of these tightly packed carriages. I could see faces of people, almost touching one another, trying to get a glimpse of the outside world. By now they could have no illusions as to the fate that awaited them. I certainly knew their true destination. Only 60 miles away, in Treblinka, they would be robbed of their belongings, stripped of their clothes and suffocated to death, like hundreds of thousands before them. And I was myself a part of the spectacle, but only by a miracle was I in the audience and not on the stage. How long could the miracle last?

I was no longer able to face this appalling sight of thousands of people driven to their execution, and for a couple of days stayed in the office at lunchtime. But then, on the third day, I suddenly felt an inexplicable urge to come out again, one more time. I fought against the cowardly desire to stay indoors. There may be somebody on the train, I thought, somebody I know, maybe even Edek himself. I left the building, crossed the road just in time to see a train approaching. It was moving extremely slowly and looked as if it was coming to a halt. Suddenly, less than 30 yards away, in one of the small windows I saw a familiar face almost pressing against the barbed wire, a face that I could never fail to recognise – yes, it was her, it was Mirka. She noticed me. She looked straight at me, smiled with a faint smile and her mouth opened slightly, as if she was saying something, but no sound reached me. There was no sign of reproach in her face. Her eyes followed me, as her wagon moved slowly out of sight. It was all over in no time. For a long while, I stood there shaking, unable to move.

When I came home from work a week or so later, my landlady looked concerned. 'The house caretaker has just been to see me. He was told that during the night the German police are to make a house-to-house search for Jews who escaped from the ghetto.'

I don't know how well I succeeded in trying to look unconcerned but could not help asking her for more details. 'How reliable is his information?'

'He does have contact with the police and he has no reason to doubt what he has heard. Many Jews apparently managed to get out of the ghetto through sewers and by other routes, and the Germans want to make certain that none are hiding in our area.'

'Will they search every house?' I just could not leave the subject alone.

'So he says.'

I hardly slept that night. Every real or imagined sound of motor engines outside, or of footsteps on the staircase; every knock on a door in the building, sent me into agonies of fear. But the night went by and nothing happened.

'They must have changed their mind,' remarked my landlady at the breakfast table.

A few days later Edek came back to the hotel. His face was badly cut and bruised. He was limping. He had a simple story to tell. He said he had been surprised in the ghetto by the resumption of deportations and the armed resistance of the fighters. He was hiding for a few days in a basement, but when the Germans threatened to burn the building he and others came out to be escorted to the *Umschlagplatz*. The SS were not interested in his papers and he was treated like every other Jew. The next morning he was pushed into a cattle wagon heading for Treblinka. The people inside the wagon were packed so tight that there was no room to move and he saw children and short people suffocating from the lack of air. The stench was unbearable and so was the wailing of children and women, many separated from their families. After half an hour, Edek, who was standing near the door, somehow managed to force it open. The sight of the ground beneath him passing by at speed was terrifying. He took a deep breath, covered his head with his hands and jumped.

When he regained consciousness he was in agony. He could hardly move one of his legs and was sure that it was broken. Yet the only overwhelming thought in his mind was his need to hide, to get away from the railway line. He dragged himself into nearby bushes and, fearing discovery, lay there motionless for hours, until night fell. With darkness coming some lights appeared in the distance and he hobbled along to discover a peasant's cottage standing a little apart from a small hamlet. A man opened the door and was shocked to see the stranger's injuries; he guessed straight away where he had come from. He took pity on Edek, his wife dressed his wounds as best she could and they let him stay in the barn for a few days until he could move around and the cuts on his face had begun to heal. The peasant managed to pass a message to Mala who had not expected to see Edek alive again; having heard the good news she came to fetch him.

In the middle of July, three months after the miraculous escape from the death train, Edek, along with his family, joined the 250 'Palestinians' – Jews who, like Edek, had revealed their identity to the Germans on the understanding that having Palestinian visas or similar documents they would be spared and eventually exchanged for the German nationals interned by the Allies. They were taken away from the Hotel Polski and loaded into passenger trains together with some 2,000 'Americans' – Jews who believed that the Central American citizenships they had recently bought would save their lives. All were sent on a journey that they expected would take them to freedom. As I found out after the war, the 'Palestinians' were taken to the Bergen–Belsen concentration camp instead, where as living skeletons they were liberated by the Allies just as they were about to be transported to the extermination camps. The 'Americans' were unlucky. They were separated from the 'Palestinians' and none of those Edek had known have been seen since.

On a visit to Mother, one day in June 1943, I was surprised by the sounds of an agitated conversation coming from the adjoining room. At the same time the faces of Mother and Hela showed concern; I could sense that something was going badly wrong. 'What's happening?' I inquired.

'Our landlady came home less than half an hour ago, when she was not expected and, no sooner had she gone into her bedroom, than she rushed out in a state of shock. From what we heard it appears that she found her husband in bed with their little daughter. She is only 11 years old!'

'How awful! But you can't stay in a household that is about to fall apart; this place isn't safe any longer. God knows who is going to be involved and what questions are going to be asked.' As more shouts and screams outside the door could be heard I decided to leave. 'I shall ask Mr Holka for some time off and come back tomorrow morning,' I promised.

When I saw Mother next morning, things seemed to have settled down. 'Our landlady was hysterical at first but she has now calmed down a little. Her husband left home last evening and has not been back since. She agrees that we ought to move out as soon as we find somewhere else to live. She actually gave me an address of a friend of hers in Milanowskiego Street, which might be an option. It's not far from your digs,' said Mother.

'I shall meet you there at 6 p.m,' I said and left to go to work.

Milanowskiego Street was only a quarter of an hour's walk from where I lived on the opposite side of Plac Narutowicza. When I arrived, Hela and Mother were already there. A charming lady called Jadwiga greeted me warmly. We went into a small living room and started talking. Jadwiga was middle-aged, of dignified appearance, and lived with her niece called Jadzia, a pretty girl of 21 who was restless, with a head of untidy blond hair. Both women listened to us with great interest and it was obvious that they understood Mother's problem all too well.

'I have a spare room in the flat. It has only a dormer window and a sloping roof but it is bright and warm in the winter. You should find it comfortable. If you like it, you can rent it from me.' The rent she mentioned was very reasonable, no more than a non-Jew would be happy to pay. 'One word of warning, though,' she said. 'My niece, Jadzia, is very much involved with the *Konspiracja*, the Underground movement, and you mustn't be surprised by what you might see here.'

'When can we move in?' Mother was not put off by the small matter of the illegal (and probably highly dangerous) activities.

'As soon as you like. Jadzia will be delighted to help you move. Won't you?' Jadzia expressed her enthusiasm with a broad smile.

We talked for a while and the subject of music cropped up. 'So you play the piano?' Jadwiga asked me. 'Come over tomorrow evening and I shall introduce you to my very close friend who lives fairly near and with whom you might have something in common.'

The next day Jadwiga took me to an apartment in Mochnackiego Street, virtually round the corner from her place. It was on the ground floor of a solidly built block of flats. We could hear the piano as soon as we reached the front door. We rang the bell, the playing stopped and two ladies came out to greet us. They were the Bogusławski sisters, Wanda and Zosia (nicknamed Dodzia). They made me immediately feel at ease. The elder of the two, Wanda, probably just over 40, was slim and quite tall, with prematurely greying hair. She wore no make-up, not even lipstick, and though neatly dressed, was not particularly smart. Dodzia, in her 30s, was quite attractive, plump and feminine and took a greater interest in her appearance. As I found out later, her husband, a Polish army officer, was a prisoner of war in Germany. We were ushered through the entrance hall into the living room which was tastefully furnished with a solid dark oak dining table and chairs, two comfortable sofas and a few armchairs. A crystal chandelier and beautifully made heavy curtains conveyed a feeling of comfortable living. An upright piano stood next to a large window that framed a view of mature poplars growing in the street outside. Wanda appeared to have heard a lot about me and was more impatient to listen to me playing than to hear of my adventures. The piano must have been recently tuned. It had a rich sound and a pleasant touch. As soon as I finished my piece she went up to a shelf, pulled down a thick volume of Beethoven's symphonies arranged for four hands and asked: 'Could you play these?'

'Let's play together and then you will get your answer.' I was good at sight-reading and it was only the approaching curfew that put an end to our music making.

Mother and Hela soon settled down in their new home. After a while, they got used to Jadzia frequently coming in and going out with a shopping bag almost bursting at its seams. Once they got a shock when, on accidentally lifting a lid covering a window seat, they saw a couple of strange-looking bulky metal objects. Jadzia, who was standing nearby smiled: 'Don't worry, they are only automatic guns.' But Mother and Hela still felt contented and secure.

I became a frequent visitor to Wanda's apartment. I thought that she was a good sight-reader – though not a wonderful pianist (but I did not tell her). She thought that I would one day make a better conductor than a pianist, and told me so. I always played the top part and she played the bass part. She had many albums of orchestral music arranged for four hands – Glucks' overtures, Handel's organ concertos, Beethoven's, Brahms', Mozart's and Mendelssohn's symphonies, and many works that I heard for the first time in my life. Our audience consisted of Dodzia, the occasional visitor, and frequently Mother and my aunt. I spent some of the happiest hours of the war years there and I believe that our music making helped brighten up our audience's existence.

When Wanda heard that Hela had a 13-year-old son, Jerzyk, she asked her to bring him over one evening. He did not look Jewish, but he had a personality problem that prevented him from having a meaningful relationship with anybody other than his parents. He was very shy and spoke little. As soon as Wanda saw him, she took a liking to him and offered him a small room in her apartment. I don't believe she charged for it. The accommodation inside the Wołowskis' cupboard being more than restricted, Jerzyk was delighted to be allowed to live in a room of his own, and one in which he could stay in peace, without the need to vanish into a wall several times a day. As I discovered one day, there was another lodger living at Wanda's in an adjoining bedroom, an elderly gentleman who kept his own company and was very rarely to be seen.

One Saturday afternoon I came to visit Wanda somewhat earlier than usual. She was not in and Dodzia, who had let me in, asked me to join her for tea in the small lounge in the part of the flat she occupied at the other side of the entrance hall, from which a door led to her bedroom. The lounge was sparsely furnished with a sofa big enough for two, a couple of matching armchairs and a low table covered with books. She closed the door and invited me to sit down on the sofa next to her. There was hardly any space between us, she was so close. She told me that her husband had been away for nearly five years and that she felt terribly lonely without him. Suddenly, I felt her arms around me and her body pressing against mine. I was completely taken by surprise.

'I am sorry,' I mumbled. 'I have a girlfriend I am very much in love with. It would break her heart if I was unfaithful to her. Please do forgive me!' She understood and I felt terribly sorry for her. We finished the tea and carried on talking about various subjects till Wanda came home. From then on, whenever I saw Dodzia I felt that I was blushing. I tried to pretend that nothing had ever happened between us.

One evening, a young woman in her early 20s came to our flat to visit my landlady and I was asked to join them for tea. She introduced herself as Mrs Samulik. A smart attractive brunette, rather short but with a perfectly shaped figure, she had black sparkling eyes. In conversation I was often seduced by her enchanting smile. My attention would be diverted from the sound of her words and I would often have to ask her to repeat them. She lived on her own in the first-floor flat just below ours and, I heard, had been separated for some time from her husband, a prosperous landowner living some distance north of Warsaw. She was witty, intelligent and fun to be with. She asked my landlady:

'Who is playing the piano in your flat? Is it Mr Stefan?'

'Yes, it is me,' I replied. 'I hope the sound does not disturb you.'

'On the contrary, I love music. Please play something for me!' I obliged, and continued playing at her request.

A few days later, in the evening, she came up again and invited me to come down to her flat for a drink. It is hard to believe, but Mrs Samulik's apartment was almost identical to ours. It was tastefully furnished and her sitting room was full of feminine touches. She must have given a great deal of thought to ensure that her silk curtains matched the upholstery of the sofa, the armchairs and the loose cushions. And all of them were in tune with the colour of the deep-pile carpet. Chinese-style lamps emitted a soft light, leaving some parts of the room in semi-darkness. There were pictures of attractive ladies in scanty clothes on the walls. On the mantelpiece stood exquisite porcelain figures, and a small cabinet housed crystal glasses and several bottles of spirits. There was a modern gramophone in the corner and a record cabinet of matching wood. The gramophone was softly playing a popular song about a couple in love. We were on our own. 'Would you like to dance with me?' she asked, with a twinkle in her eye. She was wearing a low-cut sleeveless dress revealing her beautifully sculptured shoulders. I was glad to accept her invitation – she was a superb dancer – and we danced all evening. With each successive dance I held her tighter and she made no effort to keep me at a distance. By the time I said goodnight I felt intoxicated, and not just with the drink. She asked me to come again later in the week and I started seeing her regularly. She never tired of dancing.

One night, a couple of weeks later, she came to the front door to let me in wearing a negligée. She was not well and so went to bed. I sat down on the bed next to her and, though longing to hold her in my arms, I spent all evening just talking. I was convinced that she would not resist me, but I did not dare touch her. The fear of revealing that I was circumcised held me back. I could trust no one. It was hell.

A few days later, to everyone's surprise, her husband came to stay with her. She brought him up to our flat to introduce him to my landlady and to myself. He was a big, handsome fellow in his 30s, and, from what he told me, he was fond of all the pleasures that life could offer. He had a gigantic appetite and I saw him start his breakfast with eight scrambled eggs that he would gobble up in no time. His other meals were a similar size, and yet he was not overweight, just big and powerfully built. In these days of official food rationing he must have been able to bring enough supplies from his farm so as not to be short of anything. He listened for a while to me playing the piano, then went downstairs and reappeared within minutes with two accordions. 'Would you like to try to play one?' he asked, handing me one of the beautiful instruments. This was a completely new experience for me, but after half an hour I could play some popular tunes tolerably well. He was enthusiastic. 'Let's play a duet,' he said. It was an unexpected and wonderful experience. He was very musical and almost every evening from then on we played together, improvising duets based on the popular South American tangos. Mrs Samulik, sometimes accompanied by my landlady, sat in the same room knitting, listening and telling jokes. We had great fun together. These were magical evenings. It was as if the war was an illusion.

Mr Samulik left Warsaw after a week, came back a few days later, stayed with his wife for a fortnight and then, the marriage evidently reconciled, they both returned to the country. I was sorry to see them go.

One Sunday afternoon, in March 1944, I went to see Wanda, only to find her in tears. She could not stop crying and Dodzia, though in a state of shock herself, was trying hard to console her.

'What happened?' I asked.

'Last night, soon after midnight, we were woken up by a knock on the door,' said Dodzia, while Wanda was sobbing, unable to get a word out. 'As you can imagine, we were not expecting visitors at that time of night. Four heavily armed uniformed SS men walked in and demanded to see the elderly gentleman you have met here before. I showed them his room and three of them went in – except for one, who asked Wanda if she knew that the man was Jewish. She of course denied it. He then snooped around the flat until he found Jerzyk, still in bed. He asked him if he was Jewish and when he hesitated, he made him pull down his pyjama-trousers.

'"Get dressed," he commanded and left him for a few minutes on his own.

'Jerzyk, paralysed by fear, took a long time to get ready. When the German came back, he asked Jerzyk:

'"*Wie alt bist du*? [How old are you?]"

'"*Dreizehn Jahre alt*. [I am 13.]"

'"*Du bist zu jung zu sterben* [You are too young to die]," he declared. "*Morgen fruh, verschwinde*! [In the morning, first thing, disappear!]" he said, and left.'

I never discovered what the relationship between the lodger taken away by the SS men and Wanda had been. He was never seen again. Jerzyk had left the next morning and moved back to Marysia Tylbor's flat. What with his miraculous rescue from the *Umschlagplatz*, this was his second lucky escape.

'I won't be coming round for the next few weeks,' I said as I left for home in a hurry and they both agreed that this would be safer for us all.

As 1943 was coming to an end and the Red Army was pushing the Germans back towards the old Polish–Russian frontier, the Polish Underground became increasingly active, both in the outlying districts and in Warsaw itself. Acts of sabotage became more frequent and German soldiers were being ambushed and killed. The Germans responded with their usual ruthlessness. The SS were stopping and detaining young people in the streets at random and carting them off to the notorious Pawiak prison to be kept as hostages. Each time a German was killed, 50 prisoners would be brought out and shot in public. The streets of the city became places of mass executions. Countless red posters announced the gruesome event as soon as it took place. One such mass shooting took place in Aleje Jerozolimskie, only 50 yards from Howil's shop.

With the German appetite for hostages growing insatiable, it was becoming increasingly dangerous to be out in the streets. In addition to random hostage taking, they were rounding up large numbers of people to be sent to Germany for slave labour. Nobody could be sure that they or their wife or husband, son or daughter, would get back home from work. Only employees of German firms had a reasonable chance of being spared. As for myself, this was one more danger I had to contend with.

One of my many jobs at Holka's was compilation of statistical returns on materials my firm received, processed and supplied. Since I spoke fluent German and, as some queries could be best resolved by personal contact, Mr Holka left to me the task of handing in the reports to the *Wirtschaftsamt* (the Supply Department), located in the centre of Warsaw in an imposing public building, formerly a Polish ministry. I first had to get an entry pass from the guardroom at street level. My destination was a suite of offices off a long corridor on the first floor, where I would meet the official to whom my reports were addressed.

He must have taken a liking to me, as he always greeted me warmly, and frequently discussed with me subjects that had nothing to do with his official duties. He was appalled by the atrocities committed by his compatriots and seemed almost apologetic for the way they treated the civilian population. He once pointed to me the photograph of his wife and children in a silver frame standing in the corner of his massive desk. They looked a happy, carefree family, playing in what must have been their garden. He was clearly missing them. On one of my visits I plucked up courage.

'Every time I come here,' I said, 'I take a gamble. You must not be surprised if one of these days I don't turn up when you expect me, being otherwise engaged in a Gestapo cellar, awaiting deportation to Germany or execution in one of the Warsaw streets.'

He understood my concern. 'Is there anything I can do to help?' he inquired.

'Well, yes. I believe that if I get an official letter from your department, confirming how important my work is for the German war effort and how hard it would be to replace me, I would be in much less danger.'

I spoke these words with my tongue in my cheek, but he immediately agreed. He called his secretary from the adjoining office and dictated a short letter. When she brought it back, he signed it and stamped it with the official seal, the black German eagle with the swastika under it. Another stroke of luck!

When I got back to Młocińska Street, I proudly showed the document to Mr Holka. He looked at it in complete disbelief.

'You have not forged it, you rascal, have you?' he asked, smiling.

'Of course not.'

'So perhaps you could get similar certificates for my sons, Janusz and Jerzy?' I wondered whether he was joking, but all the same I promised to do my best. The next day I presented my boss with the two certificates. It was quite an irony, probably not lost on him, that here was a Jew obtaining from a high-ranking German official documents for two 'Aryans', which one day might quite literally save their lives. Janusz and Jerzy were delighted and they could not thank me enough.

We often talked about current affairs in the office. One day in June 1944, the subject of armed resistance came up. *Pan Inżynier* was asking how well we, the young men listening to him, were prepared to fight when the time came – which might be very soon. I mentioned my two years' training with school cadets, which included the standard army drill, parades, endurance tests, night-long marches in full gear, handling and maintenance of weapons, target shooting, digging foxholes and trenches, map reading and night orientation in difficult terrain, including forests. Twice a year when we were there we went to an army camp on manoeuvres. He sounded interested and kept asking me further questions. Eventually, when we found ourselves on our own, he turned to me:

'Would you be prepared to join the Resistance?'

'I would like nothing better than to have a chance to fight, to pay back the Germans for all their bestial behaviour,' I replied. 'I'd do anything to join a fighting unit.'

'I can tell you now that I am in command of a cavalry battalion in the *Stronnictwo Narodowe* (the National Party's Underground movement). We are part of the *Armia Krajowa*, the Underground Home Army, directed by the Polish Government in Exile, in London. I could enlist you in my battalion as a cadet officer. There is no doubt that our armed struggle is imminent and we have to be ready. Every able-bodied Pole ought to be with us. You are welcome to be one of us and I shall keep you posted as to our meetings and training sessions. There are hard times ahead of us.'

The Polish Underground movement was composed of several groups, each affiliated to a different political party. The *Stronnictwo Narodowe*, as far as I knew, was on the right of the political spectrum and as a Jew I would perhaps have personally chosen another grouping. But here was the opportunity I was waiting for and I was not going to miss it.

The next day, our *Pan Inżynier* brought a blank stamped form. 'We mustn't know each other's names so we use pseudonyms,' he said. 'What should we call you? What about Hetmański? How does it sound to you?'

'It's fine with me,' I replied. He signed the certificate of my rank and handed it to me. 'If you are ever about to fall into German hands, destroy it!'

Now I had two certificates – one from the German occupier and one from the Polish Resistance. It was important to keep them in separate pockets of my jacket. In an emergency I would have to respond instantly, without confusing my pockets. I'd have to show the right certificate and destroy the other. What a ridiculous situation!

I broke the news of my joining the Resistance movement to both my parents, the only two people I could share my secret with, expecting them to be delighted with my resolve to fight for freedom and pay back the barbarians for their evil deeds. But I was disappointed. Both Father and Mother greeted the news as a disaster. In vain I tried to convince them that I was doing my duty and that it was not fair to expect other people to sacrifice their lives for our sake if we were not prepared to sacrifice ours. After what the Germans did to our people, should I not take up arms against them? They did not see it this way. 'How could you do it?' they pleaded. 'Your chances of staying alive are less than slim as things are. And now, of your own free will, you have shortened the odds even further.'

We kept on arguing every time we met, but my parents were wasting their words and their time. And so was I.

In the summer of 1944 my landlady decided to sell her flat and move to the country. Prospective buyers started coming to view it. One Sunday in late July I happened to be in the bathroom which adjoined the sitting room, when bits of the conversation between my landlady and her visitors reached my ears. At first I did not take much notice, it all sounded like the usual descriptions of the property, when suddenly the words 'him' and 'he' alerted me. I moved closer to the door and listened. What I heard alarmed me greatly. Was my landlady being stupid, irresponsible or malicious? Although no name was mentioned, she was clearly talking about me. I heard a detailed account of our conversation following the false alarm raised by the caretaker, when the Germans were supposed to make a door-to-door search for Jews hiding in the area. 'He looked frightened, and the questions he kept asking me were really telling,' she was saying. After a further short exchange (which included the amount of rent she was getting for the room) she went on: 'I got even more suspicious when he talked about his family. I clearly remember that one day he told me he had only a brother, but a few weeks later he said he had only a sister. I have never seen him go to church and nobody ever visits him. He never gets any mail and he stays at home over Christmas. It does worry me. But of course, you can easily get another lodger.'

I had no idea who the visitors were, but I became quite anxious. Even if they had no intention of doing me harm, the story could get around and end in tragedy for me. Maybe it was going round already. Rather than wait for any consequences, I resolved to move out as soon as possible. At the back of my mind was the fate that befell Wanda's unfortunate lodger. There was no point waiting for it. But the events of the next few days solved my dilemma.

9

POLISH RISING IN WARSAW

By the summer of 1944 it was obvious that on the Eastern front the Germans were being beaten and were in retreat. In Warsaw, the occupying authorities issued an appeal to all Poles between the ages of 16 and 60 to report for work, digging trenches around the city, but the appeal was virtually ignored. Instead of the expected 500,000 'volunteers' only a few elderly people and invalids presented themselves at the designated places. And yet nobody was punished! One could feel a general excitement building up in the streets of the capital.

It was evident to anyone following the news that unease and fear were building up amongst the members of the Resistance movement. The AK, short for *Armia Krajowa* (the Underground Home Army), represented the political centre ground and was working closely with the right-wing *Stronnictwo Narodowe*. The Soviets refused to have anything to do with either of them, having decided to impose their own communist regime as soon as they set foot on Polish land in pursuit of the retreating German forces. They recruited Polish communists into AL (*Armia Ludowa* – the People's Army), fighting alongside the Russian forces, and once they occupied the ancient town of Lublin, 100 miles south-east of Warsaw, they made it the seat of their own puppet Polish government. News reaching us on the grapevine and reported in the clandestine press indicated that whenever the AK, or West-oriented Underground forces came out of hiding to reveal themselves to the incoming Russian troops, they were treated as enemies and promptly arrested. It was becoming clear that what the Soviets wanted was a communist Poland ruled by the old Bolshevik guard, trained and controlled from Moscow.

With the advance of the Red Army deeper into Polish territories, the local leadership of the AK, which included the Warsaw-based delegate of the Polish Government in Exile in London, were urgently pressing their London masters to allow them to start an armed uprising against the Germans. They intended to put in place an administration friendly to the West, which, they hoped, the Russians would not challenge for fear of alienating their Western allies. The decision to start the uprising was taken in Warsaw, apparently without any clear instruction from London. (Some sources contest this.)

On Tuesday afternoon, 1 August 1944, I was allowed to leave work early, so that I could visit Father, whom I had not seen for more than a fortnight. As we sat at the table with his flatmates, waiting for Marysia to serve tea, I was struck by the pallor of their faces. They were obviously starved of sunlight. They had not been outdoors for 18 months!

'What's going on in the world outside?' asked Father. 'We often hear artillery fire, and at nights rockets light up the sky. From the Russian aircraft, I guess.'

'The Germans are in deep trouble,' I tried to describe the situation. 'I see dozens of lorries passing by. They are packed with exhausted and dishevelled soldiers. They must be running away from the Russian front.'

Sam, who always claimed to be best informed, chipped in, a solemn look on his face. 'I spoke to Leon last night. He came in a little tipsy and was giving Marysia a hard time. Still, I got out of him the latest news. Yesterday, he happened to walk past the main railway station. It was packed with German civilians. Entire families. They looked as if they were in a great hurry. They are running back home with all their belongings. Leon reckons that the Russian army is no more than eight miles away.'

Mr Tylbor, the eternal pessimist, looked more miserable than usual; he had some doubts. 'You cannot believe all Leon says, especially when he is tight.'

'So,' said Eliasz, looking pensive, 'we are going to be freed from the Germans, only to be enslaved by the Russians. Not a pleasant thought!' He had lost a lot of weight and his precariously balanced pince-nez looked as if it was about to part company with his nose.

'Yes,' I agreed, 'it's a bit of a dilemma. I'd hate the thought of having to live under the Bolsheviks.'

It was a beautiful summer afternoon and the windows were wide open; Father could never have enough of his *frische Luft*. Suddenly, a few moments after the clock struck five, sounds of gunfire broke the silence. This, of course, was not unusual in Warsaw. But this time the shooting did not stop, in fact its intensity rapidly increased. We looked at one another with disbelief. Was this what we had been waiting for all these years?

I looked out of the window. Several young men with red-and-white armbands on their sleeves were running along the street, automatic guns at the ready. They wore civilian jackets girded with belts and one or two had German helmets on their heads. On the opposite side of the street a German soldier covered in blood was lying on the ground. The men with the armbands were running in the direction of an even more intensive fusillade. The severity of gunfire was increasing from one minute to the next, at times becoming almost continuous.

'At last! We are free! We are free!' I could not keep my voice down.

We all laughed, fell into each other's arms, embracing all in turn. But I was in a hurry to leave. 'The time has come!' I shouted again. 'At long last! Now we shall pay them back for all they've done! And with interest!' I couldn't restrain myself even if I wanted to. 'Good luck to all, but my place is with the AK, with the insurgents!'

I came up to Father to say goodbye. All vestiges of laughter had left his face. He looked frightened, heartbroken. 'Don't leave me now, wait a bit to see what happens. Don't risk your life now, I beg you.'

I was not listening. I kissed him and after a quick goodbye to all the others, I ran out into the streets. There were more bodies lying on the pavements in pools of blood and their strange sweet smell with a strong admixture of gunpowder assailed my nostrils. I approached one of the men with an armband.

'I am a member of the *Stronnictwo Narodowe*,' I said, showing him my certificate. 'Where do I go? We've had no orders. Or have I missed them?' He gave me an address only a couple of blocks away.

The streets were almost deserted, except for a few frightened civilians, running, hugging the walls, their figures bent in protective postures. The wide open windows on both sides of the streets were full of people leaning out, laughing and shouting, as if about to watch a carnival. Many were waving homemade red-and-white Polish national flags.

I ran to the address. It was a big garage with a vast open forecourt. Large numbers of men and women, most of them young and all wearing the red-and-white armbands, were incessantly coming and going through wide open gates. Women seemed to be just as keen as men to sacrifice their lives. What greeted me was the loud hum of voices, people talking all at once. I saw a large pile of weapons of every sort, origin and age, and next to it heaps of ammunition, helmets and armbands. In another corner a tall, well-built man in his early 40s was sitting at a table surrounded by others, all engaged in animated conversation. Judging by the sound of his voice and his demeanour, he was the man in charge. I approached the table and showed him the certificate of my rank. He directed me to a youth standing next to the pile of weapons. The young man handed me a German helmet, an armband and a *Papasha* (a Russian automatic gun) in quite a good condition, as well as a few rounds of ammunition. I was lucky indeed! There was a dire shortage of weapons and ammunition and many volunteers would not be able to go into action for the lack of them. But I didn't have much time for reflection, as almost immediately another man came up to me, introduced himself as a lieutenant and as my commanding officer. As more and more volunteers arrived, he led me to a small group of men, with guns of various types and some just with pistols. 'This is Hetmański, your squad commander,' he introduced me briefly. Next he led us a short distance to a ground-floor flat at the corner of Żelazna and Grzybowska streets. This was going to be our base. We had hardly had time to make ourselves at home there when we were ordered to move further along Żelazna to a derelict area of badly mauled buildings, not far from the corner of Krochmalna Street. Our new position adjoined the ruins of the former ghetto. The lieutenant gave me our orders, whispered the password into my ear and disappeared. Our job was to hold the position for several hours, until relieved, and I deployed my men accordingly. If need be, I could call for reinforcements. I understood that we were now under the overall command of Captain Lech Żelazny.

First, my men and I exchanged our pseudonyms and I let them know the password. They were all about my age, full of enthusiasm, itching to fight. Then I reconnoitred the area. The entire landscape was eerie: rooms with parts of their walls missing, the standing bits still covered with patterned wallpaper; staircases that led nowhere; grotesquely twisted iron railings; balconies about to crumble; partly collapsed floors and ceilings defying the laws of gravity. I had to choose outposts for my men, which would provide a good view of all approaches to our position and yet offer reasonable protection from direct fire, stray bullets and falling masonry. Our orders were simple: any intruder was to be challenged and, if failing to stop and produce the right password, shot without any further questions. On spotting an enemy advance in force a general alarm was to be raised. I spent the next few hours walking between the individual posts and making sure that nobody was dozing off. One or two were. Exhausted with the excitement of the day and the long hours on duty, by the time the relief came late at night I too was ready to fall asleep anywhere, but back at our base in Żelazna Street a treat awaited us first: a hot meal prepared by our female volunteers.

Our own news-sheet, *Biuletyn Informacyjny* (Information Bulletin), was distributed the following day. Under the headline THE COMMANDER CHIEF OF THE HOME ARMY ISSUES BATTLE ORDERS AGAINST THE ENEMY I read: '. . . Detachments of our army are fighting the German invader in all areas of the region. I am asking the civilian population to remain calm, while giving all possible help to our fighters . . . Having overcome the enemy's resistance, we now control most of the capital . . .'

Since we were now able freely to listen to local and to worldwide news, we were overjoyed to hear that in the first three days of the Rising the Germans, taken completely by surprise, had lost many soldiers – killed, wounded and taken prisoner – and that many of their tanks had been damaged or destroyed.

Civilians were also keen to do their bit: men, women and children could be seen everywhere carting all kinds of objects and piling them high on the barricades which were, in the old tradition, being erected across the streets under our control. Soon the Germans were to start using a weapon against us: remote-controlled mines on wheels that looked like small tanks, which, propelled towards our barricades or fortified buildings, had a devastating effect. We responded with a new invention, namely heaps of pavement slabs, which when placed in front of the barricades afforded reasonable protection. As these monstrous enemy devices were called Goliaths, we christened our defensive heaps of pavement slabs *Dawidki*, or 'little Davids'.

On Friday, 4 August the Germans resumed their initiative, starting in Wola, a western district of Warsaw, and deploying newly arrived reinforcements. The SS regiments, supported by artillery, heavy machine-guns, tanks and dive-bombers, started their advance in the eastern direction, butchering the civilian population on their way and systematically burning recaptured streets house by house. Later that evening the Germans occupied St Lazarus Hospital in Leszno and killed some 1,000 people – patients as well as staff. In Wola alone they murdered 20,000 civilian inhabitants. The hospitals that were still in our hands were rapidly filling with casualties, combatants and civilians alike.

Right from the beginning of the Rising the Polish Command were pleading with our government in London for arms and ammunition to be parachuted to designated areas. Winston Churchill approached Stalin with the hope that the Russians would come to the aid of Warsaw's insurgents. After all, these supposed allies were only a few miles away, on the other side of the River Vistula. But Stalin's reply was far from encouraging. In his opinion Churchill was misinformed: the Polish Government in Exile in London had exaggerated the successes of the insurgents. He reckoned that only a few detachments had risen against the Germans, these were now fighting in several streets in Warsaw, and had no chance whatsoever of succeeding without military hardware against the four German armoured divisions. Thus the Red Army remained inactive, its political masters welcoming the destruction of potential Polish leaders. What little help we had came from the West; one night several British Halifax bombers dropped the much-needed arms in the grounds of the two cemeteries close to Młynarska Street.

On 6 August German tanks, advancing from the direction of Wola, passed north of my outpost along Ogrodowa and Chłodna streets, crossed Żelazna Street and pushed their way beyond Plac Mirowski to Plac Żelaznej Bramy, cutting us off from the ruins of the ghetto in the north and from *Stare Miasto* (the Old City) in the north-east. Our position was now part of *Śródmieście* (the City Centre), and our only communication with *Stare Miasto* was through the sewers. The Germans did not attack our barricade across Krochmalna Street, a few hundred yards from my outpost; instead they focussed on the re-occupation and destruction of *Stare Miasto*, *Żoliborz* and *Powiśle*, areas adjoining the River Vistula and thus potential bridgeheads for Soviet troops, should they decide to cross it.

In the meantime the surviving inhabitants of Wola were trying to escape. At first, singly or in small groups; and then the main body of refugees streamed towards our positions: people in torn clothes, their blackened faces distorted with fear, their belongings wrapped in blankets and sheets on their backs, babies in their arms. Our advanced posts were trying to keep them from moving towards Plac Żelaznej Bramy, straight into the murderous gunfire coming from the German stronghold. Many tried to find accommodation close to our headquarters in Grzybowska Street, but this was not an easy proposition. Several thousand refugees who had arrived earlier had already joined the permanent inhabitants of the area. As a result the cellars, where they were all seeking shelter from the bombardment, were greatly overcrowded, the newcomers trying to squeeze in anywhere with whatever possessions they had managed to save.

During the nights of 9 and 10 August several British warplanes successfully parachuted more substantial supplies over the suburb of Mokotów and over the southern part of the city centre. But the British broadcast of 10 August, warning the Germans that their crimes against the population of Warsaw and its captured fighters would be severely punished, was of little consolation to us. If it was meant as a deterrent, it failed utterly.

Many of the enemy attacks started off with an artillery bombardment from the *Fat Berta*, a giant cannon mounted on an armoured train. Its one-metre long projectiles would blow up and rip apart even the strongest reinforced concrete construction. This heavy artillery preparation would be followed by mortar fire, by deployment of grenade throwers and tank guns, preceding infantry attacks. Our soldiers fought back by letting the tanks come close to the barricades and then trying to destroy them with our few precious PIATs (the hand-held anti-tank weapons) from the parachute drops or, much more often, with Molotov cocktails – bottles filled with petrol. The PIATs were very effective and our radio station kept pleading for more of them, but in the meantime, the German tanks, the powerful Tigers, were pulverising our barricades and makeshift defences, thus opening the way for the enemy infantry. Every night, when not asleep, I kept turning my eyes towards the sky, hoping to see friendly shapes bringing precious supplies, but the sky remained dark and empty, until at last, on the night of 12 August, I woke up to streaks of luminous tracer shells criss-crossing the sky, which was reverberating with incessant anti-aircraft fire. I became very concerned for the safety of the friendly crews up there, who were risking their lives for us and who were now the targets. Unfortunately several Allied aircraft were hit and destroyed.

The next day sounds of a battle moved close to our outpost. Loud explosions followed one another in quick succession, but luckily the attacking German police forces were thrown back and did not reach our position.

In the following days we remained under constant fire. Off duty we sought shelter in the cellars of our headquarters building, in full knowledge that it would offer little protection in the event of a direct hit. German bombers hardly ever left us in peace, and it seemed safer to hide in the basement of an already partly destroyed house than to be buried by the weight of a whole collapsing building. As we had no defence against the bombers, the sky naturally belonged to the enemy, who would systematically and with impunity destroy one block after another, inflicting countless casualties amongst civilians and soldiers alike. One night I was woken up by six successive grating sounds. It was the new German weapon: a multiple mortar employed at short range, spitting out incendiary or highly explosive material from its six linked barrels. The sinister noise was like a mixture of a giant rusty clock being wound up, a heavy cupboard being dragged along a wooden floor, and a cow mournfully mooing. It would last a minute or so, just long enough to fill one with terror in anticipation of what was to follow. Then there was a long ominous silence, yet it was not long enough to for one to try and seek shelter. A deafening explosion followed, accompanied by the crash of a building collapsing like a pack of cards. One's relief at having survived was short-lived. Five more such explosions would succeed at half-minute intervals, each one coming closer. It was purely a question of chance whether you were hit by one, or whether you survived to hear the next one. This dreadful weapon, deployed regularly, both day and night, was killing, burning or burying its victims alive, and tearing our nerves to shreds. A contemporary writer, Zygmunt Zaremba,[1] described it as an antediluvian beast coming out of its lair to feed, and announcing to all and sundry in the primeval wilderness its thirst for fresh blood and its hunger for flesh. All animals, on hearing the sound, would flee in desperate panic. We humans, who survived such a salvo, were left rather ashamed at the relief that the beast had found its victim elsewhere.

Food was becoming scarce. I could divide the weeks of the Rising into time spans bearing the names of what we, the privileged soldiers, ate. The beef period came first, followed by the horsemeat one, then the dog period, the cat period – and finally the starvation period. Horsemeat had a taste similar to beef, while dogs and cats reminded one vaguely of poultry. One day, on patrolling derelict buildings, I was fortunate to discover in one of the cellars a deserted storeroom with barrels of halvah powder and bags full of sugar. By mixing the two together we made a proper halvah, a welcome supplement to our meagre diet to begin with, and our only sustenance at the end.

I spent most of my time patrolling our little patch. While in many other parts of Warsaw fierce battles were raging – whole districts fell to the enemy, were regained, fell again, and each street fought for bravely against an overwhelming force – our area saw little direct action. Ours was a war of attrition; we were under incessant aerial and mortar bombardment, we suffered daily losses without being able to inflict any on the enemy; at the same time we had to be in

---

[1] Zaremba, an active participant in the fighting and author of *Wojna i Konspiracja* (*War and the Underground Movement*), London 1957

constant readiness for an enemy assault, and the resulting tension kept us on the edge of exhaustion.

One day, while on patrol with Władzio, my second in command, walking close behind me, I heard a loud explosion and felt a sharp pain. When I opened my eyes I was lying on the ground in a pool of blood and so was Władzio. Soon, some people lifted us up and carried us to a nearby apartment. After that I must have fainted. On regaining consciousness, I found myself lying on a table and someone with what looked like pincers was pulling out bits of steel from my legs and hands. I remained conscious but the pain was not unbearable. I was told that we had both been injured by a hand grenade accidentally dropped by Władzio. Most of the shrapnel failed to penetrate deeply into the tissues, though some stayed in my fingers for many years. I was fortunate: Władzio had his foot torn off. Within a few days I was able to walk and went back to my men and our patrol duty. However, I could use only one arm, as the other was in a sling and remained so for a number of weeks.

Roosevelt and Churchill appealed repeatedly to Stalin in vain to supply the Warsaw insurgents with weapons or at least to allow Western relief planes to land and refuel on the other side of the Vistula, which would save them having to fly non-stop all the way back to their Italian bases, which greatly reduced their payload and increased casualties. Stalin was unmoved. The situation in *Stare Miasto* was now desperate. Soldiers were exhausted and supplies of ammunition were coming to an end. Our partisans normally operating in the nearby Kampinos forest had tried to break through the German lines to join the Warsaw insurgents, but this relief attempt was foiled, and the whole of the capital was under constant air bombardment and mortar fire. In the days that followed, the German efforts were concentrated on capturing *Stare Miasto*.

On 18 August the Germans called for our surrender and offered to treat us as prisoners of war. However, nobody believed their promises; hadn't they been murdering the wounded in hospitals, shooting all the captured insurgents, as well as thousands of civilians who had not even taken part in the hostilities? Furthermore, like everybody else, our leadership still believed that the Soviets were bound to launch a new offensive any day now. And thus the struggle went on.

Later that night a few Allied planes managed to parachute supplies south of *Śródmieście*, the city centre, but some fell in no-man's land, resulting in heavy fighting between the two sides, each striving to reach them first. My unit was taking the brunt of German air raids in the Krochmalna and Żelazna streets area, close to our headquarters, leaving many killed and wounded.

On 24 August the news reached us that the Allies had liberated Paris. The Germans were clearly in trouble on the Western, as well as the Eastern, front. How much longer could they withstand the assault on both?

On 30 August I heard on the radio the encouraging news that the British and US Governments had at last recognised the Warsaw fighters as combatants, thus giving us the protection of the Geneva Convention. They also warned the enemy that they would be held responsible for violating the internationally accepted rights of combatants. But would the Germans abide by the rules? So far they had shown a monumental contempt for them. So I had my doubts.

In the last days of August the bulk of the German forces were deployed on the liquidation of the remaining resistance in *Stare Miasto*, leaving us in *Śródmieście* in relative peace. That is if one ignored the bombardment. Apart from the raining bombs, our day-to-day life went on almost normally.

In another notable broadcast from London on 1 September, Mikołajczyk, the Polish Prime Minister, declared that it was primarily his decision to start the fighting in Warsaw in the name of freedom and independence. Addressing us directly he said: 'You did not get the help that you were expecting and to which you were entitled. Fate did not allow us to bring that help to you.' He pleaded with Churchill, Roosevelt and Stalin: 'Warsaw is waiting. The Polish nation is waiting. World opinion is waiting. Do all you can to bring aid and liberation to the population as soon as possible!'

On 2 September the remaining units were evacuated from *Stare Miasto*. Over 5,000 men and women managed to escape through the city sewers, but over 7,000 who were wounded and unable to make the journey had to be left behind. Some 35,000 people altogether fell into German hands. Robberies and rapes were commonplace. Many of the wounded were burnt alive; many men were stood against a wall and gunned down. Having murdered the old, the sick and those unable to make the journey, the Germans, as we found out later, evacuated the survivors to the Pruszków transit camp and they were sent to the Mauthausen and Sachsenhausen–Oranienburg concentration camps. According to a radio broadcast, the German correspondent of the *Deutsches Nachrichtenbüro* (German Press Agency) wrote: 'No town witnessed such hell. Our planes bombarded the northern parts of the city, our mortars brought destruction, our Goliaths destroyed the barricades, heavy artillery pounded the streets, creating hell that no other city had ever known.'

I came across a leaflet. It read: 'Today tens of thousands of our neighbours, our brothers, lost their homes. Fate decreed that they were the victims. The bomb could have struck us, but it struck next door instead. Our possessions were saved, but theirs went up in flames. Over the debris of crumbling masonry and broken glass, along streets divided by barricades, proceed the convoys of refugees. It is the duty of every Pole to help the homeless now, immediately, today. There should be no undamaged dwelling without accommodation for the homeless. What we have we must share with them, happy that we can do it today. It is not a favour, it is our duty. All that remains of their possessions is the bundle on their back. They don't know what to feed their children with, where to spend the night. They ought not despair. They are amongst their own. Their misery is our misery.'

During one of the air raids I was standing in our cellar next to a group of people. One of the men addressed me: 'We feel very strongly that civilians were abandoned and betrayed after the evacuation of *Stare Miasto*. Will the same happen to us?' I did not have enough conviction to reassure him. I kept hearing how despondent people there felt when they realised that the recent rumours of approaching Russian help were proving unfounded and they could see no end to their misery.

On 6 September Powiśle, a suburb on the left bank of the River Vistula, fell to the Germans. Two days later thousands of German leaflets were distributed among the inhabitants encouraging them to leave the city. Many obeyed and took the routes specified by the Germans. I don't know what their fate was.

From about the middle of September glimmers of hope were rekindled. The Germans appeared less active, having to divert more of their resources towards defence against Russian air attacks. News reached us that at long last Russian troops had entered Praga, the Warsaw suburb on the eastern side of the Vistula, and that the Germans were destroying the two bridges over the river; sounds of powerful explosions were reaching us from that direction. Also, some German units were moving back from the river along Chłodna Street towards Wola. In the bright daylight of 13 September, several Russian aeroplanes appeared overhead and dropped leaflets promising supplies of arms, ammunition and food. Indeed, late that night, low-flying Russian aircraft dropped some ammunition and arms into Żolibórz and *Śródmieście*. Unfortunately their primitive economy did not stretch to parachute drops; the sacks and crates with food and other supplies, simply jettisoned from aircraft, arrived on the ground badly damaged.

The Soviet aeroplanes returned the next night. But this time, as the planes roared overhead, bright streaks of German spotlights lit up the sky, giving us a grandstand view of the spectacular contest between clusters of luminous missiles rising from the ground and the bombs hurled towards them from the Russian aircraft. After a break of roughly two hours the planes came back, but this time there were no projectiles streaking the sky, nor was there any artillery fire to greet them. Taking great risks, the planes were coming lower and lower down, strangely not meeting any response from the ground. More sacks kept coming down and many of our boys just managed to avoid being hit by tins of food.

Late the following evening the transmission of the Polish Committee of National Liberation, the Russian-inspired Polish puppet administration, came over the air. It was broadcast from Lublin, the Polish town captured by the Russians several weeks earlier, which was the seat of the committee. 'Help is at hand,' the broadcast proclaimed, 'your suffering will end soon. The Germans will pay a heavy price. The Polish Kościuszko Division, fighting alongside the Red Army, has reached Praga. Continue your resistance with all your might.'

The next day squadrons of Russian planes appeared in the sky and

Russian artillery started bombing German targets in the city near Ogród Saski and Okęcie. At night Russian *Kukuruznik* planes dropped arms and food over different parts of the city, meeting only minimal opposition from the German side.

Our joy was short-lived, however. On 15 September the Germans launched a three-pronged attack on the district of Mokotów, surrounding it on all but one side, and the expected arrival of a large number of American planes, who were supposed to be bringing supplies after finally reaching an agreement with the Russians, did not materialise. We heard that 100 Flying Fortresses got as far as Denmark, but then had to turn back because of bad weather over Europe. In another Warsaw suburb, Żolibórz, the hand-to-hand struggle for every house and cellar resulted in enormous losses in dead and wounded and in destroyed buildings and cultural treasures. While our commander-in-chief, General Bór Komorowski described the situation in Żoliborz as critical, the remaining insurgents had to be evacuated via the sewers to *Śródmieście*.

Both the areas where Father and Mother lived in the centre of the city were now in German hands and it was impossible to get anywhere near them. I came across a man who had been stationed near Sienna Street when it had come under German bombardment. He told me that the wounded from nearby houses were taken to a hospital in Złota Street, the other side of Marszałkowska Street.

When our sector was reasonably quiet I asked for time off to look for Father in the hospital. And so, with one arm still in a sling and a large loaf of bread (a great luxury in those days) under the other, I started on an arduous journey. The streets were under constant gunfire and had become a no-go area. Pedestrians were restricted to cellars of adjoining houses, which had been linked by holes hacked in the walls between them. Most of these cellars had low ceilings and one had to keep one's head down and, at times, proceed in a crouching position. And they were crowded beyond description. In addition to people who had made them their permanent homes while battles were raging at street level, they provided shelter for the sick and wounded who lay on the floors awaiting medical attention. The flickering flames of candles and paraffin lamps contributed to the eerie atmosphere created by the pervading smell of dampness of these long-neglected cellars, and the ghost-like silhouettes and shadows of the aimlessly-moving temporary inhabitants, the walking wounded and an occasional unit of soldiers in transit to new positions. A multitude of people lived here, ate here and slept here for days and weeks on end.

At the end of each block I had to emerge into the open, at times in plain view of German tanks and, bent in half, run across the road making the best use of the flimsy protection offered by the low barricades built for the purpose. What in normal times would have been a 30-minute walk along pleasant streets, had become a perilous and strenuous endeavour taking several hours.

The greatest hazard was crossing Marszałkowska Street, the capital's main thoroughfare. It was some 100 feet wide and the intensive German fire was repeatedly wrecking the two barricades erected across it. Constructed of paving stones, rubble, tram carriages, furniture, anything that was at hand, the barricades were not strong enough to withstand the unceasing cannonade. As I came out of the basement I took a deep breath and, jack-knifed as low as I could, dashed across. A few minutes later I stood at the hospital reception desk, anxiously asking for Jan Malinowski, Father's assumed name. The receptionist seemed to take ages going through the register, while I was losing patience. At last she found the right entry.

But was it Father or some other Jan Malinowski? After all, this was a common enough name and surname. Climbing the wide staircase on the way to the ward I tried to rein in my expectations. If it was Father, how bad would his wounds be? Inside a vast ward, with little space between the closely packed beds, a nurse led me to one of them and I sighed with relief when I recognised Father. This was indeed *my* Jan Malinowski, the man I feared I might never see again. He looked pale and gaunt. His head was heavily bandaged. He was clearly taken aback by my sudden appearance. His lips trembled and I could see him holding back tears. I tried hard to hold back mine.

I kissed him.

'How did you get here?' I asked.

'Our house was hit by a bomb,' he answered. 'I lost consciousness and when I regained it I was here, lying in the hospital bed. I don't know what happened to all the other people there. None are in here.' He looked at me as if not quite sure whether he was dreaming or not.

'Do you know what happened to Mother?' He was most anxious.

'No.' I could offer no consolation. The area around Plac Narutowicza, where Mother and Hela lived, had remained in German hands throughout the Rising and since its outbreak neither of us had seen them or heard about them. My knowledge of the barbaric treatment meted out by the Germans to the civilian population filled me with foreboding, but I didn't mention it to Father.

'Are you in pain?' I asked.

'It's OK now. They might be able to remove the bandage soon.'

With a semi-theatrical gesture I put the loaf of bread on the bed in front of Father and his eyes lit up. 'I haven't seen a piece of bread since I got here. I am hungry all the time, we get very little food. I don't know how to thank you.' He looked at my helmet and Luger, the recently acquired side arm of choice for the German infantry, hanging from my belt.

'Did you risk your life to get here?'

'It wasn't that bad. Don't worry. Whatever is meant to happen will happen.'

It was hard to tear myself away. When he saw that I was about to leave, I could see a worried, anxious look clouding the unbandaged part of his face, and he could hardly control the tears gathering in his eyes.

And when finally time came to say goodbye, neither of us knew that it was to be our last parting, and that we would never see each other again.

On 17 September the London *Daily Telegraph* published a report from Warsaw: 'The fighters have to count every bullet, they don't have enough to eat, they are totally exhausted, they remain at their posts for days on end. The civilian population suffers while not taking part in any armed action. The hope is that Soviet troops will liberate the city . . . '

On 18 September something extraordinary happened: a large American air flotilla, the first we had seen since the fighting started, appeared overhead. The Flying Fortresses, over 100 planes, were flying at a very high altitude and were thus out of reach of the intensive anti-aircraft fire. The countless specks which appeared behind them turned out to be parachutes. Ignoring the danger, people were coming out of the cellars and climbing the heaps of rubble to get a better view of the spectacle in the sky. Their faces beaming with hope and joy, they were embracing one another and crying with relief. As the multicoloured parachutes came closer, somebody shouted: 'Our commandos are landing!' – but unfortunately he was wrong, they were supplies. Having dropped their cargo, the planes landed on the other side of the River Vistula, on Soviet-controlled territory. Since by now only a small part of the city remained under our control, of the 80 tons of supplies dropped from such a great height, three quarters fell into German hands. Had the help come a few weeks earlier, the outcome of the Rising might have been very different. Now it was too late.

Our daily paper, *Kurier Warszawy*, wrote: 'Stalin had planned the total destruction of Warsaw a long time ago. A vibrant city with a long democratic tradition would have been a source of constant irritation in his vast totalitarian empire. Only when he saw Warsaw almost razed to the ground, did Stalin decided to throw a few sackfuls of food to the dying few, an empty gesture designed to deceive world opinion.'

The last point of resistance to fall to the Germans was the district of Czerniaków, on the bank of the river. There, the Germans murdered some 200 wounded, and captured the remaining fighters. All over the capital they were murdering our soldiers as they were emerging from the sewers. On 26 September Winston Churchill paid homage to the 'heroism and endurance of the Polish Home Army and of the population of Warsaw, which after five years of oppression embarked on fighting that went on for nearly two months and contributed to the eventual expulsion of Germans from Poland's capital'.

By now we were aware of the critical situation. There was little ammunition left and there were no facilities for taking care of the increasing number of wounded, as the supplies of bandages and anaesthetics had run out. The lack of food was catastrophic. An increasing number of people were starving to death. Also with autumn round the corner, the lack of warm clothing combined with the greatly reduced disease resistance of the starved and exhausted people, there was a high risk of an epidemic, especially of the dreaded influenza, which in the post-First World War pandemic killed many thousands in Poland alone.

The *Biuletyn Informacyjny* of 1 October carried the following announcement:

'In view of the tactical situation, of the dwindling supplies of food and the lack of sanitation, and in order to reduce the civilian losses, the Polish authorities have accepted the German offer to evacuate the civilian population. It is to take place on Sunday and Monday, 1 and 2 October, between 5 a.m. and 7 p.m. along the designated routes leading west [one of them being Grzybowska Street]. The ceasefire will apply to both sides. Take with you your personal belongings and food, and be prepared for the difficulties of a long march. Separate instructions will follow concerning the evacuation of the sick and wounded.'

In spite of the unbearable living conditions in the cellars of the few remaining non-demolished houses, it was estimated that at first out of nearly 250,000 remaining inhabitants, only some 8,000 people, mainly women with children, accepted the offer. The rest wanted to continue sharing our common destiny as they had done during our two months of freedom. During the brief ceasefire vast crowds appeared on the streets, enjoying daylight for the first time in weeks. At the end after the rumour that negotiations for a total surrender were taking place gained more ground, the exodus gathered momentum.

In the rays of the late summer sun, like an overflowing river, a mass of people laden with bundles, the young and the old, many carrying children and newborn babies, filled the streets. They moved slowly in deadly silence. The Germans left them alone. There were no robberies or searches.

On the night of 2 October the terms for surrender were finally agreed and signed. All the participants of the Rising would be treated as prisoners of war under the Geneva Convention. The civilian population would be given complete immunity from prosecution and their evacuation would be conducted in a manner that would protect them from unnecessary hardship. The official *communiqué* issued on 3 October confirmed the agreement, but we treated it with total disbelief. Very few trusted the Germans to keep their side of the bargain.

On that day the Polish Council of Ministers in London issued the following statement: 'We have received no effective help. We were treated worse by our own side than were Hitler's allies: Italy, Romania and Finland. The Warsaw Rising collapsed while our own army was helping to liberate France, Belgium and Holland. We shall stop short of pronouncing a verdict on these events. Let God judge the dreadful wrong inflicted on our people and punish the guilty!'

The Rising, which was intended to be over in 48 to 72 hours had lasted 63 days. It had cost several hundred thousand lives. The Germans did not keep their promise of sparing the city. After all the inhabitants left Warsaw, on Hitler's direct orders, the Germans, like the conquerors of old, razed the city to the ground by fire and dynamite. Thus they destroyed most of the nation's historical and cultural heritage and left behind them an emptiness, a desert covered with rubble.

During a short official ceremony on the day before our departure I was promoted to the rank of sergeant.[2] On the morning of 4 October, as we were getting ready to leave, the sky over the ruins was heavy with clouds and there was a slight drizzle. Columns of shattered men, carrying arms and led by their officers, marched in formation from the direction of Plac Grzybowski along Grzybowska Street. Our detachment joined the main body of soldiers as they approached Żelazna Street, close to the barricade, where German soldiers were already waiting for us. Our route ran along streets bordered by heaps of rubble and lined on each side by emaciated, frequently wounded, civilian men and women. Some stood silent, some called out words of affection, of encouragement, others of anger. They had no flowers so some threw us various small objects: spoons, forks, pots, notebooks, pencils, little bundles of precious food.

Did these inhabitants of Warsaw feel that we had inflicted a terrible ordeal on them, that we had brought death or injury to their

[2] In the Polish army cadet officers were given the rank of an NCO until promoted to full officer status.

loved ones, made them abandon their homes and possessions for no good reason, and in the name of some lofty abstract idea? If we were guilty, it was because after five long years of odious, unspeakable tyranny we could endure it no longer. And neither could they. Yet did they feel bitter? A woman near me was making the sign of the cross in the air, her lips murmuring words I could not hear. Was she praying for us, blessing us?

It stopped drizzling. A short distance from the barricade, under the watchful eye of German soldiers, we threw down our arms. And what awaited us next? A concentration camp? As we marched on, escorted by soldiers, we could see the full extent of the damage inflicted on our city. There was hardly a building left standing and even those few that were, were smouldering or burning.

After an arduous march of several hours, we stopped at a place called Ożarów and spent the night on bare wooden boards. The discomfort and the intense cold kept me awake. At midday we were loaded into cattle wagons. Ours was divided into two unequal parts, the larger one reserved for two or three armed guards who enjoyed the luxury of an iron stove, which kept them warm at night. They made us remove our boots and deposit them in their part of the wagon. By the time the loading of people was finished our part was packed so closely that there was hardly any room to turn around. The doors were then locked and we were on our way: destination unknown. Soon our three guards unpacked some food and started tucking into it with great enthusiasm. Starved as I was, I resented the sight and smell of their food. Hours passed. Where are they taking us, we kept on thinking.

A few hours later the train came to a halt at a station. The door opened and a smell of food hit my nostrils. Bean soup? Was it really meant for us? What a relief! It tasted as good as it smelled and did wonders for our mood.

Late that night the train stopped again and was quickly surrounded by armed soldiers. The nameplate on the station read 'Lamsdorf'. We got our footwear back. The doors then opened to the accompaniment of loud screams and we were confronted by a horde of soldiers yelling: '*Raus, raus, verfluchte Banditen!* [Out, out, you damn bandits!]' Not a very hopeful welcome. With much pushing, shoving and an excessively generous use of rifle butts the guards marshalled us into a long column. But the abuse continued even on the move. The few stragglers who failed to keep pace with the rest of the procession were being dealt with very roughly indeed. Is this how the prisoners of war are treated, I wondered, convinced that my worst suspicions were being confirmed. My place was near the end of the column and, depending on what was happening at the unseen front end, I had either to drag my feet at a snail's pace or, roughly prodded by the guards, hurry and run fast to catch up with the body of the column suddenly speeding ahead. Hungry and tired, uncertain of what was still to come, we were getting increasingly dispirited and despondent.

Once inside the enclave, with more screaming and shoving, officers and officer cadets were separated from other ranks. I was amongst the former. We were marched to separate huts and assigned a bunk each. The two-level bunks were arranged in long rows and packed so closely together that access was difficult and, unless you were lucky enough to get either the first or the last bunk of the row, you had to climb in from the narrow front end. A long table with benches to match stood in the centre of the hut and, after depositing our belongings, at long last we were treated to barrels of potatoes and cauldrons of clear turnip soup. At this stage anything was welcome.

With the worst pangs of hunger gone, people started exploring the camp. Our first discovery was that our neighbours in the adjoining compound across the barbed-wire fence were Yugoslav army officers. Imprisoned since 1940, they were pleased to see some new faces and at last get some news from the outside world. We managed to communicate in a way – they spoke Serbian, we spoke Polish, and we just about understood one another, as the two Slavonic languages had much in common. It was from them that we learned that Lamsdorf was one of the largest prisoner-of-war camps in Germany.

There were roll-calls twice a day, during which we had to stand outside in long rows to be counted by the guards. Should the numbers not tally, due to some mistake – quite a frequent occurrence – we would have to remain standing, whatever the weather, for an hour or even more.

Another ritual we were subjected to on our arrival was the so-called de-lousing in the common shower room. It was, unfortunately, a waste of time, as the straw in our mattresses provided an excellent breeding ground for lice and we soon became adept at the technique of catching and squashing them between two thumbnails.

Once again, the mark of my Jewishness gave me some anxious moments. In the first few days I still worried that somebody might notice it in the shower room and give me away. But nobody bothered. Our guards did not care whether anyone was a Jew, nor did my companions. In captivity, for the first time in five years, I felt safe under the protection of the Geneva Convention. Actually, after a while we sensed that the attitude of our captors was becoming less brutal. However, the two main camp problems, boredom and hunger, were not subject to international conventions and Geneva did not solve them. Unlike the lower ranks, we were never taken out of the camp for compulsory labour, and with nothing to do and nothing to read, the days stretched into one long period of tedium. Our daily food ration consisted of only one fairly thick slice of bread, a small slice of margarine, a portion of turnip soup and one potato. It required some ingenuity to stretch the one slice of bread to serve both as breakfast and supper. Watching some officers dive head down into the empty potato barrels, trying to lick off the leftovers after everyone received their ration, I realised how thin our veneer of civilisation was.

Luckily, soon after our arrival, Red Cross parcels started coming at monthly intervals, one to be shared between two prisoners. A parcel contained a tin each of corned beef, Spam, dried milk, instant coffee and a large packet of cigarettes. If you did not smoke (and I didn't) you were able to barter the cigarettes for more food.

10

MY MOTHER'S STORY

The following account is taken from notes dictated to me by Mother. Her story starts on the day and the hour of my visit to Father in Leon Wołowski's apartment, when I suddenly heard the cannonade outside, the start of the Rising against the Germans.

In the afternoon of 1 August 1944, Hela and I left home to keep our dentist's appointment. Suddenly, while still in the waiting room, we heard gunfire followed by more powerful explosions coming in quick succession. We looked out of the window: people, clearly confused, were running about in all directions.

The surgery door opened and the dentist walked into the waiting room. 'Something is happening out there!' he exclaimed. 'God knows what. You'd better go home.'

We left without delay. We tried to head for home, but heavily armed German soldiers barred our way. Within minutes they rounded up a throng of people and herded us into Plac Narutowicza, where by now the crowd must have numbered thousands. We were surrounded by uniformed armed men: Germans and Ukrainians, constantly shouting and screaming their instructions, roughly pushing stragglers back into the crowd, not sparing their rifle butts. Time dragged on. We were hungry and thirsty; we had not even a drop of water to drink. In the crowd of strangers just in front of us we recognised the Dzieniakowski family[1] – a father, mother and son. Suddenly, before our very eyes, as a German policeman approached them, they seemed to panic, started backing away and then turned around and ran. '*Halt*!' he shouted, but they took no notice. He raised his gun, took aim and fired his automatic gun. They fell, all

[1] See page 95.

three of them, and lay on the ground in a pool of blood.

It was getting later and later. As night came the temperature was dropping quickly. Dressed only in our summer frocks and sandals, we were now feeling cold. One by one we lay down on the grass and tried to doze off, but fear, added to the repeated screams of guards and cries of distress coming from around us, made sleep impossible. Germans were on the prowl, looking for victims, for young girls. Should one catch their eye, they would separate her from her family and make her follow them. Their uniformed Ukrainian auxiliaries were concentrating on robbing people; they seemed to have a particular liking for watches.

In the morning, exhausted after the eventful day and sleepless night, still thirsty, cold, hungry and terrified, we were taken on a long forced march to a railway station and roughly herded into cattle wagons. The train started. At the first stop – I believe it was Pruszków – we noticed several people with Red Cross armbands on the platform. They called for the sick to come out. Hela and myself answered the call and along with others (none of them looking particularly ill) we followed the Red Cross staff, who led us to a hospital building. In the reception office, on an off chance, I inquired whether they had any trace of a Jan Malinowski. To my astonishment they did. He was actually a patient in the hospital; they let me see him and we had a chance to talk. In the bed next to Father's was Mr Landecki, Michał's schoolteacher. Father told me how you went to see him and brought him a loaf of bread after a journey through hell. 'God will help him throughout his life,' he said, 'for what he has done.' When I was about to leave, he said, 'One more thing. Mr Landecki happens to know your pre-war dressmaker, Julia. She apparently lives only a short journey from Warsaw, in Tomaszów Mazowiecki, but he does not know her exact address.' Our conversation was cut short. I had to get back to my ward in another part of the hospital.

In the evening a rumour spread that Germans were about to inspect the hospital, searching for people shamming illness. By then night was coming and we were advised that it would be best for us to leave the hospital in the morning. I managed to say goodbye to Father. I was carrying a few bulbs of garlic with me, so I gave him some to provide at least a small source of vitamins.

There was no point going back to Warsaw. The fighting was

raging there when we last saw it. We stood outside the hospital wondering which way to turn to avoid again falling into German hands. In the distance we saw a forest and in a short while we were amongst the trees, without any idea what direction to follow. You know what Polish forests are like; you can go on for miles without meeting a soul. We went on and on for hours – I cannot tell you whether we were going forwards or round in circles – till a bright light shining through the trees appeared. It was the edge of the woods: all forests must end somewhere. We were tired and sat down, letting our feet drop into the ditch. We had a long rest and then noticed a hamlet in the far distance. We were hungry. 'Let's go there and tell them that we are refugees from Warsaw,' I said to Hela. 'They may give us some bread.' When we got closer we saw a house standing some distance from the hamlet. A farmer and his wife let us in and offered us some slices of bread and water. We just began to relax when I overheard one whisper to the other: 'They must be Jews.' Needless to say, we thanked them profusely and moved on.

We must have walked several more miles along the road until a peasant cart drew up to us.

'Where are you going?' I asked the man.

'To Skierniewice.'

'Would you give us a lift? We are also on our way there. We are refugees from Warsaw.'

He stopped the horse. 'Hop in,' he said.

We did. As he dropped us in the centre of the town, I noticed a small group of people standing there in the street with bundles at their feet. They must have been refugees.

'What are you waiting for?' I asked one of them.

'We are refugees from Warsaw and a passer-by told us to wait here for some form of transport. This is the collection point. Steps are being taken to take care of the refugees. They should be coming soon. You are welcome to join us,' he said sympathetically, looking at the two of us, unmistakably homeless souls.

We joined the group. We didn't have to wait long before a large cart appeared. We got in and stopped at a hamlet called Mikołów. The man in charge of our group found Sołtys, the head of the village. He asked him if he could find us homes. Sołtys had a good idea as to who could afford what and soon distributed us all over a number of households, according to the size of each family and the space available.

Hela and I were placed with a youngish couple who had three children, a nine-year-old boy, a six-year-old girl who was still shitting in her pants, and a new-born baby. The inside of the cottage smelled of dirt and manure; it was just a single room divided by a wardrobe with a missing back panel leading into the 'living and kitchen' areas. The whole family slept in two beds. An old cot standing in the kitchen was used for storing oats for the animals housed in the adjoining barn. They let us sleep in the barn on straw in the loft and within minutes fleas were hopping all over us. There were so many that, in spite of their agility, we could catch them and squash them between our fingers. In no time our arms and legs were covered in bites and we itched non-stop. Next evening, as our hosts came home, both husband and wife would kneel down in front of the picture of the Virgin Mary and cross themselves. This was no problem, we followed suit; by then we had become quite adept in kneeling and crossing ourselves.

In the morning we decided to go to Jerzów, ten to fifteen minutes' walk from Mikołów, where we heard it was market day. Though we left Warsaw in our light summer dresses with not even a change of clothes, Father had made sure that I would not be penniless; he had given me a bundle of dollar bills which I had sewn into the lining of my bra. My first thought when we reached the market was to buy a Virgin Mary medallion or possibly a cross to hang from a chain around my neck. Then I remembered having heard rumours that for some reason Germans suspected women wearing crosses to be Jewish. Medallions were supposed to be safer, not quite as Jewish. Funny, don't you think? Hela agreed with me, having heard similar gossip. We bought two medallions and two velvet ribbons to hang them on.

As it happened Hela had a watch that did not work, so we took it to a watchmaker. When we came back to collect it a few days later, he refused to give it back to us.

'What do you mean? I left it with you to be repaired,' Hela said.

'I'm going to keep it and there is nothing you can do about it, I know you are Jewish,' was his brief answer.

I don't have to tell you how quickly we ran from his shop.

The man who sold us the medallions looked quite trustworthy, so

I asked him whether he ever went to Tomaszów. 'Yes, quite often,' he answered. 'It's not far from Jerzów. I usually go there once or twice a week.'

So I told him that I was a refugee from Warsaw and that I needed his help. 'These days one Pole has to help another,' I said. 'I have an old friend there. She is a dressmaker by trade. Could you possibly find her address for me?' I wrote Julia's name on a piece of paper. 'Tell her,' I added, 'that Guta from Łódż is looking for her.' I promised him 100 złotys if he got her address for me. He agreed and we arranged that I would meet him in Jerzów on the next market day.

He was very pleased with himself when I saw him next. He had traced Julia and he showed me with pride the note he brought from her, in which she asked me to write to her. I gave him his well-deserved reward. Then I went to the post office, arranged for a *poste restante* address, and wrote to Julia telling her how much I would like to see her. At the same time I sent a letter to Father in the hospital with nothing but my *poste restante* address in it. That was all I dared to write.

A week or so later I received a very warm invitation from Julia, which we followed up. She was a Christian. She lived in a small but comfortable apartment with a partner, whom I recognised as our pre-war client from the Poznań district. We had to give them a full account of what had happened to us since our expulsion from Łódż. Julia changed some of my dollars into złotys. She then went out shopping and bought all the clothes and blankets that we badly needed, as autumn was approaching. Back in the village, we told our peasant hosts that we had traced some of our relatives and how they had helped us get clothes, pillows and blankets.

It was essential that we acted as if we were Catholics. We went to church every Sunday, carefully watched people around us and imitated them as best we could. We crossed ourselves when they did; knelt and prayed to the Holy Virgin as they did. We took our meals together with our hosts. The Polish peasant loves swearing and some of his sayings express his sentiments precisely. One day, our hostess served us very hot soup for dinner. As her husband ate a spoonful he must have burnt his mouth. He swore, 'I'd rather drown 1000 Jews than drink soup as hot as this!'

Not long before Christmas one of the villagers appeared in the cottage. He took our host aside and they talked quietly, but we pricked up our ears and overheard the newcomer saying: 'I've heard rumours that there are some Jewish women among the Warsaw refugees. What about yours? Can you be sure who they are?'

'I've got no idea,' he replied, but we trembled and felt quite panicky. But there was nothing we could do.

As I mentioned, I sent a letter to Father. He wrote back saying that he was getting better and that he was missing me. His next letter came in late November and took me by surprise. He wrote that he could not bear to stay in the hospital any longer and that he had decided to discharge himself, had found a room locally and moved there. He gave me his address and asked me to visit him. The journey did not take long. He was renting a room in a small flat belonging to an elderly lady. He had recovered from his injuries some time ago and he looked really well. He got quite angry when I reproached him for having left the safety of the hospital. He told me that he was expecting Russian troops to arrive any day now. He was convinced that German resistance was crumbling and that we had little to fear from them now. I begged him to stay indoors as much as possible to avoid being recognised as a Jew. 'Remember, you do look like one,' I said.

We felt that if we stayed in the village over Christmas we would attract suspicion. What self-respecting Christian would have no friends or family to spend Christmas with? I picked Father's last letter up from the post office on 18 December. He was keen for us to visit him at Christmas and this was our opportunity to get away. We told our peasant hosts that we would be away for a couple of days and on 23 December took a train to Skierniewice. I was so longing to see Father that it seemed it was taking ages for his landlady to open the front door when we got there.

'Can we see Mr Malinowski?' I asked, somewhat surprised that he had not come out to greet us.

'Mr Malinowski no longer lives here,' the woman replied. 'He went out shopping the day before yesterday but did not return. That same evening three uniformed SS men came here, asked to see his room and took all his belongings away. But do come in, can I offer you something to drink?'

'No, thank you, we have to go,' I said trying to stop a flood of tears.

I must show no emotion, I kept saying to myself, as I left. 'What shall we do now?' I asked Hela when we got into the street. 'We dare not return to the village. It is Christmas. If they see us, they will know that we are Jewish.' I was standing in the street, trying to make a rational decision, while my world had just come to an end.

We got back to the station and sat in the waiting room pretending to be waiting for a connection. Trains were coming and going. How long can one wait without attracting suspicion? We decided on going to visit Julia, in spite of some new doubts. Countless thoughts were crossing my mind. Could I have given Julia a clue to Father's whereabouts by accident and was her boyfriend the person that had given him away? Julia would not have done it herself, I felt almost sure, but I worried about taking more chances. Finally, we took a train to Tomaszów. It was late in the evening when we knocked at her door. There was no reply. We kept trying again and again but had no luck. We went back to the station. We spotted an inn close to it. There was only one guest-room on offer, a kind of communal dormitory, completely bare except for a few simple beds with straw mattresses. The room had two doors, one leading to the landlord's quarters and another to the bar.

'Just as well the landlord lives here,' I said to Hela, 'it makes me feel safer.'

It was a very cold December night, so we didn't bother to undress and shared one bed to keep warm. Suddenly, in the middle of the night, a terrible racket woke us up. The door was flung open and several German soldiers burst into the inn.

'They must be looking for somewhere to spend the night, and here we are, two women, all alone!' Hela whispered in my ear, panicking.

'Let's get out of here quickly,' I answered. 'Let's go back to the station and wait for a train.'

As I was getting out of bed one of the soldiers approached me. I froze with fear.

'Please, please, can you help me?' he begged plaintively. 'Where can I get some civilian clothes to change into?'

I could not help him. And I wasn't sure whether I would have even if I had been able to.

The soldiers disappeared. For me, the war was over.

11

FREEDOM AT LAST

As Christmas 1944 approached, just before Mother's story comes to an end, the winter weather became particularly severe and thick snow covered the ground. One morning, with no warning, we were told to get ready for evacuation of the camp. We could only assume that Russian troops were not far away. We were taken to the railway station, loaded again into goods wagons and issued with some food. It was freezing cold and there was no heating in the wooden boxes. From Damsdorf the train took nearly two days to get to its destination in northern Germany, another vast prisoner-of-war camp in Sandbostel, between Bremen and Hanover. But there were no more Red Cross parcels here and we were constantly hungry, day and night. Men were lying on their bunks, hardly able to move, apathetic and morose, their limbs swollen. When the weather got warmer we sat outside the huts, trying to get at least some energy from the sun's rays. I was fortunate in that I didn't smoke, but I can never forget how many people, their bellies swollen with hunger, would still swap half their meagre bread ration for two cigarettes. The craving for nicotine must have been that much stronger than the body's need for food. At night we would listen for the roar of the hundreds of bombers flying overhead. We heard the sound of distant explosions and could not hold back our excitement: at last the Germans were getting a dose of their own medicine.

A fellow prisoner called Falk and I became great friends. He was in his early 40s, short, slim and softly spoken. One of the huts in the camp had been designated to serve as a theatre, and when volunteers were called for to take care of it and keep it clean, we both came forward. The privilege that went with it was a small room for just the two of us and we greatly enjoyed the rare luxury of privacy. The theatre was in frequent use; there were many successful performances and a lot of talent was discovered among the prisoners. It all helped to break the tedium and monotony of prison life.

One day I chatted to a young German guard who came to inspect the theatre hut; all of a sudden he was friendly and seemed keen to help us. He would drop in from time to time with a loaf of bread, a treat not to be underestimated. I was sure that he was by then expecting the imminent collapse of Germany and was trying to make friends on the winning side who were likely to prove useful once the war was over. His attempts were in vain, however, as I never saw him again after the liberation.

Ignorant of what was happening in the world, we got up as usual on 5 May 1945. A surprise awaited us in the morning: there were British soldiers at the gates of the camp, and the German guards seemed to have disappeared into thin air. We ran towards our saviours, arms outstretched. I embraced the first soldier I came across, but then had something of a shock: he was talking to me at length and I could not understand a word! Had all my English lessons been in vain? Clearly they did not stand the test of a simple conversation. I felt sorely disappointed. Just at that moment a British sergeant approached me. He was rather short, wore glasses and greeted me with a friendly smile, though his demeanour was rather formal. 'My name is Sol Polak,' he said, 'and I come from Liverpool. Tell me, can you speak English?' Strangely enough, I had no problem understanding him.

'I thought I could until a minute ago,' I answered, 'but I couldn't make out a word of what your mate was saying.'

'I wouldn't worry if I were you,' he laughed. 'He is not English, he is Scottish. Scots have their own language!' he reassured me.

I looked at Sol. There was something familiar about his features. 'Are you Jewish?' I asked. 'because I am.' He looked me up and down disbelievingly: 'You, Jewish?' he remarked. 'Never, not in a million years! Not you!'

'I'm circumcised – is that proof enough?'

'Not at all, in England lots of gentiles are circumcised, many here in the army are too. But with your looks, who would believe you were Jewish?'

The only words of Hebrew I remembered were the opening lines of the Pesach prayer Ma Nishtana and I recited them. It was only then that he believed me.

I will never know whether it was that which helped or whether he was just impressed with my English, but he went on to ask how many other languages I knew. When I told him, he took me to his commanding officer, Captain Fitzgerald.

'Sir,' he said with some pride, 'I found a man who can speak Polish, French, German, English and a little bit of Russian.'

The captain looked at me. 'What are your plans for the future?' he asked.

I had none at all. How could I make plans? In Poland the communist regime was putting Home Army soldiers in prison or sending them to Siberia, so going back was out of the question. Consequently, when he offered me the post of an interpreter with the 205 Military Government Unit that was taking full control of the area, I accepted without hesitation. My fellow prisoners were by now beginning to disperse and it was time I too left the camp and found a niche for myself in the post-war world.

I followed my new British friends to their quarters in an elegant villa in Bremenförde, a picturesque German village, where Sol and I were given a room to share. He couldn't hear enough of my account of how I survived the war. During the day I worked in an office across the road under a Major Jennings, a solicitor from London. As part of my job I had to attend meetings, adjudication tribunals, disputes, court cases and so on – as thousands of people of many nationalities, who through the vagaries of war found themselves stranded in Germany, were now trying to start a new life. To my great satisfaction I now had a motorbike at my disposal too, and could make new friends roaming round the countryside.

Soon after settling into my new job I wrote a letter to Edek's parents-in-law in Palestine and sent it to the address I remembered in Allenby Street, Tel-Aviv. To my great delight some weeks later I received a reply from Edek himself. He, Mala and Krysia had survived the latter part of the war in the Bergen–Belsen concentration camp and were now living in Tel-Aviv, where Edek was working as a taxi driver. He established contact with Mother who, together with Hela, had returned to our pre-war apartment in Łódź that January. He told me about the fate of other members of the family: Jerzyk and Eliasz Wołczyk, who survived, hidden by a Catholic priest, were also living in Łódź. My brother Michał, who fled occupied Poland in September 1939, had managed to reach England via Scandinavia. He served in the Polish army in Britain during the war, but was now ill in hospital somewhere near London. And it was from Edek that I learned that Father had been killed only a few days before the Russians arrived.

Father's death affected me badly. But I could now write directly to Mother and we established a regular correspondence. Her advice was to remain in Germany until the situation in Poland became clearer. She also sent me the address of my aunt, uncle and cousin, Jenny Kopelman, in Belgium. Jenny's mother was my late father's sister; it was her husband who had warned Father that war was imminent and advised him to prepare for it. But it was too late to do anything and, in any case, Father, having a mind of his own, did not heed the warning.

As soon as I was due for leave from my job I went to Brussels. They received me warmly. My greatest joy there was to be taken almost every night to the *Théâtre Royal de la Monnaie* – it was my first experience of live opera – and I loved it. We visited Antwerp and other places and each day brought a new exciting experience. After all the long years of deprivation I could at last enjoy life to the full.

When my commanding officer, Major Jennings, heard about my brother's illness, he arranged for me to take compassionate leave in England. I first went to Oldham, where my brother's new wife lived with her parents. It was November and my most enduring first impression of England was the cold, unheated bedroom there. It was only later that I discovered it was the norm in those days. I still shudder when I think of the cold bed with its damp sheets. From Oldham I went to Epsom and I saw Michał in hospital and two days later returned to Germany.

Five months later, in May 1946, Mother wrote to me with the news that the Polish Government had declared an amnesty for members of the Home Army and that I could safely return to Poland. I boarded a ship in Kiel and landed in Gdańsk, formerly Danzig, now in Polish hands. From there I went by train to Łódż and was reunited with Mother after almost two years. She told me in detail about her last encounter with Father. Back in Łódż, she met Mr Landecki, the man she had last seen in the Pruszków hospital in the bed next to Father's. He could not get over Father's fatal decision.

'I couldn't understand how Jakub, with his appearance, dared to leave the hospital, and of his own free will. If only he had had a little more patience and waited just a bit longer, as I did. But he was so strong-willed! That's what killed him. What a tragedy! He managed to swim across a deep, wide river but not to climb onto the shore.'

My father's factory was now naturally taken over by the communist state, but my uncle Eliasz, an experienced weaving technician, was still in charge of it. He was taking good care of Mother. The first thing Mother did when I arrived was to take me to the sitting room and show me, with pride, a beautiful grand piano, a Bechstein, a replacement for the Bluthner which the Germans had taken away. In a reversal of fortune, she'd got it from the flat next door after it was abandoned by a German family. We had to share our flat with Władysław Kendra, a famous Polish pianist and his family, but I still managed to sleep in my old room. Yet I wasn't happy back in Łódż. I felt awkward and constrained, and made my mind up to get away as soon as I could.

Mother left Poland first and went to stay in London to look after my brother. But then another tragedy struck. My brother died suddenly on 27 June 1946, at the age of 27. Michał's death presented me with an opportunity to leave Poland. As he had served with the Polish forces in Great Britain, I had no problem receiving a British visa on compassionate grounds. I boarded a British plane in Warsaw and found myself in London a few hours later. The long trek to freedom was over . . .

Mother and I went to live in Old Trafford and I completed my studies as a textile technologist in Manchester. Later I moved to London, married, had children, a career . . . but that is another story.

EPILOGUE

The Płomniks, Sam and his wife, Mr Tylbor and Marysia all survived the war.

Mr Tylbor had lived for three months like an animal in the deserted ruins of Warsaw, but eventually came out alive.

Marysia left Leon Wołowski for good and took up an acting career. She later married a politician, a minister in the Polish Government, but subsequently divorced him and emigrated to Israel.

The Holkas visited Łódż after the war. They stayed in our flat and thus Mother was able to meet them.

KRYSIA'S ACCOUNT

I was too young at the time to be able to remember what happened, so all that I know of my wartime childhood was told to me by my parents. Early in 1943 my father went to the Gestapo headquarters to ask about the provision for those Jews who could prove that they had relations in Palestine; there was talk about them being exchanged for Germans living in that country at the time. He was told very politely to return in two or three days' time. The anxiety and stress in the ghetto were such that people who could afford it were buying dubious documents permitting them to go to assorted Central American countries. My parents had to decide whether to choose that or the Palestinian option. The fact that my mother's parents lived in Palestine made them opt for the latter. The photo reproduced in this book survived because my mother somehow managed to send it to her parents, to reassure them that we were alive and well. While waiting for permission to leave Poland we stayed in Hotel Polski from April 1943 to July 1943, when we were taken to the Bergen–Belsen concentration camp. The people who had spent all their money on buying the phoney visas for Central America were all sent either to Treblinka or to Auschwitz, where their lives ended in the gas chambers, while we were sent to Bergen–Belsen as kind of hostages, pending the supposed 'exchange'. We stayed there until 13 April 1945, when we were put on a train without windows, packed so tightly that many people died on their feet. This train was taking us to one of the death camps, but on 19 April it was stopped by soldiers of the Russian cavalry. Delighted to find a child still alive they fed me cubes of sugar. The war ended soon after and in September 1945 we managed to make our way to Haifa. Having settled in Palestine, my parents changed my Polish name Krysia to the Hebrew one, Rina.

JANUSZ HOLKA'S ACCOUNT

This is a translation of the statement sent by Mr Janusz Holka from his home in Łódz to Jerzy Lando in September 2001.

My Father

My father, Edmund Holka, a businessman, was born in 1890 and lived in Gniezno, where from 1914 till 1939 he owned a wholesale textile firm. In October 1939, at the beginning of the German occupation, his business was confiscated by the German authorities. In March 1940 Edmund Holka was expelled from Gniezno to the *General Gouvernement*, where he settled with his family in Warsaw. In the spring of 1940 he established the Warsaw Recycled Raw Material Centre, which he ran till 1944, the year of the Warsaw Rising fought by the Polish Underground Army. After the Rising he went to live in Piotrków Trybunalski and in February 1945, having crossed the Soviet–German frontline, he returned to Gniezno. He died in 1972.

The Warsaw Recycled Raw Material Centre

In spring 1940, after arriving in Warsaw, Edmund Holka got in touch with a group of Jews who suggested a joint business venture. According to a note I received from Jerzy Holka, brother of Janusz Holka, their father, Edmund Holka was almost penniless when he first came to live in Warsaw in the spring of 1940. As he had a reputation for honesty, a number of Jews were happy to entrust him with their money to finance the newly-formed business. This business venture involved the collection and sale of reclaimable raw materials. The partners were:

Mr Fajwlowicz (Jewish)
Mr Hersz Gezundheit (Jewish)
Mr Edmund Holka (Christian)
Mr Roman Polirsztok (Jewish)
Mr 'Fritz' Tugenthat (Jewish)

Edmund Holka and Fritz were full-time working partners right to the end, (Roman Polirsztok until the final liquidation of the ghetto), while the others did not play an active role, apart from supplying capital. The business was located in Warsaw, first at Okopowa 76 and then at Mlocinska 14.

The office staff consisted of:

Ben

Janusz Holka

'*Pan Inżynier*'

Jerzy Lando

Zenon Rychlik

The manual work was done by a group of Jews from the ghetto. From the time the ghetto was sealed off until its final liquidation they were being brought from there each day. At some stage non-Jewish workers had to be employed. This arrangement provided a chance for smuggling Jews to the Aryan side of Warsaw.

From 1942 the firm was loosely connected with the German firm Rohstoffzentrale GmbH in Warsaw. It ceased to exist in August 1944 at the outbreak of the Warsaw Rising.

What happened to the firm's Jewish employees

Janusz Holka confirms that throughout the firm's existence Edmund Holka regularly shared the profits with all his Jewish partners, most of them in hiding, thus providing them with means of survival. Mr Fajwlowicz lived with his family in hiding on the Aryan side from 1941 onwards. After the war he emigrated to Paris[1].

Hersz Gezundheit and his family survived in hiding from 1942 and eventually emigrated to France.

Roman Polirsztok perished, probably in Sobibor.

'Fritz' Tugenthat lived throughout the war on the Aryan side of Warsaw.

Additional information

Ben perished in 1942 in Treblinka.

'Fritz' Tugenthat, who came from Bielska Biała, survived. I met him in the years 1946–7.

'*Pan Inżynier*', a former officer in the pre-war Polish Forces, survived the war. I was in touch with him in the years 1946–8.

Zenon Rychlik, a lawyer, survived the war. I met him in 1946–7. He wore the uniform of an officer in the UB (Urzad Bezpieczeństwa Department of Security).

There may be slight inaccuracies in some of the above names and locations.

---

[1] Jerzy Lando met Mr Fajwlowicz and his son on many occasions while they all lived in Paris in 1949–50. Mr Fajwlowicz, widowed at the time, proposed marriage to Jerzy's mother, which she did not accept.

The fate of the Polirsztok family: Roman Polirsztok, Lusia, his wife, and Jerzy, their son.

Roman Polirsztok was brought daily to work from the ghetto, while his wife Lusia and son remained in the ghetto. In the centre he was in charge of finances and organisation. He was the partner Edmund Holka relied on most. One day, in August 1942 (one month into the liquidation of the ghetto) Edmund Holka went home to Jasna Street for lunch. As soon as he arrived he received a phone call from the ghetto informing him that the Polirsztok family were detained at the *Umschlagplatz*. He immediately made his way there, though I cannot tell how he managed. When he arrived, the Polirsztoks were already inside a railway wagon. Edmund Holka, who could speak German like a native, approached the commandant of the *Umschlagplatz* to intervene on behalf of Roman Polirsztok, arguing that the man was an indispensable specialist in his firm. He presented documents from the Warsaw District and from the German firm, *Rohstoffzentrale Warschau*, (once sorted, the firm's produce, raw materials, were regularly shipped to Germany). Following Edmund Holka's intervention, the Germans ordered Roman Polirsztok to be let out of the wagon, but the latter would not leave without his wife and son. Further arguments followed, until the commandant was persuaded to allow the whole family to leave the train just before it departed. The following day the whole Polirsztok family arrived at the warehouse at Młocińska Street as part of the group of Jewish workers.

Roman Polirsztok went back to the ghetto each day, but Lusia and her son remained outside. Thanks to Edmund Holka's acquaintance with Father Krauze of the Priests' and Missionaries' Rest Home in Marki near Warsaw, Lusia and her son were allowed to stay in Marki until May 1943, when they left to live with friends at Jagielońska Street in Warsaw-Praga. Roman Polirsztok did not turn up for work as usual one day in February or March 1943. He had been deported and perished, probably in Sobibor. None of Edmund Holka's investigations produced any results. Lusia Polirsztok and her son survived the occupation. In 1947 they left for France and made their home in Nice. Lusia changed her name from Polirsztok to Szepetowska. She maintained contact by correspondence with Edmund Holka till 1972.